Of Cigarettes, High Heels, and Other *Interesting* Things

Semaphores and Signs

General Editors: Roberta Kevelson and Marcel Danesi

SENSING SEMIOSIS
Toward the Possibility of Complementary Cultural "Logics"
Floyd Merrell

THE SENSE OF FORM IN
LITERATURE AND LANGUAGE
Michael Shapiro

ARCHITECTONICS OF SEMIOSIS
Edwina Taborsky

OF CIGARETTES, HIGH HEELS,
AND OTHER *INTERESTING* THINGS
An Introduction to Semiotics
Marcel Danesi

Of Cigarettes, High Heels, and Other *Interesting* Things

An Introduction to Semiotics

Marcel Danesi

St. Martin's Press
New York

ISBN 0-312-21084-1 (hardcover)
ISBN 0-312-21450-2 (paperback)

Library of Congress Cataloging-in-Publication Data

Danesi, Marcel, 1946–
    Of cigarettes, high heels, and other interesting things: an
introduction to semiotics / by Marcel Danesi.
        p.   cm.
    Includes bibliographical references (p.) and index.
    ISBN 0-312-21084-1. — ISBN 0-312-21450-2 (pbk.)
    1. Semiotics.
P99.D36   1999
302.2—DC21   90-17390
                                                                    CIP

Design by Letra Libre

First edition: May, 1999
10 9 8 7 6 5 4 3 2 1

CONTENTS

LIST OF FIGURES

PREFACE

If one watched people as one might observe animals in their natural habitats, one would soon reach the conclusion that human beings are truly a peculiar lot. Why is it, for example, that certain members of the species routinely put their survival at risk by puffing on a small stick of nicotine? Why is it that some females of the same species make locomotion a struggle for themselves by donning high-heel footwear? Or is there a hidden *story* behind such ludicrous behaviors that makes the human species unique in a strange sort of way?

This book will attempt to answer the latter question and, in so doing, will make it obvious that *Homo sapiens* cannot be studied primarily in biological terms. Many of the thoughts and actions that one would probably judge as exclusively human turn out to be shaped by forces other than the instincts. Indeed, for no manifest genetic reason, humanity is constantly searching for a purpose to its existence; this search has led it not only to engage in such bizarre behaviors as smoking and wearing high heels, but also to invent myths, art, rituals, languages, mathematics, science, and other truly remarkable things that set it apart from all other species. The discipline that endeavors to understand the human quest for meaning is known as *semiotics*. Relatively unknown in comparison to, say, philosophy or psychology, semiotics probes human nature in its own peculiar way, without the usual unwieldy technical notions that other disciplines enfold. It does so by unraveling the meanings of the symbols, known more exactly as *signs,* that make up the *system of everyday life* that we call a *culture* or a *society.* My hope is that this book will engender in the reader the same kind of questioning and inquisitive frame of mind with which a semiotician would closely examine society. Perhaps the greatest skill possessed by *Homo sapiens,* literally the knowing animal, is the ability to know itself. Semiotics helps sharpen that ability considerably.

I have contrived my presentation of semiotic ideas and analytical techniques around a seemingly trivial scene, but one that nonetheless reveals a lot about the human need for meaning. The scene is a fashionable modern day restaurant—an urban courtship ground where wooing rituals are performed on a regular basis. The fictional actions in this scene allow me to tell the semiotic version of the human drama in concrete terms. I have defined in clear language any term that I felt to be understandable primarily only by semioticians, and I have kept footnotes to a minimum.

It should be said, however, that what I have chosen to write about, and how I have gone about interpreting human actions and behaviors, reflect my own particular preferences and views. Whether one agrees or disagrees with any or all of my commentaries is beside the real purpose of this book, which is to stimulate the reader to think reflectively and critically about the system of everyday life in which he or she takes part. That and that alone will have made the writing of this book worthwhile.

This book was the idea of the late Professor Roberta Kevelson of Penn State University, one of the leading semioticians of the twentieth century. She will be missed greatly. I am indebted to Michael Flamini of St. Martin's Press for having given me his support, advice, and expert help. I am also deeply grateful to Victoria College of the University of Toronto for granting me the privilege of teaching semiotics for many years. This has allowed me to learn a great deal about human nature from the always enthusiastic students I have taught over those years. Finally, a heartfelt thanks goes out to my family, Lucy, Alexander, Sarah, Danila, Chris, Danilo, and Pumpkin (our cat), for all the patience they have had with me over my incessant pontifications about semiotics. I must also ask their forgiveness for having been so grumpy and neglectful of family duties during the writing of this book.

1

CIGARETTES AND HIGH HEELS

The Universe of Signs

A cigarette is the perfect type of a perfect pleasure. It is exquisite, and it leaves one unsatisfied. What more can one want?

—Oscar Wilde (1854–1900)

It is eight o'clock on a Saturday night. Two attractive people, both in their late twenties, are sitting across from each other at an elegantly set table in a trendy restaurant/night club, located in the downtown area of a North American city. For the sake of convenience, let's call them Cheryl and Ted. Other couples are seated at tables all around them. The lights are turned down low. The atmosphere is unmistakably romantic, sustained by the soft, mellifluous sounds of a three-piece jazz band. Cheryl and Ted are sipping drinks, making small talk, looking coyly into each other's eyes, smoking cigarettes. Viewed from afar, the scenario is reminiscent of an episode from a Hollywood movie.

What Cheryl and Ted do not know is that from a hidden corner of the restaurant a semiotician, let's call her Martha, is recording their evening together as it unfolds, with a video camera. Martha's objective is to capture their actions, words, facial expressions, and other relevant behaviors on tape so that we can dissect them with the particular tools that semiotics provides.

So, let's examine Martha's tape, focusing our attention first on the smoking gestures that our two subjects made. The tape shows Cheryl taking her cigarette out of its package with a slow, deliberate movement, inserting it coquettishly into the middle of her mouth, then bringing the flame of a match toward her cigarette in a laggard, drawn-out fashion. The tape shows Ted, on the other side of the table, employing abrupt, terse movements to take his cigarette out of its package, insert it into the side of his mouth, and then swiftly light it. As the two start puffing away, the tape reveals Cheryl keeping her legs crossed, resting her arm on the table, with the cigarette between her index and third fingers pointing upwards, periodically flicking the ashes, and using her index and middle fingers to insert and remove the cigarette from her mouth, with graceful, circular, swooping motions. Occasionally, she tosses her long, flowing hair back, away from her face, looking shyly but enticingly at Ted as she does so. At the same time, the tape reveals Ted sitting with legs apart, leaning back in his chair in a regal manner, keeping his head taut, looking straight ahead during his puffing motions, holding his cigarette mainly between his thumb and middle finger, guiding it to the side of his mouth with sharp, pointed movements. The tape also shows Cheryl drawing smoke in slowly, retaining it in her mouth for a relatively protracted period (rarely inhaling it into her lungs), exhaling the smoke in an upwards direction with her head tilted slightly to the side and, finally, extinguishing her cigarette in an ashtray, "squishing" it in a tantalizing way. In accompaniment to Cheryl's gestures, the tape shows Ted inhaling abruptly, holding the smoke in his mouth for a relatively short period of time, blowing it in a downward direction (with his head slightly aslant), and then extinguishing the cigarette by pressing down on the butt with his thumb, almost as if he were effacing or destroying evidence.

CIGARETTES AND SEX

Welcome to the world of semiotics. The semiotician is, above all else, a people-watcher, an observer of how people gesticulate, of how they communicate, of how they behave typically in certain situations. The semiotician is interested in anything that reveals something pertinent about the system of everyday human life, constantly asking, what does this or that mean? So, let's start our excursion into the fascinating world of semiotics by doing exactly that—unraveling what the above smoking vignette means. The most logical point of departure is to check if there is some historically-based link between smoking and romance.

Tobacco is native to the Western Hemisphere and was probably first used by the ancient Maya peoples, who believed it had medicinal and powerful mythical properties. The Arawak people of the Caribbean, observed by Christopher Columbus in 1492, smoked it through a tube they called a *tobago*, from which the word tobacco originated. Brought to Spain from Santo Domingo in 1556, tobacco was introduced to France in the same year by the French diplomat Jean Nicot, from whom the plant derived its generic name, nicotine. In 1585 the English navigator, Sir Francis Drake, took it to England, where the practice of pipe smoking was subsequently introduced among the Elizabethan courtiers by the English explorer, Sir Walter Raleigh. Tobacco use spread quickly throughout Europe, and by the seventeenth century it had reached China, Japan, the west coast of Africa, and other areas of the world.

By the early twentieth century, smokers in the United States were consuming more than 1000 cigarettes per capita each year. The general attitude of American society was that smoking relieved tensions and produced no ill effects. During World War II, physicians even endorsed sending soldiers cigarettes, which were consequently included in ration kits. Epidemiologists soon noticed, however, that lung cancer—rare before the twentieth century—had increased dramatically, beginning about 1930. The American Cancer Society and other organizations initiated studies comparing deaths among smokers and nonsmokers, finding increased mortality rates from cancer among smokers. In 1964 the U.S. Surgeon General's report affirmed that cigarette smoking was a health hazard of sufficient importance to warrant the inclusion of a warning on cigarette packages. All cigarette advertising was banned from radio and television, starting in 1971. In the 1970s and 1980s several cities and states passed laws requiring nonsmoking sections in public and work places. In February 1990 federal law banned smoking on all domestic airline flights of under six hours. Today, there are laws throughout North America that prohibit smoking in public places, buildings, and vehicles.

Yet in spite of the dangers, 25.5 percent of the population in the U.S. currently spend nearly $50 billion each year on cigarettes.[1] So, why do people smoke? If one asks people who smoke why they started smoking in the first place, they will give a range of answers that point typically to the "sociability" of the cigarette. To the semiotician, who suspects that cigarettes are imbued with meanings that reach back into the social history of sexuality and gender, this comes as no surprise.

The restaurant scene that our semiotician, Martha, captured on tape is identifiable essentially as a courtship display, a recurrent, largely unconscious, mating ritual rooted in gesture, movement, and body signals that keep the two sexes differentiated and highly interested in each other. As Margaret Leroy has suggested, such actions are performed because sexual tradition dictates it.[2] Let's scrutinize Cheryl's smoking gestures. The sequence of holding the cigarette invitingly between her index and middle fingers, fondling it as if it were a phallic object, and then inserting the cigarette into the middle of her mouth, slowly and deliberately, is highly suggestive of coitus. At the same time, she is exhibiting her fingers and wrist to her suitor, thus displaying areas of the body that have erotic connotations in our culture. Cheryl's hair-tossing movements, slightly raising a shoulder to highlight her breasts, also constitute powerful erotic signals. These same gestures can be observed in advertising. *Sex sells,* as the expression goes.

Ted's gestures form a patterned counterpart to Cheryl's, emphasizing sexual differentiation. Her movements are slow, his are abrupt; she crosses her legs, he keeps his apart; she puffs her smoke upwards, he blows it downwards; she holds the cigarette in a tantalizing manner between the index and middle fingers, he holds it in a sturdy way between the thumb and middle finger; she puts out the cigarette with a lingering motion, he crushes it forcefully. Her gestures convey sensuality, voluptuousness, sultriness; his suggest toughness, determination, control.

The history of smoking shows that tobacco has been perceived at times as a desirable thing and at others as a forbidden fruit.[3] But in almost every era, as Richard Klein[4] has eloquently argued, cigarettes have had some connection to sex, or to something that is erotically, socially, or intellectually appealing. Musicians smoke; intellectuals smoke; artists smoke. Smoking is a symbol of both sexuality and unabashed bravado. Movies tell us that smoking is a prelude to sex and a form of relaxation afterwards; smoking seems to be the entire point of being an adult; smoking is fun. In the parlance of semiotics, smoking is a *discursive* act, because it sends out messages about who we are (or think we are). As Michael Starr puts it, "smoking is, in many situations, a species of rhetoric signifying certain qualities of the smoker."[5]

The smoking gestures that Martha caught on tape are performed in a similar gender specific way in parallel situations throughout our society as part of urban courtship rituals; they form what semioticians call a *code.*

Codes are systems of *signs*—gestures, movements, words, glances—that human beings routinely enlist to make and send out messages. The basic signs in a language code, for instance, are words, which can be combined in various ways to form spoken or written messages. The signs in a dress code are the items of clothing that can be worn in different combinations to send out certain kinds of socially meaningful messages. Codes mediate the relationship between people in a society and are, therefore, effective shapers of how we think of others and of ourselves.

The smoking gestures described above are so familiar and understandable to us because they constitute a *coded* form of behavior during courtship. The particular enactment of the code will vary in detail from situation to situation, from person to person, but its basic features will remain the same. The code provides a script for each person to assume a role in sexual acting, or flirting, affording a repertoire of gestures and postures that reinforce gender-specific models of sexual attractiveness. No wonder, then, that so many teenagers take up smoking in our society.[6] This is the period of life when sexual feelings emerge as overwhelming. To adolescents, cigarettes symbolize sexual maturity, and thus imply independence and adulthood. In a research project that I undertook a few years ago, I noticed that teenagers put on the same type of smoking performances that our restaurant protagonists did, using cigarettes as sexual props, albeit in different situations (in school yards, in malls, at parties).[7] The adolescent female typically tossed her hair, as Cheryl did, pushing it back just before inserting the cigarette into the middle of her mouth. The adolescent male, on the other hand, typically kept his head taut, inserting the cigarette into the side of his mouth, just as Ted did in our imaginary vignette. The females blew the smoke upwards, the males downwards; the females dropped the cigarette butt and stamped it out slowly with one foot; the males hurled it away aggressively. Cigarette smoking in adolescence is, in a phrase, a coming-of-age rite, a performance designed to send out signals of sexual difference, maturity, and attractiveness to peers. When I asked teenagers why they smoked, they typically gave me answers such as: "Because it makes me look big"; "To feel sophisticated"; "Because it's cool."

Smoking performances raise the more general question of the *meaning* of sex in human life. In biology, the word sex alludes to the physical and behavioral differences that distinguish individual organisms according to their role in the reproductive process. Through these differences, termed male and female, the individual members of a species assume distinct sexual roles.

Sensing the other person's sex, therefore, is a biological *mechanism,* as it is commonly called by biologists. Across species, the individual organism's sexuality—that is, its sexual state, inclination, or proclivity—is detected by another organism from the body features and signals it emits during estrus (going into heat). However, at some point in its evolutionary history the human species mysteriously developed a sexuality independent of estrus. Other animals experience chemical and physical changes in the body during estrus which stimulate desire. People, however, normally experience desire first, which then produces changes in the body. Only in the human species is sex perceived as having a recreational function.

Courtship displays are not unique to the human species. The biologist Charles Darwin (1809–82) called them "submissive," because they send out the message, *notice me, I am attractive and harmless.* Cheryl's coy glances have parallels in the females of other species as signals to prospective mates for compliance and pursuit. They are, in effect, opening gambits in a continuing series of mating negotiations. A palm-up placement of the hand on a table or a knee, a shoulder shrug, and a tilted head are other examples of submissive gestures. But human courtship is not controlled exclusively by biological mechanisms. The use of a cigarette in courtship performances, for instance, has nothing to do with evolution. A cigarette is a phallic prop. This is why a female will unwittingly manipulate it seductively, but a male will handle it stiffly. It is a key element of the code through which sexual messages are transmitted. Semioticians refer to the ways in which individuals devise their messages as *texts.* A text is, literally, a "weaving together" of the elements taken from a specific code in order to communicate something. When someone says something to someone or writes a letter, he or she is engaged in making a *verbal text;* when someone selects clothing items to dress for an occasion, he or she is making a *bodily text;* and when people employ specific gestures, body postures, and phallic props during courtship, they are making *sexual texts.*

So, the human story of sex has many more chapters in it than a purely biological version of it would reveal. The chapter on gender, for instance, has nothing to do with estrus. Throughout the world, a person's sex is not only an indication of maleness or femaleness, but also of gender, a code that emerges in specific social contexts allowing people to establish what constitutes socially sanctioned sexual behavior. Nature creates sex; culture creates gender. This is why there are no gender universals. Until recently in Western society, men have been expected to be the sex-seekers, to initiate courtship, and to show an aggressive interest in sex; but among the Zuñi Indians of New Mexico, these very same actions and passions, are expected of the women. It is informative to note that the word sex comes from the Latin *secare* (to section, divide), suggesting that the traditional Western view was fashioned by the ancient myth of Hermaphrodite, the peculiar creature with two faces, two sets of limbs, and one large body. Hermaphrodite was resented by the gods, who ended up dividing her into two biologically separate sections—male and female. Western civilization has, ever since, focused on differences between the sexes rather than on similarities, even though there are probably more of the latter.

The views people develop of sexuality and gender are stored as images in the mind. As the U.S. philosopher Susanne Langer (1895–1985) remarked, these images capture and subsequently shape our feelings, guiding our attempts to make sense of a kiss, a touch, a look.[8] Incidentally, images are not just visual. We can easily conjure up nonvisual images. To "see" what this means, think of the laugh of a friend, the sound of thunder, the feel of wet grass, the feel of a runny nose, the smell of fish, the taste of toothpaste, the sensation of being uncomfortably cold, or the sensation of extreme happiness.

People's interpretation of sexuality and gender is shaped by cultural images, which inform them how to act and behave in courtship situations. These are products of a culture's history. Consequently, across the world, views of what is *natural* in matters of sex are established by tradition and consensus of the tribe. As a case-in-point, consider homosexuality. Among the Etoro peoples of New Guinea, there exists an intense distaste for sex between males and females, because they believe that heterosexual sex shortens life. So, Etoro custom prohibits sex between males and females for more than 200 days out of the year. Homosexual relations, on the other hand, are praised and encouraged. The same is true of the Chukchee peoples of Siberia. Chukchee males can become powerful religious figures only if they assume the gender role of women and marry and engage in sexual relations with other males. Western society, on the other hand, has responded ambiguously toward homosexuality.[9] In ancient Greece, homosexual relations were permitted, and in some cases even expected, of males in certain social classes. Later attitudes toward homosexuality in the West were shaped largely by prevailing religious moral codes, which traditionally have tended to view homosexuality as immoral or sinful. Like many other sins, homosexual relations were seen by religious people as expressions of the weakness inherent in all human beings, not as pathological behavior. The latter view developed in the late nineteenth century. As a consequence, attitudes toward homosexuality during the first half of the twentieth century were overwhelmingly negative, even among nonreligious people. Homosexual activities were hidden and spoken of only secretively, and homosexual behavior, even among consenting adults, was viewed as a criminal offense in most of the U.S. Such attitudes began to change around mid-century, as homosexuals in all walks of life, growing up in all kinds of families, practicing many different religions, came out in the open. As a result, in 1973 the American Psychiatric Association eliminated homosexuality from its list of disorders and, in 1980, dropped it from its *Diagnostic and Statistical Manual.*

ENTER THE SEMIOTICIAN

Now that we have identified the smoking gestures made by Cheryl and Ted as elements of a sexual acting code, our next task is to unravel how this code came about in our society. The association of smoking with sexual attractiveness can probably be traced back to the jazz club scene of the first decades of the twentieth century. The word *jazz* originally had sexual connotations, and to this day the verb form, to jazz, suggests sexuality. Smoking was an intrinsic part of the setting—a scene captured memorably on film by Gjon Mili in his 1945 movie, *Jammin' the Blues.* In the opening segment, there is a close-up of the great saxophonist Lester Young inserting a cigarette gingerly into his mouth, then dangling it between his index and middle fingers as he plays a slow, soft, hazy kind of jazz for the late night audience. When the smoke-filled air in such a club became too oppressive, windows and doors were opened to allow some cool air in from the outside. By analogy, the slow and smooth jazz style that was performed came to be called *cool jazz. Being cool* was subsequently extended to describe any physically attractive male jazz musician or aficionado who frequented such clubs—most of whom smoked cigars or cigarettes. The makers of Camel cigarettes strategically revived this scene in their advertising campaigns of the early 1990s through the images of a camel, dressed in an evening jacket, smoking and playing the piano in a club setting, a cigarette often dangling suggestively from the side of his mouth. Those ads

were clearly designed to evoke the sexual smoothness and finesse embod-
ied by cool jazz musicians.

The sexual subtleties of the increasingly popular jazz club scene were
captured magnificently by Michael Curtiz in his 1942 movie, *Casablanca*.
Cigarettes are the dominant visual feature of Rick's café, suggesting a
"phallic control" over the people hanging around in the café, quietly involved in late-night foreplay. There is a particularly memorable incident at
the start of the movie. Swaggering imperiously in his realm, with a cigarette in hand, Humphrey Bogart goes up to Ingrid Bergman, expressing
concern over the fact that she had had too much to drink. Dressed in
white, like a knight in shining armor, Bogart comes to the aid of a "damsel
in distress," sending her home to sober up. As he talks to her, he takes out
another cigarette from its package, inserting it swiftly into his mouth. He
lights it, letting it dangle from the side of his mouth. So captivating was
this image to cinema-goers, that it became an instant paradigm of "male
cool" imitated by hordes of aspiring male courtiers throughout society. In
a scene in Jean Luc Godard's 1959 movie, *Breathless*, Jean-Paul Belmondo
stares at a poster of Bogart in a movie window display. He takes out a cigarette and starts smoking it, imitating Bogart in *Casablanca*. The cigarette
dangling from the side of his mouth, the tough-looking Belmondo ap-
proaches his female mate with a blunt, "Sleep with me tonight?" The parody of society is unmistakable.

Nicholas Ray's 1955 movie, *Rebel without a Cause*, provides visual evidence that the phallic power of the cigarette was adopted by the emerging
adolescent subculture in the mid-1950s. The "car chicken" scene is particularly memorable. Two male suitors are vying to "win over" a female
through this form of combat. There is a ritualistic rubbing of the earth.
James Dean, one of the two combatants, is behind the wheel of his car, getting ready for battle, with a cigarette dangling from the side of his mouth;
his competitor is in his own car slicking down his hair. The scene became
representative of a modern-day version of a medieval lancing joust. In
1955, one fought not with a lance or a spear, but with a car.

One of the most unforgettable cinema portrayals of smoking as sexual
acting is in Michelangelo Antonioni's 1966 movie, *Blow Up*. In an over-
powering seduction scene, Vanessa Redgrave swerves her head excitedly to
the jazz rock music that David Hemmings has put on his record player to
give her a lesson in female sexuality. He tells her to keep still, because for
female sexual foreplay to be effective, the actions she takes must be slow

and deliberate. Then he gives her the cigarette he was smoking. She takes it quickly, eager to insert it into her mouth. But, no, Hemmings instructs her, she must slow the whole performance down; she must go "against the beat," as he puts it. Leaning forward, Redgrave takes the cigarette and inserts it slowly and seductively into the middle of her mouth. She lies back salaciously, blowing the smoke upwards. She gives Hemmings back the cigarette, giggling suggestively. He takes it and inserts it into his mouth, slightly to the side, visibly overcome by the power of her sexuality.

Such scenes have become emblazoned in the collective memory of our culture. Through the movies and other media, the association of smoking with sexual attractiveness has become a part of our system of everyday life. The smoking gestures that differentiate males and females in romantic encounters are picked up from this system. This explains why, in situations that call for romance, the skillful use of the cigarette as a sexual prop increases the attractiveness of a prospective mating partner. Incidentally, the use of sexual acting in courtship reveals something extraordinary about the human species. People will do something, even if it puts their lives at risk, for no other reason than it is *interesting*. Sexual acting makes sex *interesting*. It is what sells erotic materials; it is what makes lifestyle advertising effective; and it is what can revive a marriage that has become stale. A colleague of mine once quipped that semiotics can be defined as the study of "anything that is interesting."

CIGARETTES ARE SIGNS

In semiotic parlance, cigarettes are *signs*. Like many common words, cigarettes stand for something other than themselves. To understand what this implies, think of a tree. Surely the image that you have in your mind is of a particular kind of tall, woody plant with which you have become familiar in your surroundings. It is unlikely that you have an image of the sounds that make up the word, *t* + *r* + *ee*, without conjuring up the image of that plant. So, too, when you see a cigarette you will hardly ever think of it solely in terms of its physical properties, that is, as nicotine wrapped in white paper. In courtship encounters, the cigarette functions as a sign that conjures up images of gender-coded sexual attractiveness. In other contexts, people will, of course, figure out its meaning differently. When females started smoking in the early part of the twentieth century, the cigarette was perceived as a threatening sign of equality and independence.

When a teenager takes up smoking today, he or she sees the cigarette as a sign of maturity. The cigarette, in sum, is a sign with many meanings within the system of everyday life.

The basic goal of semiotics is to identify what constitutes a sign and what its meanings are. A sign can be identified by virtue of three dimensions. First, there is a *physical* dimension—the sounds that comprise a word, the movements that define a gesture, and so on. This is called interchangeably the *signifier*, the *representamen*, or even just the *sign*. Second, there is a *referential* or *representational* dimension; that is, the actual function of the sign, by which it directs attention to some entity (object, event, idea, being, etc.). This entity is called, equivalently, the *referent, object*, or *signified*. Finally, there is a *conceptual* dimension, by which the sign evokes in different people diverse thoughts, ideas, feelings. This dimension is called, alternately, *signification, interpretation*, or simply *meaning*. The cigarette has a certain shape, feel, and taste. But, as we have seen, this is not all there is to a cigarette. In courtship displays it is perceived as a *signifier* standing for something else—a prop used in flirting (the *signified*). Of course, people also have their own views of what the cigarette means. This part of the sign's meaning encompasses the specific designations, emotions, feelings, and ideas that the sign evokes in someone at a certain point in time (*interpretation* or *signification*).

The scholar who coined the terms *signifier* and *signified* was the Swiss linguist Ferdinand de Saussure (1857–1913). For Saussure, the meanings of a sign were fixed socially by convention and, thus, were independent of any consequential variation in interpretation. Moreover, he believed that the choice of a particular sign to represent something was largely an arbitrary one; that is, he did not think that it was motivated by any attempt to make it replicate, simulate, or imitate any perceivable feature of the entity to which it referred. To understand what Saussure meant, take, as an example, the concept "object made for sitting." Surely, Saussure would have argued, such an object could be represented by any well-formed signifier, that is, by any permissible combination of sounds in a language. The nonexistent forms *vack, leat, norp* reveal a legitimate combination of sounds in English, and any one of them could have been chosen to represent the concept in question. Similarly, in the Italian language, the forms *demia, fullo, genna* could also have been chosen for the concept, since they are recognizable as Italian words (signifiers). It so happens that in English the word is *chair*, while in Italian it is *sedia*.

There is no intrinsic motivation for having coined either one to stand for "an object made for sitting."

For Saussure, onomatopoeic words—words that imitate the sound of the concept to which they refer (chirp, drip, boom, zap, etc.)—were the exception, not the rule, in language. Moreover, the highly variable nature of onomatopoeia across languages suggested to him that even this phenomenon was subject to social conventions. For instance, the sounds made by a rooster are rendered by *cock-a-doodle-do* in English, but by *chicchirichì* (pronounced "keekeereekee") in Italian; similarly, the barking of a dog is conveyed by *bow-wow* in English but by *ouaoua* (pronounced "wawa") in French. Saussure argued that such signs were only approximate, and more or less conventional, imitations of perceived sounds.

But Saussure, a brilliant historical linguist, appears to have ignored the very historical dimension of the sign. Whereas the relation of a word to its referent can be argued logically to be arbitrary, the historical record often reveals a different story. It seems that the inventors of words often attempted to capture the sounds of the things which they aimed to represent. This was, in fact, the view put forward by the U.S. philosopher Charles Peirce (1839–1914), who viewed the process of inventing signs as being tied to an innate, imitative tendency in the human species. He argued that many words are no longer perceived as imitative because time and use have made people forget how they came about. For example, the cross in Christian religions is now perceived largely as a symbolic, conventional sign standing for "Christianity" as a whole. But most people can see in the cross figure an attempt to imitate the bare outline of the actual shape of the cross on which Christ was crucified.[10]

So too, most people, whether or not they speak English and Italian, will notice an *attempt* in both the above words, *cock-a-doodle-do* and *chicchirichì*, to imitate rooster sounds. The reason why the outcomes are different is, in part, because of differences in the respective sound systems of the two languages. Such attempts, as Peirce suggested, can be easily recognized in many words, even though people no longer consciously experience them as imitations. Thus, Saussure's contention that such words can only be interpreted in social context turns out to be partially true. The English and Italian counterparts are more or less conventionally based imitations of perceived sounds. However, even those who do not speak English or Italian, but are familiar with the sounds made by roosters, will see an attempt in both these words to imitate rooster sounds.

HIGH HEELS ARE SIGNS TOO

Martha's videotape of the restaurant scene has many more insights to offer the semiotician. Let us now focus our attention on Cheryl's shoes. As you might have guessed, Cheryl is wearing high-heel pumps. Does this mean anything? a semiotician would immediately ask. In prehistoric times people went barefoot, a custom that continues today among tribes inhabiting warm regions. The first foot coverings were probably animal skins, which the peoples of the Stone Age (until about 4000 B.C.) in northern Europe and Asia tied around their ankles in cold weather. Such footwear was the likely ancestor of the European and native North American skin moccasin and the leather and felt boots still worn by certain peoples. The original purpose of shoes was, no doubt, to protect the feet and to allow people to walk on hurtful and injurious terrain. But high-heel shoes seem to contravene this function. They are uncomfortable and awkward to wear, yet millions of women wear them. Obviously, the semiotic story of high-heel shoes has other parts to it. Like cigarettes, they are most likely accouterments in sexual acting.

High heels date back to the late sixteenth-century. The fashion was encouraged by Louis XIV of France, who apparently wore them to increase his modest height. By the mid-nineteenth century, heeled shoes, low-cut, laced or buttoned to the ankle, became the fashion craze for females. In the twentieth century, according to changing fashion trends, women adopted high, spike, or low heels, with thin, platform, or wedge soles, in closed shoes or sandals. But the wearing of high heels as a sexual prop, as Cheryl did, has prevailed up to the present time.

High heels force the body to tilt, thus emphasizing the buttocks and breasts: they highlight the female's sexuality. They also accentuate the role of feet in sexuality. As the social historian William Rossi[11] has written, across many cultures feet are perceived as sexually desirable. Putting on stockings and high heels is everywhere a highly erotic act, and this is borne out by the fact that in most sexual portrayals, women are perceived as looking sexier in stockings and high-heel shoes than without them. Even in fairy tales, the "lure of the shoe" undergirds such stories as *Cinderella* and *The Golden Slipper*.

High heels are *fetishes*. The fetish is a sign that evokes devotion to itself. In some cultures, this devotion is a result of the belief that an object has magical or metaphysical attributes. In our culture, the term refers generally to objects or body parts through which sexual fantasies are played out.

Common fetishes in Western society are feet, shoes, and articles of intimate female apparel. Psychologists believe that fetishism serves to alleviate feelings of sexual inadequacy, usually among males. However, in a fascinating book on fetishism, Valerie Steele[12] points out that we are all fetishists to a large extent, and that the line between the "normal" and the "abnormal" in sexual mores and practices is vague. Fashion designers, for instance, steal regularly from the fetishist's closet, promoting ultra-high heels, corsets, pointy bras, frilly underwear, latex cat suits. The appropriation has been so complete that people wearing such garments and apparel are unaware of their fetishist origins.

To a male, high-heel shoes are erotically exciting. In terms of the courtship ritual that our two protagonists are performing in the restaurant vignette, the high heels worn by Cheryl allow her to send out powerful sexual signals, including a sense of domination tinged with sensuality.

THE SYSTEM OF EVERYDAY LIFE

Cigarettes and high-heel shoes are props that allow human beings to act out their constantly varying roles on the stage of everyday life. Perhaps the most interesting part of the semiotician's job is to explain the nature of the script that is used by people to act on that stage. The sociologist Erving Goffman (1922–82) drew attention to the idea that everyday life is very much like the theater,[13] because it involves a skillful staging of character. The two protagonists in our imaginary scene are indeed "staged characters," individuals who know how to utilize facial expressions, bodily gestures, and various props to impress and attract each other. They are both the cast of characters and the audience. The Latin term for "cast of characters" is *dramatis personae,* literally, "the persons of the drama," a term betraying a theatrical origin to the very concept of *personhood.* Indeed each one of us seems to be bent on preparing our individual *persona* or *self* for presentation to spectators. Gender-coded differences in bodily schemas (posture, facial expression, rhythm or pace of gesturing, etc.) are understandable because they are part of a recognizable social *script.*[14] An intriguing 1976 study by Mary Jenni demonstrated how these schemas show up even in something as trivial as the ways in which individuals carry books.[15] She noticed that females tended to clasp books against their bodies with one or both arms wrapped around the books, whereas males almost always carried their books in one hand at the side of their bodies.

This gender-coded manifestation of unconscious bodily schemas illustrates how deeply rooted the influence of culture is on patterns of behavior. We do indeed think and act routinely as if all life was a stage, as William Shakespeare so aptly put it.

The question of how our systems of everyday life came into existence is an intriguing one. The scientific record suggests that life in early hominid groups revolved around duties associated with hunting, crop-gathering, and cooking. These were shared by individuals to enhance the overall efficiency of the group. As the brain of these early hominids developed, their ability to communicate their thoughts increased proportionately. Plaster casts of skulls dating back around 100,000 years, which allow scientists to reconstruct ancient brains, reveal that human beings had brains of a size similar to ours. Archeologists record the first appearances of cave art shortly after this time, and linguists speculate that human language had also started to emerge, a development that would come to have profound implications for all aspects of human activity. About 10,000 years ago, plants were domesticated, followed shortly by the domestication of animals. This agricultural revolution set the stage for the events in human history that eventually led to civilization.

The first human groups with language developed an early form of culture, to which scientists refer as the *tribe*, a fully functional system of everyday life to which even modern humans seem instinctively to relate. In complex societies, where various cultures, subcultures, countercultures, and parallel cultures are in constant competition with each other, and where the shared territory is too large to allow for members of the society to come together for key ritualistic purposes, the tendency for individuals is to relate instinctively to smaller tribal-type groups (communities, clubs, etc.). This inclination towards *tribalism*, as the communications theorist Marshall McLuhan (1911–80) emphasized, reverberates constantly within humans, and may be the source of the sense of alienation that many people who live in complex and impersonal social settings experience.

The early tribes were distinct from previous hominid groupings because they organized their daily life through a *signifying order*—a system of signs that gave stability and continuity to group life because it allowed members to pass along what they had learned from one generation to the next. Archeological evidence suggests that as the members of the early tribes became culturally more sophisticated, that is, as their signifying orders, expressive capacities, and technological systems grew in complexity, they sought larger and larger territories in order to accommodate their growing needs. The tribes thus grew in population and diversity, cooperating or amalgamating with other tribes in their new settings. The anthropologist Desmond Morris calls the complex tribal systems that came into existence as a consequence of expansion and amalgamation, *super-tribes.*[16] The first super-tribes date back only 4,000 to 5,000 years, when the first city-states emerged.

A modern *society* is a super-tribe, a collectivity of individuals who do not necessarily trace their ancestral roots to the founding tribe, but who nevertheless participate in the signifying order of that tribe as it has evolved over time. Participation in that order allows individuals to inter-act in both spontaneous and ritualistic ways that are perceived as "nor-mal." Unlike tribes, however, the mode of interaction does not unfold on a personal level because it is impossible to know, or know about, every-one living in the same super-tribe. Moreover, a society often encompasses more than one signifying order. Consider what people living in the soci-ety known as the U.S. call loosely "American culture." The signifying order underlying American culture traces its origins to an amalgam of the signifying orders of the founding tribes of European societies who settled in the U.S. American society has also accommodated aboriginal and other parallel cultural systems, with different ways of life, different languages, different rituals. Unlike his or her tribal ancestor, an American can there-fore live apart from the dominant signifying order, in a parallel one, or become a member of a subculture; he or she can also learn and utilize dif-ferent signifying orders, each with its own communication and lifestyle codes. But like tribal systems, American society still defines the "normal" through the primary signifying order; those living apart from this order will typically face risks, such as being subjected to various forms of ridicule, censure, and even ostracism.

THE SCIENCE OF SIGNS

Although the primary task of semiotics is observing and documenting how the world's many systems of everyday life provide different scripts for so-cial living, its ultimate goal is understanding the human need for a *master script* (or *master playwright*), a theme captured skillfully by Luigi Pirandello (1867–1936) in his great play, *Six Characters in Search of an Author* (1921). Aware that a direct path to the *master script* is unlikely to be found, semiotics is content to glean its insights into the human meaning-quest from a study of the distinct meanings that are generated through the world's various systems of everyday life. This book will take you through some of the many pathways that make up such systems. From the beginnings of time, these have given reassurance to our species that there is continuity, purpose, and meaning to life.

In its oldest usage, the term *semeiotica* was applied to the study of the physiological symptoms induced by particular body states and changes. Hippocrates (460?–377? B.C.), the founder of Western medical science, defined symptoms as the *sema* ("signs" in Greek) of these states and changes. Hippocrates' term was introduced into philosophical inquiry by the British philosopher John Locke (1632–1704) in his *Essay Concerning Human Understanding*, published in 1690, in which he defined *semeiotics* as the "doctrine of signs." At the start of the twentieth century Saussure used the term *semiology*, instead, to refer to the science that he thought would eventually study all kinds of signs systematically.[17] Today, Hippocrates' original term, now spelled *semiotics*, is the preferred one.

An interesting definition of semiotics was provided by Umberto Eco (1932–) in his 1976 book, *A Theory of Semiotics*. Eco is the author of the best-selling novel, *The Name of the Rose*, which has stimulated a lot of interest in semiotics in recent years. He defined semiotics as "the discipline studying everything that can be used in order to lie," because if "something cannot be used to tell a lie, conversely it cannot be used to tell the truth; it cannot, in fact, be used to tell at all."[18] Despite its apparent facetiousness, this is a rather insightful statement. It implies that signs do not tell the whole story, or the whole "truth." Humans, in fact, talk convincingly all the time about things that are entirely fictitious, with no back-up empirical evidence. In a sense, culture is itself a big lie—a break from our biological heritage that has forced us to live mainly by our wits. As Prometheus proclaimed prophetically in Aeschylus' (525–456 B.C.) drama *Prometheus Bound*, one day "rulers would conquer and control not by strength, nor by violence, but by cunning."

The definition of semiotics that has become the most widely adopted is that put forward by Peirce, who, along with Saussure, is a founder of the modern study of signs. Like Locke, he defined it as the scientific "doctrine" of signs—the term *doctrine* as used by Locke and Peirce refers to a theoretical system of knowledge based on carefully worked out principles, taught or advocated by its adherents. Since Peirce, the field of semiotics has become truly enormous. It now includes, among other things, the study of how animals communicate, of body language, of the arts, of metaphor, of myths, of media messages—in sum, of anything that makes human life *interesting.*

By and large semiotic method has been defined as *structuralist,* because of its focus on systems of meaning as reflexes of innate psychic structures. The premise that guides semiotic research is, therefore, that the recurring patterns of meaning that are captured and expressed by means such as languages, narratives, and works of art are culture-specific reflexes of universal patterns in the human psyche. Cultures are seen as huge *templates,* each with its own particular configuration of openings through which these patterns take on specific *forms.* The forms produced by the different templates may be dissimilar, but the psychic substance, or *content,* from which they issue forth is the same. In the late 1960s, however, the French semiotician Jacques Derrida (1930–) rejected this premise, proposing a counter-approach that came to be known widely as *post-structuralism,* by which he denounced the search for universal patterns of meaning behind the cultural templates. Derrida's theory has had particular impact on the field of literary criticism. But, on the whole, semioticians continue to endorse structuralist principles and, thus, the idea that there are basic meaning structures in the human species.

The view of semiotics as a *science* is not the traditional one. In the Western world this term has, since the times of the philosopher and geometer Pythagoras (582?–500? B.C.), designated the objective knowledge of facts of the natural world, gained and verified by exact observation, experiment, and ordered thinking. The question as to whether or not human nature can be studied with the same objectivity has, however, always been a problematic one. Indeed, many semioticians refuse to call their field a science, for they believe that any study of the human mind can never be totally objective, preferring instead to characterize it a *rhetorical* science.

This view of scientific method is not unique to semiotics. When the German physicist and Nobel laureate Werner Heisenberg (1901–76) put forward his now famous *uncertainty principle* during the first part of the twentieth century, it became the view of all physicists. Heisenberg's principle can be illustrated in concrete terms as follows. Suppose that a physicist born and reared in the United States observes a previously unknown natural phenomenon and then jots down his or her observations on a notepad in English (his or her native language). At the same instant that the American physicist observes the phenomenon, another scientist born and reared in the Philippines observes it and then also writes down his or her observations on a notepad in Tagalog (his or her native language). Now, the question becomes: Will the observations recorded on the two notepads coincide? Or will they be significantly different? Whose observations will be more "accurate" or "true"? Clearly, it will be impossible to decide *objectively* which notepad will contain observations that are closer to the "truth." This is why physicists no longer envisage the discovery of absolute truths. They now prefer to talk about approximate truths and observer-dependent realities.

PRINCIPLES OF SEMIOTIC ANALYSIS

Three general principles underlie semiotic analysis. The first is that all systems of everyday life have tribal roots, no matter how modern they may be. The first task of the semiotician is, therefore, to wrestle out the original tribal features from such systems. Our imaginary restaurant vignette shows that modern societies have hardly eliminated the tribal need for sexual acting in courtship. As in tribal rites, modern courtship continues to involve a presentable body image, sexually signifying postures, appropriate garments, and so on. As anthropologist Desmond Morris has aptly written, the modern human being refuses "to lose its tribe."[19]

The second principle states that systems of everyday life tend to influence people's notions of what is *natural* in human behavior. The second task of the semiotician is, thus, to sift out the truly *natural* from the *conventional.* In North America it is perceived as "natural" for women to wear high heels and put on lipstick, but "unnatural" for men to do so. In reality, the classification of a clothing item or a cosmetic technique in terms of gender is a matter of historically-based convention, not of naturalness or lack thereof. In the Baroque seventeenth century, high heels, as we saw above, were the fashion craze for noblemen and male aristocrats generally, who obviously considered it quite "natural" to wear them.

The third principle asserts that systems of everyday life influence world-views. Consider the concept of health. In our culture we say that disease "slows us down," "destroys our bodies," or "impairs" body functions. Such expressions reflect a mechanistic view of the body in Western culture. Tagalog, the indigenous language of the Philippines, has no such equivalents. Its expressions reveal a holistic view of the body as connected to spiritual forces, to the social ambiance, and to nature. As a consequence, people reared in English-speaking cultures are inclined to evaluate disease as a localized phenomenon, within the body, separate from the larger social and ecological context. Tagalog people, on the other hand, are inclined to evaluate disease as tied directly to that context.

The foregoing discussion does not imply that there are no objectively determinable symptoms or diseases. Humans the world over have an innate physiological warning system which alerts them to dangerous changes in body states. Many of the symptoms produced by this system have, of course, been documented by the modern medical sciences. But in daily life, the human being's evaluation of, and response to, the body's warning signals are mediated by culture. In a remarkably perceptive book, *Illness As Metaphor,* the well-known writer Susan Sontag demonstrated eloquently how culture intervenes in people's interpretation and evaluation of diseases.[20] Using the example of cancer, Sontag pointed out that when the disease was first diagnosed, the very word *cancer* would kill some patients who might not necessarily have otherwise succumbed to the malignancy. This was due to the fact that cancer was conceived as an evil, invincible predator, not just a disease; therefore, most people with cancer did indeed become demoralized by learning what disease they had. Sontag's point is that health cannot be defined ahistorically, aculturally, or in purely objective terms. The ways in which a tribe or society understands and defines health will largely determine how it views and treats disease, what life expectancy it sees as normal, and what features of body image it considers to be attractive, ugly, normal, or abnormal. Some cultures view a healthy body as being a lean and muscular one, others a plump and rotund one. Certain cultures perceive a healthy lifestyle as one that is based on rigorous physical activity, while others perceive it as one that is based on a more leisurely and sedentary style of living. The list could go on and on.

Medical practitioners, too, are not immune to cultural world-views. The body is as much symbolism as it is organic substance, and this can have serious consequences for the practice of medicine. A few years ago, psychologists found that medical specialists trained in private schools were more likely to achieve distinction and prominence by working on the head as opposed to the lower part of the body, on the surface as opposed to the inside of the body, and on the male as opposed to the female body.[21] This comes as no surprise to the semiotician, who knows that parts of the body or its sex possess a symbolic significance that influences world-view.

It is subjects such as cigarettes and high heels, which might at first appear to be trivial, that expose implicit world-views. Semiotics ultimately allows us to filter the implicit meanings and images that swarm and flow through us every day, immunizing us against becoming passive victims of a situation. By understanding the images, the situation is changed, and we become active interpreters of signs.

2

WHAT DOES IT MEAN?

How Humans Represent the World

> The whole visible universe is but a storehouse of images and signs to which the imagination will give a relative place and value; it is a sort of pasture which the imagination must digest and transform.
>
> —Charles Baudelaire (1821–67)

Martha's videotape of the restaurant scene contains many more interesting episodes for the semiotician to digest and ponder. In one segment, Ted's attention is caught by a pin that Cheryl has on her dress. Noticing its unconventional shape, he inquires: "What an interesting design. What does it *mean?*" Cheryl answers as follows: "It *represents* a water spirit in Chinese culture. The water spirit symbolizes the vitality of life."

Such questions and answers are common in human affairs, even though we rarely give them much consideration, beyond the fact that they allow us to satisfy our curiosity. But human curiosity is a remarkable thing. The crux of semiotic analysis is, in effect, to unravel what something *means,* or more accurately, *represents.* It is the *science of representation,* and its primary objective is to develop notions and ideas that can be applied to deciphering the meanings of even seemingly trivial things like cigarettes and high heels. As we saw in the previous chapter, notions such as *sign, code,* and *text* allow us to understand with much more accuracy how we extract meaning from the things and actions that we come across routinely in our society.

These also made it quite evident that even something as ordinary as flirting can hardly be considered random behavior. Rather, it unfolds as a recognizable form of behavior inherited through the channel of cultural history. Semiotically, culture can be defined as a *container* of the *meaning-making strategies* and *forms of behavior* that people employ to carry out their daily routines. Culture is the phenomenon that sets the human species apart from all other species. Humans transmit what they have learned, not through the genetic code, but through the *cultural codes* that undergird the customs, traditions, languages, art works, and scientific practices that fill the world's *cultural containers*. These may differ substantively in contents, and may show considerable variation from one historical epoch to another, but at their core they are all reflexes of a universal need for meaning.

The ability to create and make use of a vast repertoire of signs can be traced to the development within the human species of an extremely large brain, averaging 1400 cc/85.4 cu. in., more than two million years ago. The brain's great size, complexity, and slow rate of maturation, with connections among its nerve cells being added through the pre-pubescent years of life, has made it possible for humanity, in effect, to step outside the slow forces of biological evolution and to meet new material demands by means of conscious rapid adjustments rather than by force of genetic adaptation. This is why humans have the ability to survive in a wide range of habitats and in extreme environmental conditions without further mutations. However, on balance, the prolonged juvenile stage of brain and skull development in relation to the time required to reach sexual maturity has exposed newly born human beings to an unparalleled risk among animals. Each new infant is born with relatively few innate traits yet with a vast number of potential behaviors and, therefore, must be reared in a cultural setting to achieve its biological potential. Without such rearing, survival is unlikely. So, while culture may have taken over from biology in charting humanity's future course, it has done so at a considerable risk. No one really knows why this has come about in our species, although there certainly are no lack of theories attempting to explain it.

The world's *sign* systems provide key pieces of evidence for solving the riddle of culture and for probing the mystery behind the human *meaning quest*. But, what is *meaning*? As it turns out, the word has many *meanings* itself. In 1923 two scholars, C. K. Ogden and I. A. Richards, found 16 common meanings for this word in English:[1] In a sentence like "Does life have a meaning?" for instance, the term is equivalent to "purpose." This is a universal concept which reveals that the human animal, aware of its mortality, is distinguished by its need to know if its life has a purpose. The human meaning search is a real phenomenon. It is what art, philosophy, and religion have always sought to understand. However, in sentences such as "What does love mean to you?" or "A green light means go," the term *meaning* is equivalent to "conveyance" or "indication." This is what we called *referential* or *representational* meaning in the previous chapter. In general, when we ask "What does it mean?" we are really asking, "What does it *stand for* or *represent?*" *Representation* is literally "presenting again" (re-presenting) some aspect of the world through signs, codes, or texts.

Representation implies *classification,* that is, the organization of the meanings captured and conveyed by signs, codes, and texts into *categories.* This makes the world much more understandable in human terms. But classification does not tell the whole truth, and is in fact highly variable across cultures. To get a firmer grasp of what this means, consider the world of plants and animals. In theory, human beings are capable of classifying this physically perceivable world by simple trial and error into *edible* (non-perilous) and *non-edible* (perilous)—that is, people living anywhere on earth are capable of classifying any species of plant or animal that they find by experimentation to cause disease or death as non-edible, and any species that does not as edible. But, in practice, the inclusion of a particular non-perilous species in one or the other category is a culture-specific decision. Rabbits, many kinds of flowers, and silkworms, for instance, would be classified by and large as non-edible by North American society, even though they cause no harm to health. On the other hand, many Europeans regularly consume rabbit meat and various types of flowers and Mexicans eat cooked silkworms with no adverse physical reactions whatsoever. But if any of these were to be presented to North Americans in a cooked form, chances are that they would react adversely if told what they were about to eat. Thus the *meaning* of "rabbit" or "silkworm" is clearly different from culture to culture. World-views are built up from the acquisition of such meanings, or categories, in specific cultural contexts.

The fact that a particular culture predisposes its users to attend to certain meanings does not imply that members of other cultures are incapable of perceiving the world in similar ways. Indeed, although people from a different culture might construe a cigarette differently from how we defined it in the previous chapter, they can easily understand what it means in our culture if we simply explain to them its meaning as a sexual prop. They might react with surprise or consternation, but they will nevertheless be able to grasp its meaning. Practical *knowledge* of the world is culture-specific, built on the categories used to classify the world that an individual acquires in social context; but the capacity for knowing is limitless, and can easily transcend the very culture-specific categories that commonly guide it.

The act of *representation* entails a corresponding act of *interpretation*. Simply defined, this is the ability to extract an appropriate meaning from some sign or text. Although interpretation is subject to much individual variation, it is not an open-ended process; it involves familiarity with the meanings of signs in specific contexts, with the type of code to which they belong, and with the nature of their referents—concrete referents are less subject to variation than are abstract ones. Without such familiarity, communication would be virtually impossible in common social settings. In essence, interpretation is a purposeful selection of specific meanings among the boundless meanings of which the human mind is capable. In art and performance, one talks of interpretation as if it were less than the original creation of the work of art. But this is not correct. The interpreter is a creator of meanings as well. The late Canadian pianist Glen Gould was no less an artist for not having composed *The Well-Tempered Clavier,* which he so masterfully played. He effaced himself the better to serve Bach's model. The more successful was he at his task, the more deeply involved did he become in Bach's art form. Every touch, every turn of phrase, became a mirror of his own creative imagination.

TYPES OF MEANING

Now, let's take a closer look at the process of *representation,* the way a semiotician would. First, there are two levels of representation—the *denotative* and the *connotative.* You already have a sense of what this involves when you use everyday words. Think of the word *red.* What does it mean? At one level, it refers to a color at the lower end of the visible spectrum, but at another level, it refers to such things as an emotional state ("I'm red with anger"), a financial predicament ("I'm in the red"), or a political ideology ("He's been a red communist all his life"). Virtually all words have such levels of meaning. So, the discussion that follows will not be totally foreign to you. It is intended simply to formalize what you already know intuitively.

A sign represents something observed, perceived, felt, or thought. This is what it *denotes,* or calls attention to. The word *red* denotes a color on the spectrum. The word *house* denotes a "structure for human habitation." The kind of "habitation structure" that it refers to is not specific, but rather, prototypical (a perfect example of a particular type). The word *house* can thus be used to denote many different types—large, small, cubical, spherical. In our society, this word will normally evoke the image of a cubical, rather than a spherical habitation structure, because that is the typical shape of our houses. But, in others, such as the Dogon society of the Sudan or the settlements of Zambian herders, the equivalent words will denote a spherical or conical structure.

A sign can also have a different level of meanings, known as *connotative.* The uses of the word *red* to refer to an "emotional state," a "financial predicament," or a "political ideology" are examples of connotative meanings. These allow people to use a manageable set of signs to represent a large array of potential meanings. There are three basic kinds of connotative processes: *extensional, emotive,* and *symbolic.*

The additional set of meanings that a sign acquires through usage are its *connotative extensions.* The word *house* connotes a "legislative quorum," an "audience," and a "dormitory" by *extension,* as can be seen in such sentences as "The house is in session," "The house roared with laughter," and "They sleep in one of the houses at Harvard University." These new meanings are *extensional* because they presuppose "structures" of certain kinds that are "inhabited" in some specific way by "humans."

The emotional nuances that can be conveyed through a sign are called its *emotive connotations.* The word *yes* in English denotes "affirmation," but one can communicate doubt or incredulity through this same word by simply raising one's voice as in a question: *Yes?* Similarly, one can convey conviction by stressing it: *Yessss!* The same kinds of emotive connotations can be imparted through the word *house:* "Are you sure that's a house? It looks more like a garage" (= incredulity); "Yes, it's a *house,* not a garage!" (= conviction).

The additional meanings that a sign acquires in specific social contexts at particular moments of its history are its *symbolic connotations.* In the expressions "the house of God" and the "house of ill repute," *house* connotes a church and a prostitution establishment respectively. These differ from the extensional connotations of *house,* discussed above, because they cannot be figured out solely in terms of the word's prototypical meaning, but must be learned from their use in social context. The meanings of cigarettes, high heels, perfumes, brand names of cars and of clothes, and other such things, are all similarly symbolic.

In 1957, the psychologists C. E. Osgood, G. J. Suci, and P. H. Tannenbaum developed an interesting technique for fleshing out the connotations of words, known as the *semantic differential.*[2] By posing a series of questions to subjects about a specific concept—Is it good or bad? Weak or strong?—as seven-point scales, with the opposing adjectives at each end, they were able to sift out any general pattern from them using statistical techniques. As an example, suppose you ask a group of people to evaluate the concept *U.S. President* in terms of categories such as young–old, practical–idealistic, modern–traditional, attractive–bland, friendly–stern, each on a scale of 1 to 7, as shown in figure 2.1.

Those who feel that the President should be modern, would place a mark towards the corresponding end of that scale. Those who believe that the President should not be too young or too old would place a mark near the middle of the young-old scale. People who think that the President should be bland-looking, would place a mark towards the corresponding end of the attractive-bland scale, and so on. If you were to ask larger and larger groups of people to rate the President in terms of such scales, you would then be able to draw a profile of the presidency in terms of what it connotes to people. Remarkably, research utilizing the semantic differential has shown that, while the connotations

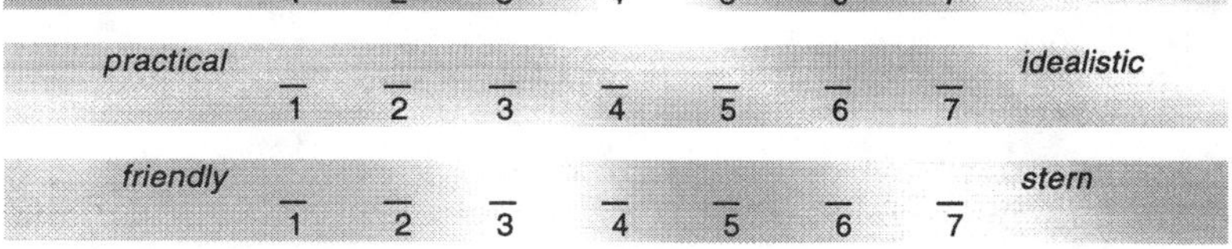

Figure 2.1: Connotations of "President"

of concepts are subject to personal interpretation and subjective feelings, the range of variation is rarely a matter of randomness. In other words, the experiments using the semantic differential have shown that connotation is constrained by culture, and thus prototypical. For example, the word *noise* turns out to be a highly emotional concept for the Japanese, who rate it consistently at the emotional ends of the scales presented to them; whereas it is a fairly neutral concept for Americans who place it in the mid-range of the same scales.

In a fundamental sense, the semiotician is a "scientist of connotations," as the French semiotician Roland Barthes (1915–80) claimed throughout his career. The aim of our analysis of Cheryl and Ted's smoking performance in the previous chapter was, in fact, to sift out the sexual connotations that cigarettes and high-heel shoes have in specific situations. Recall that it would not have been possible to decipher those connotations without taking into account the physical and social *context* of the scene. If you came across a crumpled up and discarded cigarette package on a sidewalk on a city street, you would interpret it as a piece of rubbish. But if you saw the very same package encased in a picture frame, hanging on a wall in an art gallery, autographed by some artist, and given the title *Waste,* then you would hardly perceive it as garbage. You would interpret it in a markedly different way—as a symbol of a "throw-away society," as a metaphor of a "materialistic culture," or as some other symbol. Clearly, the package's *context* of occurrence—its location on a sidewalk versus its insertion in a picture frame displayed in an art gallery—determines the kind of meaning you will extract from it. But note that the *meaning* of the context, too, is determined by culture. Only those living in cultures with art galleries in it will know enough to interpret the cigarette displayed on the gallery's walls as a "work of art."

The art gallery is a perfect example of a *code,* because it entails recognizing what a painting is, how paintings differ from each other, and how they can be arranged (on walls, in sections of the gallery). A code is an organizing grid of signs; it is what allows individuals to extract meanings from signs. There are many codes in a culture. These regulate how the members of the culture make messages and meanings together. Indeed, semiotically speaking culture itself is one huge code, or *macrocode,* constituting a *signifying network* that unites individual signs into a cohesive circuitry of intertwined meanings. Signs are linked to each other in this network as circuits are linked in an electrical system.

A face-to-face conversation, for instance, is a code-based event, involving not only the deployment of a language code, but also gestural, facial, and other nonverbal codes. When people talk to each other, they not only use words, but unconsciously use hand gestures, facial expressions, and other kinds of body language. The verbal message is "woven together" with the resources of different codes into a *text*. Not only routine conversations, but musical compositions, stage plays, dance styles, and ceremonies, are also the products of our *text-making* capacity. The terms *message* and *text* are not synonymous. A message refers to *what* one wishes to communicate; a text refers to *how* the message is constructed.

TYPES OF SIGNS

Much work within semiotics has been devoted to identifying and understanding the main types of signs of which the human brain is capable. The American semiotician Thomas A. Sebeok has identified six types—*symptom, signal, index, icon, symbol,* and *name.*[3] Although some semioticians would exclude symptom and signal from their purview of investigation, Sebeok correctly insists that their inclusion would force semiotics to consider the relation of biological factors to cultural ones more seriously in its investigation of *semiosis*—the ability to produce and comprehend signs.

Let's consider this idea a little further. Symptoms are bodily signs that are indicative of physical states or conditions. But their identification as such is filtered culturally. Facial acne, for example, is recognized as a chronic disease of the skin afflicting adolescents and young adults, linked in large part to lifestyle factors (diet, stress, etc.) in Western cultures. The symptoms associated with this condition are pimples (furuncles) on the face, back, and chest. But the appearance of pimples on the face is not seen as indicative of disease in other cultures, as attested by the lack of words equivalent to *acne* in many of the world's languages. The Inuit tribes in northern Manitoba do not recognize the physical conditions associated with *rickets*—a softening and, often, bending of the bones usually caused by a lack of vitamin D and insufficient exposure to sunlight—as symptomatic. As their lack of a word for this condition testifies, the people living in those cultures do not perceive this pattern of bone formation as indicative of an abnormality of the skeletal system. This is akin to our lack of recognition of the syndrome that Malaysian, Japanese, Indonesian, and Thai peoples call *latah,* which results from sudden fright. Lacking an equivalent term for this state, we simply do not recognize it as a condition, although it clearly exists (as people living in these other cultures would avow). As such examples show, the whole process of diagnosing a disease is a semiotic one, since it involves deciphering and establishing what constitutes a symptom in cultural terms.

A *signal* is a bodily emission (sound, odor, etc.) or movement (head tilt, eye wink, etc.). In most species, signals have the primary function of identifying the sex and species of an animal's potential mate. For example, a fish called the stickleback uses a system of interlocking releasers to orchestrate its mating. When its breeding season arrives, the underside of each male turns bright red. This color attracts females, but also provokes attacks by other males. Red objects of almost any description will trigger male stickleback aggression. A female responds to the male's red signal with a curious approach posture that displays her swollen belly full of eggs. This incites the male to perform a zigzag dance that leads the female to the tunnel-like nest he has built for her. The female snuggles into the nest, whereupon the male touches her tail with his nose and quivers. The ensuing vibration causes the female to release her eggs for the male to fertilize. If the male fails to perform the last part of the dance, the female will not lay her eggs. Vibrating the female with a pencil will also work perfectly well, but the male in this case, not having gone through the last stage of the ritual, will refuse to fertilize the eggs and eats them instead.

Signaling can, of course, have other functions. Worker honey bees, for instance, are endowed with a sophisticated system for signaling the location of a cache of food to their hive members. Upon returning to the hive from foraging trips, these bees have the extraordinary capacity to inform the other bees in the hive, through movement sequences, about the direction, distance, and quality of the food with amazing accuracy. This signaling system is known as a dance because its movements resemble the actions of human dancing. The remarkable thing about bee dancing is that it is representational, thus sharing with human signs the feature of conveying information about something in the absence of the thing to which it refers. Several kinds of dance patterns have been documented by zoologists. In the "round" dance, the bee moves in circles, alternating to the left and to the right. This dance is apparently used by the bees to signal that the cache of food is nearby. When the food source is farther away, the bee dances in a "wagging" fashion, moving in a straight line while wagging its abdomen from side to side and then returning to its starting point. The straight line in this dance points in the direction of the food source, the energy level of the dance indicates how rich the food source is, and the tempo provides information about its distance from the hive.

Despite their noteworthiness, such examples of signaling are hardly ever deliberate in the human sense. They are instinctual, even though they sometimes do not appear to us to be so. A classic example of how easily we are duped by our own perceptions of animal signaling is the well-documented case of Clever Hans. Clever Hans was a world-famous German "talking horse" who lived at the turn of the twentieth century. He appeared to understand human language and communicate human answers to questions by tapping the alphabet with his front hoof—one tap for *A*, two taps for *B*, and so on. A panel of scientists ruled out deception by the horse's owner. The horse, it was claimed, could talk! Clever Hans was awarded honors and proclaimed an important scientific discovery. Eventually, however, an astute member of the committee of scientists who had examined the horse, the Dutch psychologist Oskar Pfungst, discovered that Clever Hans could not talk without *observing* his questioners. The horse decoded signals that humans transmit and over which they have no conscious control. Clever Hans sensed when to tap his hoof and when not to tap it in response to inadvertent cues from his human handler, who would visibly relax when the horse had tapped the proper number of times. To show this, Pfungst simply blindfolded Clever Hans who, as a consequence, ceased to be so clever. The "Clever Hans phenomenon," as it has come to be known in the annals of psychology, has been demonstrated with other animals—for instance, a dog will bark in response to inadvertent human signals.

Many human signals are also instinctual. Psychological studies have shown, for instance, that men are sexually attracted to women with large pupils, which signal strong sexual interest and make a female look younger. This might explain the vogue in central Europe during the 1920s and 1930s of women using a pupil-dilating crystalline alkaloid eye-drop liquid derived from the drug known popularly as *belladonna* ("beautiful woman" in Italian) as a cosmetic to enhance facial appearance. But human beings also have the ability to send out signals consciously and intentionally. A look or tilt of the head can be used to indicate to someone the presence in the room of a certain person; a wink of the eye can be used to communicate the need to maintain secrecy or sexual interest; and so on.

INDEXES, ICONS, AND SYMBOLS

The power of human *semiosis* (sign-making) lies in the fact that it is not limited to instinctual signaling. The signs that humans make allow them to carry the world "around in their heads," because they permit the recall of the things, beings, events, feelings, to which they refer, even if these are *displaced* in space and time, that is, not physically present for the person to observe and perceive. This *displacement* property of signs has endowed the human species with the remarkable capacity to think about the world beyond the realm of responses to stimuli to which most other species are constrained, and thus to reflect upon it at any time or in any context whatsoever.

Consider, for instance, the action of pointing a finger at an object, say, a ball. This action will invariably direct someone's eye to its location. The pointing index finger is an example of a remarkable type of sign known, logically enough, as an *index*. But there is more to *indexicality* (the capacity for indexical representation), than just finger-pointing. Words such as *here, there, up, down,* are also indexical signs. When someone says "I am here, you are there," he or she is referring to the relative position of persons to each other. Personal pronouns such as *I, you, he, she* are also indexes because they refer to different people in relation to where they are located in the line of sight—*I* is the origin, *you* is closer to the origin than is *he,* and so on.

In addition to such forms, there are many examples of abstract forms of indexicality in languages across the world. Take, for instance, the English expressions *think up, think over,* and *think out:* "When did you think up that preposterous idea?" "You should think over carefully what you just said"; "You should think out the entire problem." Even though these refer to abstract ideas, they nonetheless refer to them in ways that presuppose location and movement: *think up* elicits a mental image of upward movement, portraying the activity of thinking as if it were an object being extracted physically from a kind of imaginary mental terrain; *think over* evokes the image of an internal eye scanning the mind; *think out* suggests the action of taking a deeply buried thought out of the mind so that it can be held up, presumably, for the mind's eye to see and examine.

The presence of such expressions in languages across the world suggests something rather intriguing about the possible origins of language. Representing abstract concepts in accordance with the laws of physical perception suggests an evolutionary link between language, cognition, and the senses. Languages across the world show the same feature of representing ideas as if they were objects in time and space, with physical properties: in Sanskrit the word *maya* (perceiving form in thought) contains the particle *ma* (to measure or lay out); in Italian, the verb *pensarci* (to think about something, to think over), is constructed with the indexical particle *ci* (here, there); in English, *perceive* derives from Latin *cipio* (to seize) and *per* (through), *examine* from *agmen* (to pull out from a row) and *ex* (from), and *prospect* from Latin *spectus* (looking) and *pro* (forward, ahead).

Now, consider the ball again. If location is not a requirement of the situation, one could alternatively refer to the same object by *showing* what a ball looks like. To do this, one could use gesture, cupping one's hands and moving them as if one were "drawing" the ball in space: that is, moving the left hand in a counterclockwise circular motion and the right one in a clockwise motion at the same time. One could do virtually the same thing on a piece of paper with a pencil in each hand. In both cases, the sign that results is a circular figure resembling the outline of a ball. This type of sign is known as an *icon.*

An icon is a sign that simulates, replicates, reproduces, imitates, or resembles properties of its referent. A portrait, for instance, is contrived as a reproduction of the actual face of a person from the perspective of the artist; a perfume scent is made chemically to simulate a natural aroma or fragrance; words such as *drip, bang, screech* were obviously coined as attempts to imitate certain sounds. *Iconicity* (the capacity for iconic representation) is clearly based on sensory knowledge. Its presence in the system of everyday life is so pervasive that people are hardly aware of it. If you have a Macintosh computer or a Windows program for your IBM, you will see icons displayed on a screen, representing available functions or resources in a visual way. On the doors of public toilets, you will see figures representing males and females also in a visual way. If you listen carefully to Beethoven's *Pastoral* symphony or Rossini's *William Tell Overture,* for instance, you will hear musical icons that are evocative of the sounds found in nature (bird calls, thunder, wind). Icons are everywhere.

One of the key figures of semiotics, Charles Peirce, who was introduced in the previous chapter saw iconicity as the primary, or default, way of representing the world, precisely because it is tied to sensory knowledge. This is why its handiwork shows up even in prehistoric etchings, small sculptures, and relief carvings of animals and female figures found in caves throughout Europe that go back some 30,000 to 40,000 years. The appearance of such art is probably the end-result of something that is not much different from the kind of hand gesture made to represent the ball described above. With some cutting, sculpting, or drawing instrument in one's hands, it would be a fairly straightforward task to transfer the imaginary picture of the ball made through gesture onto some surface, using the same kinds of movements. Indeed, this is probably what happened in human prehistory. It was only at a later point in time that the hand movements used to make those works of art became more abbreviated. At that point, figures became more condensed and abstract, leading to the invention of picture writing. Archeological research suggests, in fact, that the origins of alphabetic writing lie in symbols previously made out of elemental shapes that were used as image-making objects—much like the molds that figurine and coin-makers use today. Only later did they take on more abstract qualities.[4]

The persistence of gesture in human communication is also a testament to the ancient origins of iconicity. Although vocal language is our primary mode of communication, the evolutionary link between speech and gesture is still clearly noticeable. The linguist David McNeill has shown that when people speak they gesture unconsciously, literally "drawing" the concepts they are conveying orally.[5] Over a ten-year period, he painstakingly examined how individuals—of different cultures, children as well as adults, some even neurologically impaired—invariably represent mental images in terms of gesture. For instance, when people talk of "large" things, they typically cup their hands moving them outward in imitation of a swelling motion. When they talk of "small" things, they typically cup their hands moving them inward, mimicking a shrinking motion. McNeill's research suggests that, although vocal language has become the dominant form of communication in humans, the use of the hands has not vanished, but remains a functional subsystem. The story of gesture as a servant of vocal communication is, however, incomplete. Indeed, gesture persists today as the default form of communication when an interaction is otherwise impossible. This happens typically when two people speak different languages. Of course, in individuals with impaired vocal organs, gesture constitutes the primary mode of communication.

This innate "drawing" capacity is also evident in the development of children. The ability to draw the outlines of rudimentary figures emerges at approximately the same time as the first verbal utterances. If a drawing instrument is put in a child's hand at this point in life, he or she will instinctively make random scribbles on a surface. As time passes, the scribbling becomes more and more controlled; shapes become suggestive of geometric figures which, with adult prompting, are soon labeled as "suns" or "faces." At first, children do not appear to draw anything in particular, but instead spontaneously produce forms, which become refined through practice into precise, repeatable shapes. They draw for the pleasure of it, without larger or more explicit associations of meaning. Drawing in early childhood is, in effect, an example of "art for art's sake."

In a generic sense, indexes and icons are types of *symbols,* because they can be used to represent something *displaced,* that is, not physically present for the person to observe and perceive. In semiotic parlance, a sign becomes increasingly *symbolic* the more it has this property of *displacement.* In such cases, its meaning can be gleaned only in terms of convention. Consider the ball again. The easiest and most efficient way to refer to the object in question is to use the word *ball.* But this can be done only if one knows the English language. The word ball is, in fact, a symbol, a sign that stands for a referent in an arbitrary or conventional way and which, therefore, must be learned in social context. Words, in general, are symbolic signs. But any signifier—an object, a sound, a figure—can be used symbolically. A cross can symbolize the concept "Christianity," a "V" configuration made with the index and middle fingers can symbolize the concept "peace," and so on.

The interconnection between symbols and other kinds of signs is not always evident. Take, for instance, a word such as *flow.* It probably was coined as an icon, because the sounds that comprise it suggest an attempt to represent the sound made by moving water. Indeed, a word made with other kinds of sounds would seem, intuitively, to be inappropriate for referring to a stream—*klop, twing, yoot,* for example, do not seem suitable; but *flow* does. The reason why the word flow sounds more "natural" is because it is more *representative* of the sound made by water. Over time, the word has become detached from its sonority and is now understood mainly *symbolically.* Time dims the sounds that many words attempt to capture when they are first coined—a story that repeats itself with virtually every kind of human sign. Practically everything in human representation tends towards the symbolic. This is why the twentieth-century philosopher Ernst Cassirer (1874–1945) characterized the human animal as a *symbolic animal.*

As Charles Peirce also argued, signs are often amalgams of iconic, indexical, and purely arbitrary modes of representation, because they tend to enfold more than one way of referring to something. Take, as an example, the common traffic sign for a crossroads, as seen in Figure 2.2.

The "cross" on this sign is both an icon and a symbol. It is iconic because its form visually represents the outline of a crossing. However, since the cross figure could be used to represent a church in other contexts (with minor changes to its shape), it is also conventional insofar as we need to know that it has been chosen to refer specifically to a crossing. Finally, the sign is an index because when it is placed near a railway crossing it indicates that we are about to reach it. In parallel ways, most signs are amalgams, and will be interpreted as more or less iconic, indexical, or conventional, depending on their uses, their forms, and their purposes.

Nowhere has the use of symbols borne more remarkable fruits than in mathematics and science. Mathematical symbols have given us a unique opportunity to represent the physical world in abstract (displaced) ways, and then experiment with it in a purely intellectual and imaginary fashion. The results of this mental experimentation can then be redirected to the

Figure 2.2: A Railroad Crossing Sign

real world to see what they yield. Often, this leads to real discoveries about that world. Symbolic reasoning in such areas of human thought carries the burden over intuition.

One of the early impressive examples of what this type of reasoning can achieve is the calculation of the earth's circumference by the Greek astronomer, geometer, and geographer, Eratosthenes (275–194 B.C.). Standing, during the summer solstice, at Alexandria, and knowing that it was due north of the city of Syene, with the distance between the two cities being 500 miles, Eratosthenes used an ingenious method for measuring the earth's circumference—without having to physically measure it. At the summer solstice he knew, as an astronomer, that the noon sun was directly overhead at Syene, shining directly down upon it. Thus, he drew a diagram, showing the earth as a circle, labeling the center of the equator with the letter **O** and the cities of Alexandria and Syene with **A** and **B**, respectively, as shown in Figure 2.3.

He then represented the *direction of the sun* (**S'**) over Syene as **BS'** and he reasoned that joining this line to the earth's center **O** would form the

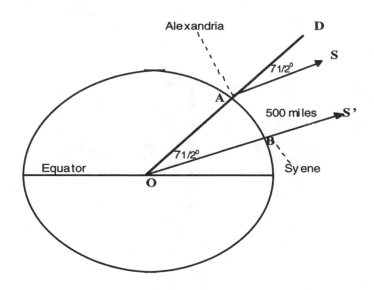

Figure 2.3: Eratosthenes' Representation

straight line **OBS'**, since at that instant the sun was shining straight overhead: that is, at Syene the *overhead direction* and the *direction of the sun* were coincident. At the same moment in Alexandria, he argued, the *direction of the sun* (**S**) could thus be represented with **AS**, a line parallel to **BS'** because, as he knew, sun rays are parallel to each other. Then, on the diagram he extended the line **OA**—the line joining the center of the earth to Alexandria—to an arbitrary point **D**. The line **OAD** thus represented the *overhead direction* at Alexandria. Now, Eratosthenes reasoned, since **AS** was parallel to **BS'**, the angles **DAS** and **AOB**, formed by the line **OAD** cutting the two parallel lines **AS** and **OBS'**, were equal by a theorem of Euclidean geometry. On the basis of this knowledge, Eratosthenes had only to measure **DAS**, which he was able to do easily, being in Alexandria, by measuring the angle of the shadow made by a well near which he was standing. This was the difference between the *overhead direction* and the *direction of the sun* at Syene. He found it to be 7½°. This, then, was also the size of angle **AOB** on the diagram. Moreover, Eratosthenes reasoned, this angle is 7½° of 360° since the earth is virtually a sphere and therefore forms almost a 360° angle. Thus, he proved the angle **AOB** as being ⅟48 of the entire angle at O (7½° of 360°), the circumference of the earth. From another fact of geometry, Eratosthenes knew that the arc **AB**, the distance between Alexandria and Syene, was also ⅟48 of the circumference. Therefore, Eratosthenes concluded, the circumference was 48 times the length of that arc: 48 × 500 = 24,000 miles. His calculation of 24,000 miles was, in fact, in close agreement with the modern value of 24,844 miles.

This classic episode in the history of science shows how powerful symbolic representation is. Symbols can replace physical intervention, allowing humans to model the world in abstract ways and then discover real properties of that world. But it must not be forgotten that the reason why representations such as the one by Eratosthenes produce the results that they do is because they are extrapolations of experiences and observations. The derivation of the term *geometry* is "measuring the earth," and this is, in fact, an accurate description of what the early geometers did: they measured the size of fields and laid out accurate right angles for the corners of buildings. This type of empirical geometry, which flourished in ancient Egypt, Sumer, and Babylon, was refined and systematized by the Greeks. It was in the sixth century B.C. that the Greek mathematician Pythagoras (580?–500? B.C.) laid the cornerstone of scientific reasoning by showing that the various measurements made by geometers held a hidden pattern in them. When he tied three pieces of string or rope together to form a right-angled triangle, the square on the hypotenuse of the triangle was always equal to the sum of the squares on the other two sides. Pythagoras' great achievement was essentially to develop a convenient shorthand for this pattern and demonstrate its generalizability.

NAMES

There is one kind of symbol that merits separate consideration—the *name*. The name is a word-symbol that identifies a person, place, or by connotative extension, a brand, an animal, a tropical storm, etc. At first thought, names would seem to be like other symbols, having no particular emotional significance. But that is not the case. It is, in fact, impossible to think of a human being without a name—if an individual is not given a name by his or her family, then society steps in to do so. Names define the human person. This is why children tend to become rather upset when someone calls them by a name other than their birth name, or else makes fun of that name.

The personal name, known technically as an *anthroponym*, constitutes a truly significant chapter in the history of the human species. Throughout the world a newly born child is not considered a full-fledged member of this species until he or she is given a name. In Inuit cultures an individual is perceived as having a body, a soul, and a name; a person is not seen to be complete without all three. This is true, to varying degrees, in all cultures. A few decades ago, a British television program, *The Prisoner,* played on this theme. It portrayed a totalitarian world in which people were assigned numbers instead of traditional names—Number 1, Number 2, etc. The idea was that a person could be made to conform more submissively and to become more controllable if he or she did not have a name. The use of numbers to identify prisoners and slaves throughout history has constituted an act designed to negate the humanity or the existence of certain people. *The Prisoner* was, in essence, a portrayal of the struggle that humans feel to discover the meaning of self.

Naming is an intrinsic feature of a society's *signifying network,* mentioned above, that unites all forms of representation into a congruous system of intertwined meanings. In our culture, for instance, given names are commonly derived from the names of the months (April, June), precious stones (Ruby, Pearl), popular personalities (Franklin, Liza), flowers (Rose, Violet), places (Georgia), legendary figures (Diana, Jason). Although name-giving is very much influenced by vogue and fashion in Western cultures, rather than exclusively by tradition, modern societies vary widely in this respect. Britain and the United States permit all kinds of names, but in some countries there are approved lists of names that must be given to a child if he or she is to be legally recognized. In Brazil, for example, a child must be given an appropriate Christian name before he or she will be issued a birth certificate.

Sometimes one name is not sufficient to identify individuals. Historically, *surnames*—literally "names on top of names"—became necessary when name duplications in growing societies made it difficult to differentiate between people. Surnaming accomplished this typically by representing an individual with reference to his or her place of origin, occupation, or descendancy. In England, for example, a person living near or at a place where apple trees grew was called *John* "where-the-apples-grow," hence, *John Appleby*. Regional or habitation names, such as *Wood, Moore, Church,* or *Hill* are products of the same kind of surnaming process. Surnames denoting an occupation are *Chapman* (merchant or trader), *Miller,* and *Baker.* Parentage surnames in Scotland or Ireland are often indicated by prefixes such as *Mac, Mc—McTavish, McManus,* etc.—or in England by suffixes such as *son—Johnson, Harrison,* and *Maryson* (son of John, son of Harry, son of Mary). Compound surnames are also used in some countries where retaining both family names is the custom. Thus, in Spain, Juan the son of Manuel Chávez and Juanita Fernández would be named *Juan Chávez (y) Fernández.* The surname is also an index of ethnicity, since it reveals to which family, society, or culture the individual probably belongs— the surname *Smith* indicates that the person is of Anglo-American heritage, *Bellini* (Italian), *Lamontaigne* (French), and so on.

The story of naming does not stop at surnames. People create *nicknames,* for instance, to emphasize a physical characteristic (*Lefty*) or a personality trait (*Cranky*), and *pseudonyms* (false names) to conceal sex (*George Sand,* pseudonym of Amandine Aurore Lucie Dupin), the past (*O. Henry,* pseudonym of William Sydney Porter), or simply as a personal whim (*Mark Twain,* a Mississippi River phrase meaning "two fathoms deep," pseudonym of Samuel Clemens). Some pseudonyms have become better known than the real name, as in the case of *Mark Twain* or *Lewis Carroll,* whose real name was Charles Dodgson.

People also name things other than human beings. Throughout the world, people give names to deities, vehicles (ships, boats), and to geographical spaces and formations—countries, states, islands, rivers, streets, houses, fields, mountains, valleys—known technically as *toponyms*. Toponyms may have historical significance (*Washington,* a city named after the first president of the United States), religious significance (*Santa Cruz* means "holy cross"), or some other kind of culture-specific connotation. Some are simply descriptive: *Honolulu,* "safe harbor," *Dover,* "water," *Doncaster,* "camp on the Don." A rough estimate is that 3.5 million place names exist in the United States alone, one for each square mile. Many of these reflect Native American influence (*Niagara, Potomac, Tennessee*). Others are of various origins: Spanish (*Florida, Santa Fe*), French (*Lake Champlain, Baton Rouge*), Dutch (*Brooklyn, Harlem*), Russian (*Kotzebue, Tolstoi Point*), and so on. Nations typically have regulatory agencies that supervise and recommend geographical names. In the United States, the agency is the Board on Geographic Names of the Department of the Interior.

In modern cultures, naming has been extended in a variety of ways—to identify products (*brand names*), to recognize teams (*New York Yankees, Dallas Cowboys*), to name tropical storms (*Hazel, Harry*), and so on. Aware that a product with a name has a more personal quality to it, marketing and advertising people pay close attention to the choice of a brand name. The intentional creation of a name for a product engenders a personality for that product that is meant to appeal to specific consumers. Sometimes the brand name becomes so well-known that it is used to represent the whole category of products: *Scotch tape* for adhesive tape, *Skidoo* for snowmobile, *Kleenex* for facial tissue, and so on. The names given to cosmetics and beauty products are created to elicit desirable connotations such as natural beauty (*Moondrops, Natural Wonder, Rainflower, Sunsilk, Skin Dew*), scientific authority (*Eterna 27, Clinique, Endocil, Equalia*), or masculinity (*Brut, Cossak, Denim, Aramis, Devin*).

STRUCTURE

Recall Ted's question at the beginning of this chapter regarding the meaning of the design of the pin Cheryl was wearing (a Chinese water spirit). In terms of semiotics, Ted asked that question because he did not recognize the design as meaning anything in the framework of any of the codes he knew. For any sign to bear meaning, it must have some *differential* physical feature that individuals recognize as code-based. What does this imply? Consider words such as *pin, bin, fun, run, duck, luck.* As a speaker of English, you will instantly recognize these as separate, meaning-bearing words because you perceive the initial sounds of successive pairs (*p* versus *b* in *pin-bin, f* versus *r* in *fun-run, d* versus *l* in *duck-luck*) as *differential.* In technical terms, this *differentiation* feature in the make-up of signs is known as *paradigmatic structure.* For any sign to bear meaning, it must have some physical feature in its make-up that individuals recognize as keeping it distinct within some specific code. People are intuitively aware of this feature of signs, even though they may never have consciously reflected upon it. It is the reason why, for example, people can easily recognize (a, b, . . .) and (1, 2, 3, . . .) as pertaining to separate codes (the *Roman alphabet code,* the *positive integer code*) and as distinct elements of each code.

Words such as *pin* and *bin* are not only recognizable as distinct signs through their differing initial sounds, but also by the way in which their constituent sounds have been put together. In technical terms, this *combination* feature in the make-up of signs is called *syntagmatic structure.* For any sign to bear meaning, it must not only have some physical feature in its make-up that keeps it distinct, but also be constructed according to some recognizable pattern. The word *pin* is recognizable as a legitimate English word because of the way in which its constituent sounds, *p + i + n,* have been linked. On the other hand, the form *pfin* is not recognizable as an English word because the sequence *p + f + i + n* violates English combinatory (*syntagmatic*) structure. So, too, the integers (1, 2, 3, 4, 5, . . .) can be combined to form numerals larger than nine according to specified rules of *horizontal* combination—12, 345, 9870, etc.; but they cannot be put one under the other *vertically,* because we do not form numerals in that way. In sum, paradigmatic structure involves *differentiation,* syntagmatic structure involves *combination.*

The notion of *structure* is a crucial one. So, it is worth mulling over with an analogy to solitaire. Solitaire is the term applied to a variety of card games that can be played by one person. In all versions, the cards are dealt to the table according to a plan or pattern, known as a *tableau.* The game develops out of the undealt portion of the deck, known as the *hand,* which is turned up one card or more at a time. The object of most solitaire games is to build columns of cards in ascending or descending order. The rules of play may require that these be built-up in one color, in alternating colors, in some number-value arrangement, or in one suit alone. Playing solitaire, therefore, entails both the ability to recognize the distinctive features of cards (suit and number value) and knowledge of how to put the individual cards together in vertical columns. In other words, solitaire is a *code* in which the various cards (signs) are distinguishable *paradigmatically* from each other by suit, color, and number, and placeable *syntagmatically* into columns in certain specified ways.

To summarize, forms are recognized as legitimate meaning-bearing signs when they fit *structurally* into their respective *codes*—language, number systems, card games, etc. Signs are like pieces of a jigsaw puzzle, which have visible features on their faces that keep them distinct from each other, as well as differently shaped edges that allow the puzzle-solver to join them together in specific ways to complete the overall picture. The words *pin, bin, fun, run, duck, luck* are acceptable words in English not only because they are kept *distinct* by different initial sounds (paradigmatic structure), but also because the sound *combinations* that were used to construct them is consistent with English syllable structure. Codes can be thought of as formatted computer disks. The *speech code,* or more precisely the *sound system,* of a language, has a format that permits only certain types of sounds along with a finite set of sound-combination patterns in the formation of syllables; a specific type of *dress code* has a format that allows the wearing of only certain clothing items that can be worn in specific combinations.

Codes are both restrictive and liberating. They are restrictive in that they impose upon individuals born and reared in a specific culture an already-fixed system of meaning; this system will largely determine how they will come to understand the world around them—that is, through the *structure* of the language, music, myths, rituals, technological systems, and the other codes to which they are exposed in social context. Code-based *structure* influences beliefs, attitudes, world-view, and even sensory perception. To grasp how a particular type of *visual code* to which you have become accustomed can influence your own visual perception, look at figure 2.4.

People reared in Western cultures are typically fooled by these lines. Lines AB and CD are actually *equal* in length, but the *orientation* of the arrowheads fools the Western eye into seeing AB as longer than CD. As psychologists have found, many people living in non-Western cultures do not experience the same illusion. The reason why people from Western cultures see one line as longer than the other is because they have become

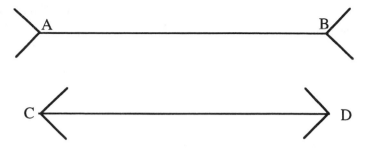

Figure 2.4: A Visual Illusion

conditioned by their upbringing to view drawings in a certain *perspective.* Perspective refers to the ability to create an illusion of depth or length. Visual artists in our culture, from painters to graphic designers, learn how to manipulate and guide perspective by means of line, shape, color, value, and texture so as to induce a specific range of interpretations to their visual texts. Their craft dates back to the Renaissance (from the fourteenth to the sixteenth centuries) when the Italian artist Filippo Brunelleschi (1377–1446) discovered and popularized the technique of perspective. Since then, the Western eye has become accustomed to reading pictures in terms of Brunelleschi's technique. Pictures are thus perceived as having depth, figures within them as being far or near, and so on. This way of seeing is a consequence of Brunelleschi's *visual code,* which now structures our experience of viewing visual texts.

The story of culture does not end on the rather worrisome note that we are all caught in a predetermined cultural system of perception. Paradoxically, the very same *perception-structuring* system of signification in which we are reared is also liberating because it provides the means by which we can seek new meanings. The great artistic, religious, scientific, and philosophical texts to which we are exposed in cultural contexts open up the mind, stimulate creativity, and engender freedom of thought. As a result, human beings tend to become restless for new meanings, new messages. For this reason, codes are constantly being modified by new generations of artists, scientists, philosophers, thinkers, and others to meet new demands, new ideas, new challenges. Therein lies the paradox of culture.

3

MAKE-UP

Why Do We Put It On?

God hath given you one face, and you make yourselves another.

—William Shakespeare (1564–1616)

Now that the onerous technical matters of semiotic theory are behind us, it is time to get back to the other semiotically interesting parts of Martha's videotape. Incidentally, the smoking code, which was the focus of our attention in the first chapter, is just one of many such codes, known as *nonverbal,* that make up the *system of everyday life.* The nonverbal mode of message-making involves gesture, posture, facial expression, and other bodily-based forms of signaling. In its most rudimentary forms, it is probably the only mode that permits meaningful interaction between humans and other species. We instinctively touch cats and dogs to send out messages of affection to them, and they rub against us when they are content or when they want something. Sharing the same living space, and being dependent on each other for affection and companionship, we do indeed develop a negotiated system of nonverbal communication with our cats and dogs. Our tone of voice, posture, hand gestures, and other kinds of nonverbal signals convey specific meanings to them ("It's time for food," "Come here," "Go away,"); in turn, we can interpret feline or canine sounds, stares, and postures fairly accurately in certain situations. This kind of interaction between species is grounded in *empathy*—the ability to sense the moods and mental states of another animal through the nonverbal signals it emits. But there is no guarantee that the signals humans direct to animals, or vice versa, will be interpreted in ways that resemble each other. Moreover, if the anatomies and brains of two species are vastly different, it is unlikely that any form of interaction can be realized. This is why we do not even attempt to enter into any communication with, for instance, reptiles, insects, or fish.

Individuals born and reared in a specific culture will come to perceive the world around them through the *structure* of the codes that they acquire from their ambiance. This includes nonverbal codes. In North American culture, for instance, childbirth is widely regarded as a painful event, but in others, there is no distress whatsoever associated with it. This in no way means that North American women are making up their pain. It indicates, rather, that the *code of childbirth* in their culture influences them to view childbirth as a painful and possibly life-endangering event.

Returning to the smoking scene on Martha's videotape, we can now ask a follow-up question: Does sexual acting in human courtship involve reliance on other *nonverbal codes?* The semiotician would answer this question with a resounding "Yes," since human interaction is based much more on nonverbal intercommunication than people might imagine. Worldwide research has established that, as a species, we transmit most of our messages, not through words, but through the body, and especially the face. We have the capacity to produce up to 700,000 distinct physical signs, of which 1,000 are different bodily postures, 5,000 are hand gestures, and 250,000 are facial expressions.[1] Psychologist Paul Ekman has even linked particular emotions to specific facial patterns—eyebrow position, eye shape, mouth shape, nostril size, and so on.[2] When someone is telling a lie, for instance, the pupils tend to contract, one eyebrow may lift, and the corner of the mouth may twitch. To cover up the lie, the person might use such strategies as smiling, nodding, and winking, which seem to be incongruent with the other facial patterns.[3] In short, Ekman has shown that it is possible to write a "grammar of the face" that shows less cross-cultural variation than do the grammars of languages.

Conveying emotional states through ear, mouth, and lip actions is a trait that cuts across species. Dogs prick up their ears during an alert mode; lynxes twitch them in conflicted or agitated states; cats flatten them when they are in a protective mode. Many animals constrict their mouths and bare their teeth to convey hostility. Following intense sexual sniffing, various primates expose their upper teeth, making themselves appear to be overwhelmed by their sexual urges. Many of our own emotional states are conveyed in similar ways: when we bare our teeth, for instance, we invariably signal aggressiveness and hostility. In our species, the face is not only a source for the display of emotions, but also a primary source for defining and presenting the self in social situations. *Making-up* the face by putting on cosmetics, removing (or growing) facial hair, and wearing decorative trinkets such as earrings and nose rings is, in fact, designed to do something that is entirely alien to other species—to communicate who we are to others or what we want them to think we are. Make-up can announce social class or status, as is the case in India where a caste mark on a person's face lets others know his or her place in society; it can mark the coming of age; it can function to enhance attractiveness in sexual acting; and the list could go on and on. Make-up is clear evidence that we have cut the link to our biological past, and transformed the face into something more than a carrier and conveyor of emotional states.

Does Martha's videotape reveal anything pertinent to the theme of make-up? Of course it does! The tape shows that Ted, our male protagonist, has shaved himself and has slicked down his hair with lotion for the occasion. It also shows that Cheryl, our female protagonist, has put on red lipstick, mascara, facial powder, and long pendant earrings. Martha has also made some interesting notes for us which are relevant to the matter at hand. Her notes inform us that Ted had doused himself with musk cologne and Cheryl had applied sweet lavender perfume.

Given our previous analysis of the restaurant scene as a courtship performance, it should come as no surprise that the semiotician would see cosmetics, lotions, and perfumes as elements of a *grooming code* which, like the *smoking code,* is gender-specific and, thus, designed to enhance the sexual attractiveness of the actors in the performance. To the semiotician, the *signifiers* that comprise the grooming code provide further insights into human courtship, and more generally, into human meaning-making.

MAKING–UP THE FACE

Psychologists have found that, at puberty, an individual will respond sexually or amorously only to particular kinds of faces. The source of this response is hardly biological but, rather, appears to be the kinds of experiences he or she had during childhood. At puberty, these generate an unconscious image of what the ideal love-mate's appearance should be like, becoming quite specific as to details of physiognomy and facial features. This finding of psychology only confirms what tribal peoples have known intuitively all along. This is why tribal cultures have always marked the coming-of-age with elaborate rites involving cosmetic decorations designed to highlight the face as the primary focus of sexual attention. For instance, the pubescent males of the Secoya people who live along the Río Santa Naría in Peru wear a sprig of grass through their nasal septum for the traditional coming-of-age rite. This allows them to keep their faces "poised" to exude confidence and sexual control. This "sexualizing" of the face has parallels in all cultures. Even in our own, where formal society-wide puberty rites are lacking, adolescent females, for example, sexualize their faces, typically, by putting on lipstick, mascara, and earrings.

The cosmetic make-up that has become so widely used today in consumerist cultures has, as the archeological record confirms, a long and unbroken connection with tribal customs that go back considerably in time. As anthropologist Helen Fisher has remarked, even in the prehistoric Cro-Magnon era, during the last glacial age, humans spent hours decorating themselves, plaiting their hair, donning garlands of flowers, wearing bracelets and pendants, and decorating their tunics and leggings with multi-colored fur, feathers, and beads.[4] Our contemporary cosmetic and fashion practices are really no more than modern versions of such ancient courtship and fertility customs. The colors used in lipsticks and eye decorations, as well as the rings people put on their ears, nose, lips, eyebrows, and even tongue are signifying props in the contemporary sexual *grooming code.*

References to face-painting appear throughout the Old Testament. Archeologists speculate that the Jewish people probably adopted their facial make-up practices from the Egyptians. Indeed, one of the earliest records of cosmetic use in ancient civilizations comes from the First Dynasty of Egypt (ca. 3100–2907 B.C.), where unguent jars, some of which were scented, have been found in the tombs of that era. These were probably used by both men and women to keep their skin supple and unwrinkled in the dry heat of Egypt. The women of Egypt also developed the art of eye beautification by applying dark-green color to the under-lid and by blackening the lashes and the upper lid with *kohl,* a preparation made from antimony or soot. By the middle of the first century A.D., cosmetics were widely used by the Romans, who employed rouge, depilatories, *kohl* for darkening eyelashes and eyelids, chalk for whitening the complexion, and pumice for cleaning the teeth. The almost universal use of commercially manufactured cosmetics in modern times was begun in the nineteenth century by the French, who made more and better cosmetics available at low cost.

The reason why Cheryl wore red lipstick can now be broached from a semiotic standpoint. As a physical phenomenon, the color red can be defined as a band on the light spectrum with a specifiable wavelength. As a signifier, red has its own fascinating symbolic history. More often than not, it connotes "life" and "beauty." To the Pawnees of North America, for example, painting one's body red is the symbolic embodiment of life associated with the color of blood; in Hebrew the name of the first man, Adam, means "red" and "alive"; in languages of the Slavic family red signifies "living, beautiful."[5] In the case of red lipstick, there seems to be little doubt that it is suggestive of female life, beauty, and even the color of female genitalia. This is the reason why in advertising (and in erotic pictures and movies) close-ups of female lips, painted red, slightly parted, have a powerful erotic effect on viewers.

Styling and cutting one's hair have also been an important part of grooming since ancient times.[6] Members of the Mesopotamian and Persian nobility, for instance, curled, dyed, and plaited their long hair and beards, sometimes adding gold dust or gold and silver ornaments for embellishment. Egyptian men and women shaved their heads to combat the Egyptian heat. Hebrew men were prohibited by Biblical law from cutting their hair or beard, but orthodox women, upon marriage, were expected to crop their hair and wear a wig, a custom that is still practiced to some extent.

Among the ancient Greeks, boys under the age of 18 generally wore their hair long; men were clean shaven and wore short hair, often curled in small ringlets. Greek women, on the other hand, wore their hair long, parting it in the middle and drawing it back into a knot or chignon. Curling became so popular in Athens that it gave rise to the first professional hairdressers. In Rome, men were also beardless and short-haired, and women wore their hair elaborately curled and braided. In the same era, the men of Germanic and Celtic tribes of northern Europe wore their hair and beards long; short hair was considered a mark of slavery or of punishment.

Since the French Revolution of the late eighteenth century, women's styles have moved back and forth from the simplicity of the ancient Greek chignon, to curls, ringlets, and fringes. It became fashionable for women after World War I to wear bobbed hair, often permanently waved. In the 1980s and 1990s female hairstyles fluctuated primarily between a long, flowing style (like Cheryl's) to shorter, trimmed styles. The closely cropped crew cuts adopted by men for obvious practical reasons during World War II gave way to longer hair and untrimmed beards in the 1960s and 1970s. Shorter, shaped hairstyles and neatly trimmed beards reappeared in the late 1970s. In the 1980s and 1990s men in Western cultures have tended to wear their hair short (like Ted's), or even shave their heads. Today, the wearing of short or long hair by males and females in our society is a mix of fashion trend and personal taste.

Given the long history of cosmetic make-up and hairstyles, it is now a straightforward matter to understand in semiotic terms why Cheryl wore her hair long (which was the "in" style for women at the time of Martha's videotaping), put on red lipstick, mascara, and facial powder, while Ted wore short hair (the "in" style for men), shaved himself cleanly and put on styling lotion to keep his hair in place. Make-up and hairstyling allow prospective mating partners to highlight their sexual differences and their sexual attractiveness through the deployment of the appropriate grooming props and techniques. Like the use of make-up in the theater, everyday cosmetics are part of the process of successfully staging a character in such situations—a character whose primary intent is to be admired.

Perfume is part of the *grooming code* too. This is why Cheryl sprayed on a sweet lavender perfume and Ted, a musk cologne. Although the sense of sight has largely replaced the sense of smell for sexual arousal—modern humans are more inclined to respond to erotic images than to bodily scents—the need for olfactory-based sexual stimulation has not disappeared completely from the species. The *sense ratio,* as Marshall McLuhan preferred to call it, may have shifted towards the visual,[7] but the previously dominant sense of smell is still latent in sexual desire. Like other animals, humans continue to respond sexually to odors and scents that are emitted by prospective mates. In our consumerist culture, perfume has become the artificial surrogate for biological scent and, therefore, is quite apt to make a long-lasting impression. Years after our first infatuation we seldom fail to recognize the perfume fragrance that was worn by the person with whom we "fell in love," as the expression goes.

Grooming codes are not restricted to sexual acting situations. They have many more social functions. In general, they provide people with the appropriate techniques for "presenting an acceptable self" in society, as the sociologist Erving Goffman emphasized.[8] Throughout the world, people equate the self with the face. This idea is, in fact, implicit in the word *person*. In ancient Greece, *persona* signified a mask worn by an actor on stage. Subsequently, it came to have the meaning of "the character of the mask-wearer." This meaning still exists in the theater term *dramatis personae* (cast of characters), literally "the persons of the drama." Eventually, the word came to have its present meaning of "self." The association between personhood and the theater is still very much alive in Western cultural thinking. This is why we routinely use expressions such as *playing roles in life, interacting with others, acting out our feelings, putting on a proper face* (mask), and so on. The self is the total image that the individual chooses to present in the theater of social life, the total impression he or she wishes to make on a social audience. But in the same way that an ancient actor would change the theatrical mask for effect, we can, and often do, change the self we present to others. The *persona* we present in a workplace setting, for example, will be different from the one we present to a prospective mate in a courtship display.

The association of masks with living entities and personality traits is an ancient one. Since at least Paleolithic times, people have used masks to cover the face, the entire head, or the head and shoulders for magical effect, because they were thought to represent deities, mythological beings, good and evil spirits, spirits of ancestors, animal spirits, and other entities presumed to possess power over humanity. In many tribal cultures, the shaman wears a mask during religious, healing, or curative rites, and is believed to be transformed into, or possessed by, the spirit inhabiting or represented by the mask. Masks of human ancestors, or *totems* (beings or animals to which a clan or family traces its ancestry), are often objects of family pride, and may be honored with ceremonies and gifts. In early agricultural societies, masks were worn to entice the heavens to send the rains; in hunting societies, animal masks were worn in rituals to ensure a successful hunt. Some tribal societies think that masks are potentially dangerous unless handled with the proper rites. The Iroquois, for instance, carve their masks from a living tree, which must be ritually asked to grant permission for the carving and then must be offered tobacco.

This whole line of investigation raises the question of what is the *self*. The self, like a mask, is a *sign* standing for the human individual. The *signifiers* of this sign are shaped by an amalgam of biological, emotional, and social forces. As the American philosopher and social psychologist George Herbert Mead (1863–1931) stressed, in cultures the world over the primary problem of life is solving how to construct these signifiers in terms of the social system into which one is born and reared; that is, how to present a *persona* that conforms to the expectations of this system. Every child learns relatively early in life that gaining the acceptance of his or her social audience entails fashioning a *persona* that will allow him or her to conceal certain habits, views, idiosyncrasies from public view, while exposing and highlighting others. However, as the child matures the question of "Who am I?" becomes problematic, as he or she realizes that it cannot be resolved in purely social terms. At this point, the search for the "real self" begins, a search that lasts throughout the lifecycle. In the history of the human species, this very search has been the inspirational source of some of the world's greatest religious, philosophical, and aesthetic works.

PORTRAITURE

The worldwide perception of the face as a conveyor of self is also borne out by the universality of the art of portraiture. The great portrait artists have focused on the face as the bearer of *persona,* as a symbol of humanity, as a model of beauty. Portraits are probes of the face, aesthetic interpretations of the many meanings that the "human mask" is capable of conveying.

The first portraits of identifiable individuals date from Egypt around 3100 B.C. These were mainly funereal representations of pharaohs and nobles. The subjects were seated in rigid, staring poses, communicating eternal authority. The ancient Romans also made death masks of ancestors (worn by survivors in funeral processions) which were remarkable in capturing the individuality of their subjects. Roman law required that portraits of the emperor be present in order for court proceedings to take place. Early Christian art, dating from the third to the seventh century, included portraits in mosaic and sculpted form. Known as *imago clipeatae,* the images of the subjects were generally stylized, relying on a standardized depiction of the face and the figure to convey authority. Medieval gospel books included portraits of the gospel authors, shown writing at their desks. During the same era, the portraits of donors became a means of verifying patronage, power, and virtue. The Renaissance marked a turning point in the history of portraiture. In that era artists started to become fascinated by the "facial mask" worn by the average individual. Among the portraitists of that era were some of the greatest visual artists of all time—Sandro Botticelli, Leonardo da Vinci, Raphael, and Titian. Their portraits explored the "poetry" of the face, seeking to extract from its expressions of sadness, humor, joy, and tragedy, the meaning of the human condition. Rather than seeing portraiture as an art of and for exceptional people, these artists saw it as a vehicle for exploring the mask worn by the common individual. They saw it as an aesthetic means of exploring universal human proclivities behind that mask.

The focus on individuality that the Renaissance spawned was not a unique historical development of Western culture. In China, murals depicting portraits of common people have existed since the Han Dynasty (206 B.C.–220 A.D.). These convey the subject's character not only through facial features, but also through clothing, pose, gesture, and the position of the figure in relation to others. The stone heads by the Maya peoples, the "laughing clay sculptures" of the Veracruz region in Mexico, the effigy vessels and funerary vases of the Mohican tribe, and many other examples of Native American portraiture also display powerful images of individuality.

The art of portraiture took a technological turn during the late nineteenth and early twentieth centuries when photography made it possible to make this art form more realistic. But photographic artists, like canvas portraitists, have hardly shown an interest in merely capturing the actual appearance of their subjects. The American photographer Dorothea Lange (1895–1965) was among the first to exploit the photograph's power to portray the poignancy of everyday life through the faces of real people in unadorned settings by recording the Great Depression of the 1930s. Diane Arbus (1923–71), also an American, was pivotal in showing how photography could be used to capture the ebb and flow of impressions, feelings, and thoughts in the minutiae of the human face, transforming the inner lives of human beings, and their otherwise average circumstances, into extraordinary events.

KISSING

Let's return to Martha's videotape. In another segment of the tape we see Cheryl and Ted making oscular contact—a form of nonverbal communication we commonly call kissing. Needless to say, kissing is one of those things that a semiotician would find highly interesting and relevant to understanding human nature. Humans kiss for a variety of reasons: to greet each other, to show love and affection, to convey sexual feelings.

Throughout history, kissing has served a variety of social functions in different cultures. In early Christian times the kiss was regarded as spiritual rather than sexual. It represented the exchange of breath between two people, and was thus thought to contain the soul of each. This idea was extended to marriage ceremonies, with the nuptial kiss symbolizing the spiritual union of the bride and groom. Kissing became a common greeting protocol during medieval times when it was regarded as a sign of trust. It was in Renaissance poetry and romantic lore that kissing was assigned a more erotic meaning. By the eighteenth and nineteenth centuries kissing was viewed more narrowly as vulgar and reprehensible. Today, kissing during courtship is felt, by and large, to be a necessary part of the courtship ritual to show affection and sexual desire.

Archeological findings suggest that kissing may have originated as a sexual act in ancient times. Representations of sexual kissing have been found, for instance, on 2000-year-old Peruvian pots and vases. Some psychologists argue that the origin of sexual kissing lies in the need to transfer *sebum,* the substance that lubricates our skin and hair, so that mating partners can achieve a form of chemical bonding. Others believe that we kiss because the lips, tongue, and interior of the mouth are highly sensitive erogenous zones connected to the limbic system, the oldest part of the brain and the source of sexual pleasure. Whatever the case, it is clear that kissing, like smoking and grooming, constitutes a *code* that allows the partners in courtship performances to communicate sexuality. In a sense, erotic kissing is mock-suckling or mock-feeding, implying vulnerability, closeness, and romantic sensuality. This is perhaps why prostitutes may be willing to perform a variety of sexual acts for hire, but frequently draw the line at kissing.

Erotic kissing is not universal. It is not common in China or Japan, and is completely unknown in some African tribal societies. In Inuit and Laplander societies, mating partners are more inclined to rub noses than to kiss. The semiotician Michel Foucault (1926–84) argued that erotic kissing is a product of historical forces. The Puritans of England saw kissing and touching during sex as necessary evils. Many other traditions glorify these sexual activities as crucial to romance and courtship. Obviously, what is abnormal or obscene behavior in one system of everyday life, is normal or virtuous in another.[9]

GAZING

Martha's videotape has still many more relevant insights on nonverbal communication to offer the semiotician. For example, as Cheryl and Ted smoke and chat away at their table, they gaze intently and steadily at each other, as if they were in a state of wonder or expectancy. This, too, fits in nicely with our analysis of the scene as a courtship performance. The distinct ways in which Cheryl and Ted look into each other's eyes clearly reinforce their different sexual acting roles. Gazing is actually part of a vast repertoire of eye signals that humans deploy to send out various messages: *staring* suggests a challenge, *making eyes* a flirtation, *eyebrow constriction* thoughtfulness, *eyebrow elevation* surprise. The presence of numerous words in our language to describe the ways we look at each other—*glower, gawk, glance, watch, gaze, scan, peep, wink, observe, peek, peer, inspect, scrutinize, ogle, gape, sneer, grimace, scowl*—bears testimony to the fact that we perceive eye contact and signaling as a crucial means for conveying, regulating, and "fine tuning" the flow of emotional meanings between individuals.

Gazing is particularly powerful as a signal for initiating a sexual relationship. *Looking* and being *looked at* are sexual acting strategies that depend not only on the directness of the eyeline, but also upon head and facial movements, the orientation of the body, and the sex of the gazer. *Gazing* is clearly a *code* that informs individuals involved in sexual acting how to use their eyes to send out signals of invitation and compliance, or the contrary.[10]

In Western pictorial representations, such as paintings, sculptures, and advertisements, men are shown as being in control of the gaze, and women controlled by it. Men are the *lookers,* women the *looked at.* Although the changes in social roles that the feminist movement has brought about since the late 1960s have had some effects on altering this code, it is still largely operative in courtship situations. Some psychologists claim that it is a remnant of an ancient animal (limbic) mechanism connected with courtship displays. Whether this sexually-based pattern of looking has a biological source or whether it has been passed on by history and tradition, is open to discussion. To the semiotician, finding an answer to this question involves documenting the structure of gazing codes, reporting on how gazing manifests itself across cultures, recording what kinds of behavioral effects gazing produces. Only after all the cultural information has been amassed and analyzed can one theorize on what are the plausible implications of the presence of gazing codes in human sexual behavior.

BODILY SCHEMAS AND DECORATIONS

The details of skeletal structure distinguishing *Homo sapiens* from its nearest primate relatives—the gorilla, chimpanzee, and orangutan—stem largely from a very early adaptation to a completely erect posture and bipedal (two-legged) striding walk. The uniquely S-shaped spinal column places the center of gravity of the human body directly over the area of support provided by the feet, thus giving stability and balance in the upright position. This biological development is the physical source of ritualistic posturing, and of other *bodily schemas* of which human beings are capable.

In human affairs, the body has always been an issue of high moral, social, and aesthetic significance. In ancient Greece it was glorified as a source of pleasure; in Rome as the root of moral corruption, and in the Christian Church as both a temple and an enemy of the soul. Since ancient times, Western philosophy has constantly debated the nature of the relation of the body to the soul and the mind. The French philosopher and mathematician René Descartes (1596–1650) even went so far as to suggest that God had created two classes of substance that make up the whole of reality: one was thinking substances, or *minds,* and the other was extended substances, or *bodies.*

Overall, Martha's videotape lends itself as a classic study of bodily schemas. Because these are coded, they tend to appear comical to outsiders. To those who know the code, they are seen as crucial sexual acting strategies to be performed at key stages in mating rituals. As part of the code, the body is perceived to be the physical "costume" that people wear to accompany the facial "mask" they present to a partner or, more generally, to a social audience. So it, too, must be prepared and decorated for presentation. This view of the body explains why people in the West seem to be preoccupied with "getting into shape." The association of thinness with attractiveness is learned from media images. The opposite is true in other cultures, where the slim look of Westerners is judged to be self-inflicted emaciation or culturally-conditioned malnutrition.

An interesting case-in-point of body decoration is *tattooing,* which has existed throughout history and across cultures. Tattooing was practiced by

the Egyptians as early as 2000 B.C. to indicate social rank, affiliation, or al-
legiance. Sailors introduced the practice into Europe during the Age of Exploration (in the sixteenth and seventeenth centuries). Throughout the
twentieth century in North America, tattooing remained popular among
sailors. But since mid-century, the practice has gained popularity with
many groups, including fashion models, youth gangs, and prison inmates.
It was propelled into mainstream American culture in 1981 by the album
Tattoo You by the rock group the Rolling Stones. As a result, tattooing in
Western culture has paradoxically become both fashion statement and
counter-cultural declaration.

Decorating the body to present an appropriate *persona* also involves
putting on trinkets and jewelry. Rings, for instance, convey specific types
of messages that can be interpreted only in cultural contexts. In Western
cultures they are worn to convey things such as educational status (gradu-
ation ring), institutional affiliation, marital status, athletic prowess, social
status (diamond ring), group affiliation, and personal interests. Some ornaments, such as cross chains, beads, and amulets, are worn to convey religious or superstitious meanings. But, more often than not, the wearing
of jewelry has a courtship objective. When a Zulu woman falls in love, she
is expected to make a beaded necklace resembling a close-fitting collar
with a flat panel attached, which she then gives to her suitor. Depending
on the combination of colors and bead pattern, the necklace will convey a
specific type of romantic message: a combination of pink and white beads
in a certain pattern would convey the message "You are poor, but I love
you just the same."[11]

EXTENDING *PERSONA*

Across cultures people manifest a tendency to extend *persona* typically to
encompass personal objects and possessions. We see ourselves not only in
terms of the make-up we wear or the jewelry and bodily trinkets we put
on, but also in terms of those objects that we use on a daily basis. These
too are part of self-image.

A modern-day object that is felt widely as extending one's *persona* is the
automobile. At a *denotative* level, the automobile is definable as an invention that has considerably extended the function of body locomotors (of the
legs and the feet) in mechanical ways. But at a *connotative* level, it is experienced as a body. In the public world of traffic, the automobile extends the

body's armor and is therefore perceived as inviolable as the body itself. No wonder drivers become so upset and prone to "road rage," as it is called. A challenge or transgression committed against the car is a challenge against the person driving it.

Parenthetically, the association of the automobile with the body is not confined to Western culture. The anthropologist Keith Basso found that the Apache tribe of east-central Arizona also perceive the car as a metaphorical body.[12] This is why they have named the parts of the automobile in terms of body parts: the hood is called a "nose," the headlights "eyes," windshield "forehead," the area from the top of the windshield to the front bumper "face," the front wheels "hands and arms," the rear wheels "feet," the parts under the hood "innards," the battery "liver," the electrical wiring "veins," the gas tank "stomach," the distributor "heart," the radiator "lung," and the radiator hoses "intestines."

As an extension of sexual *persona*, it should come as no surprise to find that the car plays a role in courtship. As the social critic Barry Richards has aptly remarked, it is experienced as both a male body, "punching its way through the traffic," and a graceful, nurturing female body, depending on the sex of the driver.[13] When I started dating during my adolescent years, I remember clearly that I was often asked what kind of car I drove, before my offers to date were taken seriously into consideration. I remember dreaming frequently of owning and driving a convertible "Chevy"—which I certainly could not afford at the time—probably because I saw myself as a sporty, happy-go-lucky guy.

DANCING

Before leaving the topic of the body, there is another segment on Martha's videotape that requires some semiotic commentary here, namely, the footage where Cheryl and Ted can be seen engaged in a bodily embrace called a *dance*, moving in rhythmic synchronism to the musical sounds made by the jazz band in the restaurant. Bodily locomotion has a biological source. This is probably why it is virtually impossible to remain motionless for any protracted period of time. Indeed, when we are forced to do so, our body reacts against it. During the performance of a lengthy, slow movement of a classical piano sonata, it is almost impossible to keep perfectly still or not to cough, even though one might be enraptured by the music. The need for almost constant movement during our waking hours is probably a remnant of an ancient survival mechanism designed to keep us moving, so as not to be easy prey for enemies. At some point in human history, however, our instinctual survival movements gave way to something vastly different—the expression of meanings through the dance.

Dancing is common to all cultures. It involves *spatial gesture* (the shapes made by the moving body and the designs in space made by the limbs), *tempo,* and *bodily schemas* (heavy or limp movements, tense, restrained, or bound movements, freely flowing motion). These may have no meaning in themselves, as in some classical ballets and European folk dances, or else they may allow dancers to express emotions, moods, ideas, tell a story, or simply experience movement that is pleasurable or exciting in itself. In some situations, dancing may lead to trance or some other altered state of consciousness. This is often interpreted as signaling possession by spirits. In tribal societies, for instance, shamans dance in trance in order to heal others physically or emotionally. The modern field of dance therapy has evolved from such ancient reasons for dancing.

Many animals perform dance-like movements in situations similar to human courtship. However, these appear to lack the conscious control that is present in human dancing. It is not known when people began to dance. Prehistoric cave paintings from more than 20,000 years ago depict figures in animal costumes who seem to be dancing, possibly in hunting or fertility rituals or perhaps merely for entertainment. Written as well as visual evidence of dance has survived from the ancient civilizations of the Mediterranean region and the Middle East. Egyptian tombs depict people who seem to be dancers, often in acrobatic positions. These figures probably represented professional slave entertainers. Dancing was an integral component of agricultural and religious festivals in Egypt, such as the one enacting the cyclic death and rebirth of the god Osiris (symbolizing the seasonal cycle of the Nile). Religious dances, especially those honoring Dionysus, the god of wine, are believed to be the motivation for the dance in Greek drama, in which the chorus used symbolic gestures and dance steps to accompany the spoken or sung verse. In ancient Rome, professional dancers, pantomimists, jugglers, and acrobats worked as traveling "sexual entertainers," very much like the erotic dancers of today. This is perhaps why the Christian Church, which at first allowed dancing as a part of worship and religious celebrations, denounced dancing as immoral during the Middle Ages. Dancing continued among the peasants, however, both in communal festivals and as a form of entertainment. Variations of medieval peasant dances continue today as folk dances. Some peasant dances, taken over and adapted by the aristocracy, became courtly dances that, in turn, evolved into classical ballet. The latter originated in the courts of Italy and France during the Renaissance, becoming a professional art form by the late seventeenth century. Since that time, ballet has remained a major category of the Western performing arts. Its style and subject matter continue to evolve as modern-day dance artists experiment with new ways of expression through dance. Some forms of dancing have developed around work activities, as in the Japanese rice-planting dances or in the Swedish weaving dances, which make working more pleasant.

Throughout the world, the significant stages of an individual's life, such as birth, puberty, marriage, and death, are typically marked and celebrated by rituals involving the dance. Weddings, for instance, provide one of the most common occasions for ritualistic sexual dancing. The bride and the groom may dance together to show bonding, or else they may perform separate dances—the bride's reel of northern England, for example, is danced by the bride and her attendants. Dance is also perceived by many societies as part of their rites of passage. Indeed, in some societies organized dances may be the only events at which young people of different sexes can meet and socialize. The movement of two sexually alert bodies in rhythmic coupling is a passionate act.

WHAT DOES IT ALL MEAN?

The semiotic study of *nonverbal codes* is a study in how people experience and define themselves through their bodies. In most cultures, self-image is carved out and conveyed primarily as body image. In Western society the slim and lean look is nowadays a strategic characteristic of attractiveness for both males and females. The margin of deviation from any idealized thinness model is larger for males than it is for females; but males must additionally strive to develop a muscular look. Females also perceive the size of their breasts as part of their self-image. This is why adolescent girls are highly conscious of their breasts as being either too big or too small. The same kind of sensitivity is felt by male teenagers with respect to height, with the general principle being "the taller, the more masculine." This oversensitivity to idealized body prototypes is the reason why adolescents tend to become discontented with their bodily appearance.[14]

The theme of this chapter has been the constant interplay that exists between biology and culture in the human species. The semiotician's concern over the meanings associated with the face and the body is hardly a trivial or purely theoretical one. The inability to present a socially acceptable body image can have dire consequences for people, leading to the ostracism of individuals from the tribe, to their confinement, or to various forms of marginalization. The increase in eating disorders such as anorexia nervosa and bulimia among young females in North American society since the 1950s is compelling evidence of how emotionally powerful the slim and lean look perpetrated by media images has become. The concern over virtually every facet of body image, from hairstyle to body shape, is a clear signal that humans invest enormous meaning in the body as personal statement and as a primary source of self-definition. This results through a process of learning in childhood how one's body fits into the system of everyday life. Semiotics provides a key for the individual to unlock the meanings and messages hidden within this system and, thus, to emotionally protect himself or herself against it.

4

TELL ME ABOUT YOURSELF

What Is Language?

Language is the mother of thought, not its handmaiden.

—Karl Kraus (1874–1936)

Needless to say, Martha's videotape contains much more footage that is of interest to semiotics. Now, let's focus on an early segment where Ted can be heard asking his date, "Tell me about yourself," to which Cheryl replies with the following words: "There's not much to say. I was born here, and I've lived here all my life. I majored in math at college. I now work for IBM." A semiotician never fails to be intrigued by such seemingly trivial forms of discourse because, in their essence, they reveal many interesting things about the vital functions of language in the system of everyday life, ranging from its use for making courtship chatter to its utilization as a tool for gaining and storing knowledge. In courtship, the function of conversation is clearly similar to that of theatrical discourse, complementing and reinforcing the nonverbal components of the ongoing courtship performance. Like smoking, grooming, and gazing, discourse constitutes a *code* supplying the verbal resources for presenting an appropriate *persona*. Whereas the grooming code allows Cheryl and Ted to present an attractive face and body to each other, discourse allows them to present an "attractive intellect."

Since the dawn of civilization, human beings have had an abiding fascination with language—the ability to use the tongue and other organs of the vocal tract to represent the world through sounds. Language has served humanity well. All the world's cultures have oral myths and legends to explain their roots. Knowledge and skill are passed on in all societies through stories, oral explanations, and books that record thoughts and ideas for posterity. It is no exaggeration to say that the very survival of civilization depends on preserving language. If somehow all the knowledge captured and stored in verbal texts were to be irretrievably destroyed overnight, the next morning people the world over would have to start anew, bringing together story-tellers, writers, scientists, educators, law-makers, and others to literally "retell" and "rewrite" knowledge; otherwise civilization as we know it would soon disappear. Those texts constitute humanity's collective memory.

No wonder, then, that across the world language is felt to constitute the faculty that, more than any other, sets humanity apart from all other species. There is a deeply embedded conviction within us that if we were ever able to solve the enigma of how language originated in our species, then we would possess a vital clue to the mystery of human existence itself. The Bible starts off with the phrase "In the beginning was the *Word,*" acknowledging the close connection that exists between the birth of language and the origin of sentient, sapient life. The ancient Greek philosophers defined it as *logos,* the faculty they claimed had transformed the human being from an insentient brute into a rational animal. But they also saw language as a potentially dangerous weapon for inflicting harm upon others. Indeed, to this day, there is a tendency in many societies to blame language for many of the world's ills, from conflicts between individuals to wars between nations. If we all spoke the same language, avoided insulting each other verbally, and employed our languages constructively, so the story goes, then we would avoid many of our problems. If we were to purify all languages of the favoritisms and biases that they have acquired throughout their histories, we would be able to set the world right.

LEARNING TO SPEAK

Language is truly a wondrous phenomenon. It has endowed humans with the unique ability among species to refer to events that have not, as of yet, occurred, to formulate questions about existence, to propose answers to them, to make up fictitious worlds, to frame important thoughts and actions. Just as remarkably, it comes *naturally* to humans.

The only requirement for learning any language is adequate exposure to samples of it from birth to about two years of age. Noam Chomsky (1928–), perhaps the most influential linguist of the second half of the twentieth century, has even gone so far as to claim that there is an organ in the human brain that is especially designed to detect and reproduce language. This would explain why humans acquire language without any training or effort during infancy, and why attempts to teach a human language to the higher primates, who do not have such an organ, have turned out to be unsuccessful.

To the semiotician, however, there is no reason to posit a special organ or mental system for language. Language is really no more than one of the many forms that *semiosis* (the ability to produce and understand signs) takes in the human species. The psychological record shows that verbal and nonverbal forms of semiosis emerge in tandem during childhood. So, Chomsky is partially correct. Language is undoubtedly a species-specific faculty; but so are the nonverbal *representational* abilities that set humanity apart from other species (art, music, etc.).

Before proceeding further with the discussion, it is essential to differentiate between *speech* and *language*. Speech is a physiological capacity, involving the intentional use of the vocal organs (tongue, teeth, lungs, etc.) for producing sounds. Language, on the other hand, is a mental code, consisting of signs and exhibiting the same structural properties that characterize any code. Verbal messages can be conveyed as sound sequences (speech), but they can also be communicated in other ways, through writing or gesture. One can have language without speech (as do individuals with impaired vocal organs), but one cannot have speech without language because it is dependent on the categories of the language code.

The physiology of speech is made possible by the lowering of the larynx (the muscle and cartilage at the upper end of the throat containing the vocal cords). During their first months of life, infants breathe, swallow, and vocalize in ways that are physiologically similar to gorillas and chimpanzees, because they are born with the larynx high in the neck. It is found in virtually the same position in the neck of other lower primates. Some time around the third month of life, the larynx starts to descend gradually, dramatically altering how the child will use the throat, the mouth, and the tongue from then on. The new low position means that the respiratory and digestive tracts will cross above the larynx. This entails a few risks: food can easily lodge in the entrance of the larynx; simultaneously drinking and breathing can lead to choking. In compensation, the lowered larynx permits speech by producing a chamber above the vocal folds that can modify sound.

How do children learn to speak? When infants come into contact with an unknown object, their first reaction is to explore it with their *senses,* that is, to handle it, taste it, smell it, listen to any sounds it makes, and visually observe its features. This exploratory phase of knowing, or *cognizing,* an object produces *sensory models* which allow children to *recognize* the same object the second time around without having to examine it again with their sensory system. As infants grow, recognizing more and more objects, they start to engage in *representational* behavior that transcends the early sensory phase: they will start pointing to the object they recognize, or else imitate the sounds it makes. At this point in the child's development, the object starts to assume a new mental form of existence; it has, in effect, been transferred to the physical *sign* (manual gesture or vocal imitation) used to refer to it. This is a quantum leap in development that probably has no parallels in any other species since, as the American semiotician Charles Morris (1901–79) remarked, from that point on the sign will replace the object for the child.[1] As rudimentary as they might seem, these early physical signs allow human infants to refer to virtually anything they notice or find interesting in their immediate world.

Soon after, children start imitating the words they hear in context, repeating them as single syllables (*mu, ma, da, di,* etc.). These are not mindless imitations: they are early *signifiers* in search of *signifieds.* The Russian psychologist L. S. Vygotsky (1896–1934) called them "small works of art" because, like poetic images, they are attempts to make sense of things through sound and tone. By the age of six months the child's repertoire of one-syllable words increases at a rapid rate. At around eight months the child starts reduplicating words (*dada, mama,* etc.) and using elementary intonation patterns. By the end of the first year the first true words emerge, as the child realizes that words are powerful tools for naming and thus remembering things, for expressing actions or a desire for some action, and for conveying emotional states. At that point in his or her development, the child seems to become mesmerized by the fact that words evoke thoughts. By simply saying the right word, a thought appears "inside the head" as if by magic! The psychologist Julian Jaynes has suggested that this feeling of amazement is an ancient one, dating back to when the first sentient human beings must have become overwhelmed by the "magic" of articulated words to conjure up images in their minds of things not present for the eyes to see.[2] The magical aspect of words is certainly evident in the fascination children show toward words, repeating them over and over as if to "test their magic." Words make children aware that there is a dimension to life beyond the purely sensory—a dimension that connects the *body*, the *mind*, and the *world* through language.

At around 18 months of age children start using language creatively, often talking to themselves as they play. My grandson was barely 15 months of age when I observed him use language creatively. I knew at the time that he could refer to many objects in the house with the appropriate words, but he had not learned the words for colors. Remarkably, one day he referred to the orange color of our household cat in a way that can only be called "a small work of art," as Vygotsky put it. He pointed to the cat's hair, hesitating for an instant as he searched his mind for an appropriate word. Not finding one, he came up with his own—*juice*—a word he had been using to refer to the orange juice he drank at breakfast on a daily basis. Examples such as this one, which we take for granted, reveal the presence of a "creative fantasy" in children which provides them with the means to make images and to move them about inside their heads in new forms and arrangements. The human *fantasia*, as the philosopher Giambattista Vico (1688–1744) called it, is a truly unique faculty. It has allowed the human species to know from the inside, and thus to transcend the limitations imposed upon other species by the senses.

LANGUAGE AND THOUGHT

Language provides perhaps the most significant clues for understanding how the *knowing animal* actually comes to *know* the world. The words a society uses are the *logical building blocks* of its "edifice of knowledge." One of the earliest efforts to link these blocks to knowledge can be traced back to around 400 B.C. when the Indian scholar Panini showed how words in the Sanskrit language were constructed systematically and what meanings each of their parts carried. Another early attempt to study verbal logic is that by the Greek scholar Dionysius Thrax (late second century B.C.) whose work, the *Art of Grammar,* became the model for many Greek, Latin, and (later) modern European grammars. Not only did he deal with the forms and structure of words, their arrangement in phrases and sentences, but also with the rules for correct speech. Throughout the centuries, interest in grammar (the study of structural patterns in language) never waned. With the spread of Christianity and the translation of the Scriptures into the languages of the Christians, medieval scholars began thinking about how to compare different languages. Their comparisons, however, were haphazard, and it took many centuries for scholars to develop more systematic methods for studying the world's languages and for examining the nature of grammars scientifically. It was after the publication of Saussure's *Cours de linguistique générale* in 1916 and the work of the American anthropologist Franz Boas (1858–1942), who documented and studied the native languages of North America in the 1920s, that *linguistics* emerged as a "science of language."

Since the 1930s, linguists have studied and documented many fascinating things about language, describing with precise detail its basic structural properties. Perhaps the most remarkable finding is the intrinsic link that exists between words and the concepts that inform a culture's system of everyday life.[3] Words are not just convenient labels for already-existing concepts. Rather, they make specific kinds of concepts available to the members of a culture. Consider a "device for keeping track of time." Given that it is a human-made object, there really should be little or no variation in the ways different peoples refer to it. In English, for example, there are two basic words for this device, *clock* and *watch*. The difference lies in the fact that a watch is carried or worn (around a wrist, around the neck), whereas a clock is placeable in specific locations (on a table, on a wall) but cannot be carried. This double classification has a historical *raison d'être*. The word watch appeared in northern Europe several centuries ago when people started strapping timepieces around their wrists, so that they could literally "watch" time pass and thus maintain appointments with precision. The subsequent manufacturing of watches (portable timepieces) on a large scale in the nineteenth century signaled a radical change in the perception of time management. In Italy, on the other hand, the double classification was never introduced into the language. The single Italian word *orologio* still refers to any type of timepiece. This does not mean that, in Italian, there is no verbal way for signaling the distinction that English makes. After all, Italians also wear watches. It implies, rather, that Italian culture did not go through the same historical process that introduced the categorical distinction in English. The Italian language can also refer to a clock's location or portability, as does English, but it does so in a linguistically different way, namely, with the structure *da: orologio da polso* =

wristwatch (watch for wrist), *orologio da tavolo* = table clock (clock for table), and so on. This structure allows Italian speakers to refer to a timepiece's location if the need should arise. In English, on the other hand, it is built into the double classification and is therefore something that speakers of English perceive as somehow necessary.

Thus it can be seen that differences in language reflect differences in cultural thinking and, ultimately, in cultural behavior. Indeed, Italians have a subtly different approach to time management than do North Americans, although differences between these two industrialized societies are becoming less marked as they assume more and more of a "global cultural structure" through media access, travel, and socioeconomic interaction. As the psychologist Robert Levine recently discovered in his travels, a fixation with being "precisely on time" is typical of cultures that distinguish between clocks and watches, but less so of others which do not.[4] Burmese monks, for instance, know more or less that it is time to get up in the morning when there is enough light to see the veins in their hands. They are not as compulsive about time-keeping as we are, thus avoiding many of the stress-related syndromes that afflict us in the West.

The intrinsic bond that exists between words and the structure of concepts is fairly easy to discern, as the above example shows. It exists as well in a less obvious fashion at the level of sentence structure. Consider the difference between the active sentence, "Alexander ate the carrot," and its passive equivalent, "The carrot was eaten by Alexander." In traditional theories of grammar, the passive is considered to be a stylistic option of the active. Why, then, are there sentences that seem conceivable only in the passive form, such as, "The Bible was written at the dawn of time"; "My work is still unfinished"? If we consider the sequence of the mental images that active and passive sentences elicit, we will soon realize that the two types are hardly just stylistic variants. Because the *subject* (Alexander) is first in an active sentence, it appears in the foreground of the mind's eye, whereas the *object* (the carrot) comes into view in its background. A change from active to passive reverses this mental view, so that the object (carrot) now becomes visible in the foreground, and the subject (Alexander) in the background. Both sentences say the same thing, but the way in which they portray perspective is significantly different. The passive sentence emphasizes the object at the expense of the subject. This emphasis on the object is the reason why the passive form characterizes Western scientific writing. The aim of science is *objectivity*. In language, this translates into an emphasis on the *object,* so as to de-emphasize the *subjectivity* of the human scientist and all the undesirable connotations (error, unreliability, etc.) that this entails. This is why a passive sentence such as "The experiment was conducted in support of the theory," sounds much more objective, and thus more credible in our culture, than an active sentence such as, "I conducted the experiment in support of the theory."

Examples such as these suggest that language is a modeling system, that is, a system of representation that attempts to model the world in some concrete way. The active versus passive distinction demonstrates how syntactic structure (the organization of words in a sentence) provides a *perspectival* model of a specific type of scene.[5] This was the view of the philosopher Ludwig Wittgenstein (1889–1951), who argued that words in sentences show how things are related to each other, in ways that parallel physical vision. Modeling is not restricted to providing visual perspective; it can also, for instance, be based on sound properties. In a classic study conducted by the American psychologist Roger Brown, native English speakers were asked to listen to pairs of opposites from a language unrelated to English and then to try to guess which foreign word translated into which English word.[6] The subjects were asked to guess the meaning of the foreign words by attending to their sounds. When Brown asked them, for example, to match the words *ch'ing* and *chung* to the English equivalents *light* and *heavy,* Brown found that about 90 percent of English speakers correctly matched *ch'ing* to *light* and *chung* to *heavy.* He concluded that the degree of translation accuracy could only be explained as indicative of a primitive kind of *sound symbolism,* an instinctual tendency to link sounds and meanings. Sound symbolism is a perfect example of linguistic modeling based on sound imitation.

The view of language as a modeling system is not a twentieth-century one.[7] It goes back to ancient Greece, when some philosophers claimed that words were constructed on the basis of the way their referents looked or sounded (although others maintained that words were arbitrarily related to their referents). This perspective was championed in the nineteenth century by F. Max Müller who proposed that humanity's first words tended to be instinctive, expressive sounds uttered in response to an emotional state—anger, surprise, pain, pleasure, relief.[8] Remnants of this tendency, he claimed, can be found in all the world's languages. In English, interjections such as *Huh?, Ouch!, Wow!,* which are uttered in response to different emotionally charged situations, and words referring to sonorous referents, such as *dip, rip, sip, crack, click, creak, rub, jab, blob, rustle, bustle, trickle, ooze, wheeze, squeeze, puff, huff, cough,* are obviously such remnants.

The German philologist Wilhelm von Humboldt (1767–1835) went further than anyone before him in linking language to mental and emotional states. Indeed, von Humboldt claimed that the structure of a particular language constrains the thought and behavior of the people using it. In the twentieth century, von Humboldt's outlook was pursued first by Edward Sapir (1884–1939) and then by Sapir's pupil Benjamin Lee Whorf (1897–1941). Sapir asserted that human ideas, concepts, feelings, and characteristic social behaviors were rooted in the structures of language. Sapir never carried out an extensive research program to test his idea rigorously and systematically. That fell on the shoulders of his brilliant student Whorf, whose work on the language of the Hopi tribe, a native people occupying pueblos on reservation land in northeast Arizona, led him to believe that the language an individual learns in cultural context constitutes a mental filter through which he or she comes to perceive and understand the world.

The Whorfian perspective raises some fundamental questions about the connection between social inequalities and the language that encodes them. Did terms like *chairman* or *spokesman* predispose speakers of English to view social roles as gender-specific? Feminist social critics maintain that English grammar is organized from the perspective of those at the center of the society—the men. This is why, not long ago, we said that a woman *married into* a man's family, and why, at traditional wedding ceremonies, expressions such as "I pronounce you man and wife" are still common. These define women in relation to men. Others, such as *lady atheist* or *lesbian doctor,* are exclusionary of women, since they insinuate that atheists and doctors are not typically female or lesbian. In the Iroquois language the reverse is the norm—the language favors the female gender.[9] This is because in Iroquois society the women are in charge: they hold the land and pass it on to their heirs in the female line, are responsible for agricultural production, control the wealth, arrange marriages, and so on.

The foregoing discussion in no way implies that language constrains or stifles the imagination. On the contrary, language is a malleable code which can be put to any use the human imagination desires. Should the need arise to create a new word-category, all we have to do is be consistent with the structural requirements of our language's sound system. Imagine a concept roughly involving "all preadolescent boys who have a missing front tooth." You certainly have seen such boys, but you have not thought of them as a *category*. This is because there is no word in the English language that calls attention to them as such; by simply making up a word— say, *forbs*—we will *ipso facto* have created that category. If English-speaking people started using the word *forb* routinely, then after a while they would start "seeing" or "recognizing" *forbs* everywhere, eventually believing that the category must have some necessary existence. This example shows exactly what Sapir meant when he said that language is both limiting and limitless.

Nowhere is the intrinsic relation between language and thought more evident than in the area of color categorization. Color is a sensation produced through the excitation of the retina of the eye by rays of light. Physicists point out that, in theory, millions of color gradations can be discriminated by the human eye, but no more than twelve color terms have been found in any of the world's languages. The colors of the spectrum are produced by viewing a light beam refracted by passage through a prism, which breaks the light into its wavelengths. If one were to put a finger at any point on the spectrum, there would be only a negligible difference in gradation in the colors immediately adjacent to the finger at either side. The organization of so many potential gradations into a limited number of categories has an obvious purpose: without it, people would have to refer to all possible gradations by coining and memorizing millions of words. There is, however, a trade-off. While a limited set of color terms makes it possible for people to refer to color gradations efficiently, those very terms also predispose them to recognize the categories that they entail. To put it in semiotic terms, people recognize only those color signifieds that the signifiers of their native languages have encoded.

English speakers distinguish six basic color categories, known as the focal colors: *purple, blue, green, yellow, orange,* and *red*. In color theory, *white* and *black* are not considered colors. The sensation of *black* is that of a complete lack of stimulation of the retina; that of *white* is of complete stimulation. English speakers might disagree on exactly where on the spectrum one category ends and another begins but, by and large, the disputed range would be minimal. This is because the above terms have established the color categories for speakers of English; they have, in effect, *structured* the content of the spectrum in specific ways. However, there is nothing inherently "natural" about this organizational scheme. The specific color categories that speakers of English have learned to recognize are part of the structure of English, not of nature.

By contrast, speakers of other languages are predisposed to see other color categories on the same spectrum. Speakers of the indigenous African language Shona, for instance, divide the spectrum into *cipswuka, citema, cicena,* and *cipswuka* (again), from left to right, and speakers of Bassa, a language of Liberia, dissect it into just two categories, *hui* and *ziza,* from left to right. When an English speaker refers to something as *blue,* a Shona speaker would refer to it as either *cipswuka* or *citema,* and a Bassa speaker as *hui.* The Bassa speaker would refer to *green* also with *hui;* while a Shona speaker would refer to it with *citema* or else with *cicena.*

In 1969, the psychologists Brent Berlin and Paul Kay conducted a study which has since become a point of reference in color psychology. They found that differences in color terms are merely superficial matters that conceal general underlying principles of color perception.[10] Using the judgments of the native speakers of 20 widely divergent languages, Berlin and Kay came to the conclusion that there are "focal points" in basic (primary) color systems which cluster in certain predictable ways. They identified 11 universal focal points, which correspond to the English words *red, pink, orange, yellow, brown, green, blue, purple, black, white,* and *gray.* Not all the languages they investigated have separate words for each of these colors, but there emerged a pattern that suggested to them the existence of a fixed way of categorizing color across cultures. If a language has two color terms, then the focal points are equivalents of English *black* and *white.* If it has three color terms, then the third one corresponds to *red.* A four-term system adds either *green* or *yellow,* while a five-term system has both of these. A six-term system includes *blue;* a seven-term system adds *brown.* Finally, *purple, pink, orange,* and *gray,* in some combination, are found in languages with more than seven color terms. Berlin and Kay found that no language has a four-term system consisting of, say, *black, white, red,* and *brown.*

This study, however, raises some questions. For one thing, the fact that the 11 focal points discovered by Berlin and Kay correspond to the color terms of their own language (English) has raised some doubts. The linguist N. McNeill noticed, for instance, that the 11-term Japanese system posited by Berlin and Kay dated only from the time of Japanese contact with the West, beginning in the 1860s.[11] The traditional Japanese system had five focal points: *black, white, orange, turquoise,* and *yellow,* which does not fit in with Berlin and Kay's theory.[12]

Whatever the truth about color, the semiotician would emphasize that color terms constitute a *code* which, like any code, will condition its users to perceive the world in specific ways. However, as mentioned above, this does not imply that color schemes close up the mind. The specific color categories acquired in cultural context in no way preclude people from discerning those established in other cultures, if they so desire. This is, indeed, what a student of another language must learn to do when he or she studies the color system of the new language. Moreover, in all languages there exist verbal resources for referring to more specific gradations on the spectrum if the situation should require it. In English the words *crimson, scarlet, vermilion,* for instance, make it possible to refer to gradations within the category *red*. However, these are still felt by speakers to be subcategories of red, not distinct color categories in themselves.

There is one more point to be made here about color. While the psychological research would lead one to surmise that color categories are established arbitrarily in a culture, the historical record tells another story. Color vocabularies originate out of specific needs and experiences. In Hittite (the language of an ancient people of Asia Minor and Syria), for instance, words for colors initially designated plant and tree names such as *poplar, elm, cherry, oak*. Many English terms, too, were not coined to indicate colors: *green* originally meant "to grow," *yellow* "to gleam," *purple* "a type of shellfish," and so on.

As the research on color suggests, vocabularies offer up only a portion of what is potentially knowable. The British writer of children's books, Lewis Carroll (1832–98), showed this by inventing his own nonsense language, which he called *Jabberwocky*. He argued, by poetic illustration, that there were gaps in the English vocabulary for concepts such as "the time of broiling dinner at the close of the afternoon," "smooth and active," "a species of badger with smooth white hair, long hind legs, and short horns like a stag," and "side of a hill." So, he provided his own words for these concepts—*bryllyg, slythy, tove,* and *wabe,* respectively. Even though such gaps exist, language provides the means to fill them any time we wish, just like Carroll did.

WRITING

As mentioned above, language is expressed not only through vocal speech but also through *writing,* that is, through the use of visual signs, known as *characters,* transferred to some surface. The characters that we use to write English words have a more or less fixed correspondence to the sounds of the language. These comprise a type of *writing code* known as an *alphabet.* Alphabets allow their users to unambiguously write any concept that can be expressed in vocal speech. This is why in an alphabet-using culture like ours a distinction between speech and writing is rarely made. History shows, however, that writing systems did not start out as visual means of recording spoken language. Rather, they originated as systems of pictorial representation that were largely independent of vocal language. Picture forms of writing are still in existence today, even in alphabetic cultures: images of males and females on bathrooms, figures indicating public telephones, and many other types of *pictographic signs* are all around us. The Chinese continue to view their writing code as both a means of representing speech and as a pictorial art form.

Systems in which images represent word concepts are called *pictographic* or *logographic.* The combinations that result when several pictographs are used to represent ideas are called *ideographs.* In Chinese, for instance, the pictographs for *sun* and *tree* are combined to form the ideograph for *east.* Pictographic and ideographic signs frequently coexist alongside alphabet characters in modern writing systems. For example, in English the pictographs *1, 2, 3,* etc. exist alongside the spelled forms, *one, two, three,* etc. The earliest systems of writing were largely pictographic. Among those of which we have preserved a record is the *cuneiform* system of the ancient Sumerians, Akkadians, Assyrians, Babylonians, and Persians, the *hieroglyphic* systems of the Egyptians and the Mayans, and the pictographic systems still used by the Chinese and Japanese.

Writing systems using signs to represent syllables, rather than concepts, are known as *syllabic.* Such systems allow for greater economy in representation because, rather than having one picture sign stand for one concept, or class of concepts, the same sign can be used to stand for syllables that recur in different concepts. This reduces the number of signs that must be used, and thus memorized, to write a language.

The most efficient writing code is, of course, alphabetic. The idea of using signs to represent consonant sounds probably originated with the Phoenicians around 1000 to 1500 B.C. The Greeks took the final step of separating the consonants from the vowels and writing each separately, thus arriving at full alphabetic writing about 800 B.C. As the communication theorist Marshall McLuhan argued, the invention of the alphabet principle brought about the first *cognitive revolution* in the human species. In pre-alphabetic oral societies, words elicited sound images. Knowledge was processed and remembered in an auditory form. With the invention and spread of the alphabet, this gave way to a visual form of processing and remembering knowledge.

Alphabetic writing is a truly remarkable achievement. It has made possible the recording and transmission of knowledge in an efficient and constantly reusable way. Indeed, in Western culture to be *literate,* or "alphabetized," is to be *educated.* So close has the link between the two been forged that today we can scarcely think of knowledge unless it is recorded in an alphabetic form and preserved in books for posterity. The story of writing informs us that in every alphabetic symbol we now use to record our thoughts, there is an ancient pictorial history that has become dim or virtually unseeable because our eyes are no longer trained to extract visual meaning from it. Alphabets did not start out as symbol-for-sound systems of representation. They evolved from pictographs that became so condensed and stylized through repeated usage that their pictorial relation to the world was severed. They became units of an abstract system for recording sounds. It was the Greeks who called each symbol by words, *alpha, beta, gamma,* etc., which were imitations of Phoenician/Semitic words: *aleph* (ox), *beth* (house), *gimel* (camel), etc. Note that the word *alphabet* comes from the Greek words for the first two letters (*alpha* + *beta*). Alphabet characters represented the initial sounds of the spoken words denoted by the pictographs. Thus, a pictograph representing a *house,* for which the Semitic spoken word was *beth,* eventually came to symbolize the initial *b* sound of *beth.* This Semitic symbol, standing originally for the entire word *beth* and later for the sound of *b,* ultimately became the *b* of our alphabet.

Although the alphabet principle implies establishing a fixed correspondence between a character and a sound, most alphabetically written languages are highly unphonetic, largely because the system of writing remains static while the spoken language evolves. The spelling of the English words *knight, knave, knot,* for instance, reflects the pronunciation of an earlier period of the language, when the initial *k* was pronounced as it continues to be in German (*Knopf* "head"), a sister language of English.

Cultures that have alphabetic writing systems, tend to perceive them as sacrosanct and inviolable. This is why attempts to reform spelling or eliminate inconsistencies in writing conventions meet with strong resistance. In early cultures, writing systems were often attributed to divine sources. Indeed, in many societies religious principles and laws are preserved in the form of sacred written texts. The Ten Commandments were inscribed on two stone tablets directly by God. The sacred revelations that Muhammad received from Allah (God) were recorded and compiled shortly after Muhammad's death in 632. The principles of Hinduism were written down in four collections of hymns, detached poetic portions, and ceremonial formulas. The first significant example of a written legal code comes from ancient Rome—a code, incidentally, that has influenced most of the legal systems of the modern world. In the eighth century B.C. the law of Rome was largely a blend of custom and interpretation by magistrates of the will of the gods. The magistrates eventually lost their legitimacy as the plebeian classes threatened to revolt against their discriminatory practices. This led to one of the most consequential developments in the history of civilization— the Twelve Tables of Rome, a set of laws engraved on bronze tablets in the fifth century B.C. Concerned with matters of property, payment of debts, and appropriate compensation for damage to persons, these tables are the source for the widespread modern belief that fairness in human affairs demands that laws regulating human conduct be formulated in writing.

DISCOURSE

So far our semiotic story about language has focused on how it is learned and on how it allows humans to model and classify the world. Language has another crucial function in the life of human beings—*discourse*. The most common form of discourse is face-to-face oral dialogue. The actors in the dialogue must know how to start and end the conversation, how to make themselves understood, how to respond to a partner's statements, how to be sensitive to a partner's concerns, how to take turns, and how to listen. All this implies knowledge of the appropriate *discourse code*. This informs people what to say and how to say it in specific situations. Take, as an example, the social function of leave-taking. If the speaker were a male adolescent and the interlocutor a male teacher, then he would say something like "Good-bye, sir." If the interlocutor were his mother, however, then he would say something else, like "See you later, ma." If the interlocutor were a peer, he would say something else again, like "I gotta' split, man." Note that the three formulas are not interchangeable. Each one is appropriate to the situation and to the interlocutor.

There are, in fact, several factors that will shape how discourse will unfold in human dialogue. First and foremost, there is the social situation itself. The utterance "Good-bye, sir," cited above, is a highly ritualized, formalistic one; the other two are more casual. Discourse spans the whole range of formality, from highly ritualistic to highly intimate. Second, there is the setting (time and place) in which discourse occurs. Greeting someone in the morning entails a "Good morning," while in the evening it requires a "Good evening," instead. Third, there is the function or purpose of the discourse: to make contact, greet, gossip, inform, praise, blame, persuade, advise, urge into action, entertain, congratulate, agree, disagree, vent frustrations, and so on. This entails not only level of formality, but also mode of delivery (voice tone, rate of speech). In a situation such as our imaginary restaurant scene, the appropriate tone of voice of the participants would be low and their rate of speech, drawn out and deliberate. Fourth, there is the mood of the participants. This makes the discourse event construable as serious, jovial, ironic, and so on. Fifth, there is the relationship of the participants to each other (intimate, distant, etc.). Greeting a stranger entails a "Hello," while greeting a friend entails a "Hi'" instead.

As was the case with nonverbal codes (Chapter 3), the discourse code also provides resources for presenting the self to a social audience. These include verbal negotiation, manipulation, suasion, and other forms of "verbal acting." Discourse is, more often than not, the purposeful and artful use of language to deal with others.[13] People talk not just to convey information, but to evaluate events and others in ways that are relevant to the larger life patterns in which they are engaged. I once heard a colleague say, "I've faced admiring eyes for 25 some odd years." This person did not simply say, "I've been teaching for 25 some odd years," but rather wanted to reveal in the content of his message something relevant about his life, namely, that he has enjoyed teaching at the university because of the amount of attention he has gotten over the years. Similarly, my dentist uttered recently in a humorous vein, "I've looked inside stinky mouths for nearly 30 years," attempting to convey to me that her work as a dentist was not as pleasant as was mine. This kind of humorous discourse reflects a deeply ingrained need to draw attention to one's feelings and attitudes, deliberately imploring a partner to focus momentarily on one's life experiences. This is why the linguist Deborah Tannen has defined discourse as a way of achieving the understanding of others through verbal involve-ment.[14] In a sense, discourse is performance art. As in a play, where the au-thor's feelings and perspective shape the form and content of the dramatic dialogue, so too in common discourse the moods and perspectives of the participants shape the form and content of everyday dialogue.

The type of conversation that transpired between Cheryl and Ted in our restaurant scene is an intrinsic part of sexual acting, reinforcing the nonverbal components of their courtship performance. Talk is probably more crucial to human courtship than is grooming. Indeed, an error in discourse is likely to be more harmful to the success of the performance than is an error in make-up. The discourse *code* for lovemaking supplies sexual actors with the appropriate verbal scripts for presenting an attrac-tive *persona*. This is why Cheryl recited strands of her life story that estab-lished both who she was socially ("I was born here; I've lived here all my life") and intellectually ("I majored in mathematics at university; I now work for IBM"). Her response reveals that in human courtship, sexual in-terest is not limited to the desire of the other's body, but includes a keen interest in his or her mind and social background. This is because in the human story the ultimate goal of courtship is not simply copulation, but also cohabitation and the social interaction that comes along with it. In-deed, the latter becomes increasingly important as the frequency of sexual intercourse declines the longer the mating partners stay together.

There is more to the language of courtship than sexual acting, provid-ing as it does a key to unlocking the enigmatic nature of *romantic love* in the human species. The love poems, songs, and stories that people have written throughout time and across cultures tell as much, if not more, about the nature of love and courtship than do the reams of papers and monographs written by psychologists and cognitive scientists. Stories about mythical lovers like Dido and Aeneas, Anthony and Cleopatra, Romeo and Juliet, and others delight and intrigue us because in them we try to evaluate the actions and experiences of the love partners in terms of our own actions and experiences. We try to determine why they do what they do and what they will do next, comparing it to what we would do in a similar situation. We ask ourselves, "What is he trying to do?" "What's her motivation?" "Why did he do what he just did?" in an attempt to de-cipher the deeper meanings of love and to understand why imperfection seems inevitable in every human love story.

RITUAL AND LANGUAGE

As discussed above, language has a crucial role to play in cultural rituals such as courtship performances. The role of such rituals in the system of everyday life is not to create new meanings, but to assert communal meanings and to impart a sense of cultural cohesion. This is why most people love to hear the same speeches, songs, and stories at specific times during the year (Christmas, Easter, and so forth). Societies are held together as a result of these rituals.

The link between language and ritual reaches far back into the origin of human culture when certain words were felt to have awesome magical powers. That same feeling of awe is still manifest in children's eyes when they listen to a magician's *abracadabra,* or when they read about the power of a magical spell or formula, such as the *Open Sesame* formula used by Ali Baba in *Arabian Nights* to open the door of the robbers' cave. Incidentally, the word *abracadabra* derives from the letters arranged in the inverted pyramid design of an amulet worn around the neck in centuries gone by. In each line of the pyramid there was a letter. Each letter was supposed to vanish magically until only the *A* remained to form the vertex of the triangle. As the letters disappeared, so purportedly did the disease or problem of its wearer.

Word magic is an ancient and universal phenomenon. In tribal societies, shamans were thought to possess knowledge of magical words that allowed them to control objects, people, spirits, and natural events, and thus cure disease, ward off evil, bring good or harm to another person. In some cultures, knowing the name of God was thought to give the knower great power. Such knowledge was often a closely guarded secret, if indeed it was allowed to be known by anyone but a select few. In ancient Egypt, the sorceress *Isis* tricked the sun god *Ra* into revealing his name, allowing her to gain power over him and all other gods. In Native American cultures, the given name is thought to bring with it all the spiritual qualities of the individuals who have shared that name. These are thought to cast a magical, protective spell on the child given the name. This is why many Inuit will refuse to say their name out loud, fearing that this "senseless" act could break the magical spell. The Inuit also believe that a newborn baby cries because it wants its name, and will not be complete until it gets it.

In all cultures, ritualistic speech is an intrinsic part of religious ceremonies, practices, and beliefs. At a Roman Catholic mass, for example, the speaking of the words "This is My Body" identifies the moment when the communion bread is changed into the body of Christ. In all Christian liturgies, the invocations and supplications pronounced by the clergy, alternating with responses by the choir or the congregation, are thought to have the power to influence the will of God.

The feeling that certain words are sacred or magical has become largely unconscious in modern societies, but the residues of word magic can be found in everyday discourse. We take oaths to fulfill a pledge, calling on God or a sacred object as witness. We tell our children "Just say the *magic* word, and what you want will appear." When someone sneezes, we utter "Bless you," no longer realizing that the words are meant to ward off sickness. Expressions like "Oh, God" and "Thank Heaven" have become so common that we scarcely think of them any more as sacred formulas.

The other side of sacredness is profanity. Most societies look down upon profane or vulgar language, viewing it in the same way that they would an immoral or criminal act; most societies have *taboos* against its use. The word *taboo* comes from the tribal Polynesian language, Tongan, where it means "holy, untouchable." Verbal taboos exist in all cultures. For example, among the Zuñi of New Mexico, the word *takka* (frogs) is prohibited during religious ceremonies because of its vulgar connotations. In our own culture, so-called four-letter words are generally considered obscene, and considered taboo in sacred places like churches and sanctuaries. In our common law it is a misdemeanor to speak or publish words that vilify or ridicule God or the Bible. The manner, rather than the content, of the utterance or publication renders it blasphemous. Thus, a statement of opinion, no matter how heretical it may be, is not punishable as blasphemy. Language that offends or provokes a public disturbance is also held to be in violation of the law.

SLANG

The language spoken in a society is rarely homogeneous, especially in large societies. Certain people or groups within the society may use, on a regular basis, a version of the language called *slang,* which implies the use of nonstandard words and phrases, generally shorter lived than the expressions of ordinary colloquial speech. However, slang is hardly an inconsequential form of "vulgar" speech (note that originally *vulgar* meant "of the common people"); rather, it constitutes a powerful form of discourse because it bestows a recognizable identity on group members, embodying their attitudes and values as a group. Slang suggests that language is like make-up, smoking, and other codes; it is a code that provides the props (verbal in this case) for defining and presenting a *persona* to a specific social audience.

Although the larger society may find slang undesirable and boorish, it is not immune from it. If the slang-using group has enough contact with the mainstream culture, some of its figures of speech might become forms known to the whole society, usually because they may provide a name needed for an object or action (*walkie-talkie*). Sometimes, slang terms become accepted as standard speech with an altered, tamed meaning (*jazz*, as you might recall from Chapter 1, originally had sexual connotations). Slang also finds its way into the cultural mainstream through the work of writers who use it to convey character and ambiance. Shakespeare, for instance, brought into acceptable usage such slang terms as *hubbub, to bump*, and *to dwindle*. In the twentieth century, television and cinema have been instrumental in spreading slang usage. For instance, the words *pot* and *marijuana*, which were part of a secret criminal jargon in the 1940s, became, through the media, common words in the 1960s when they were adopted by rebellious youth.

The speech of adolescents is quite different from regular slang. It constitutes a kind of social dialect with specific traits that set it apart from adult forms of slang. For this reason, a term such as *pubilect* (the dialect of puberty) is perhaps more appropriate for designating adolescent language.[15] Pubilect provides an outlet for teenagers to express the whole gamut of emotions they feel in social situations. This is why adolescents tend to overstress words—"He's sooooo cute!" "She's faaaaar out!" "That's amaaaazing!"—or talk with emphatic intonation patterns—"We called her up (?) (intonation contour like a question) . . . but, like, she wasn't there (?) (same contour) . . . so we, like, hung up (?) (same contour)." Named colloquially by the media as "uptalk," the second pattern is an implicit *tag questioning* strategy. A *tag* is a word, phrase, or clause added to a sentence to seek approval, to ascertain some reaction: "She's coming tomorrow, *isn't she?*" "That was a good meal, *right?*" The uptalk of adolescents is, in effect, a tag questioning strategy without the tag, indicating an unconscious need to ensure the full participation of interlocutors, to seek their approval, and to enact emotions verbally.

Perhaps the most outstanding feature of how adolescents use language is the tendency to coin descriptive words, most of which are intended to mock, shock, or satirize. In the mid-1980s, words such as *loser, gross out, air-head* and *slime-bucket,* for instance, were in widespread use in North American pubilect. In the 1990s, *vomatose, thicko, burger-brain, knob* gained some currency. Regardless of the generation, the psychological motivation is the same: an unconscious need to describe others and meaningful social situations in highly derisive, satirical, ironic, or sarcastic ways. During childhood the individual's modes of interaction with the social world are centered upon a constantly developing consciousness of self. The child is typically concerned with learning about how the self fits into the scheme of things. At puberty, however, the child's social consciousness comes to dominate his or her thinking and actions. While human beings of all ages are influenced by their relation to others, and tend to conform to behavioral models that are acceptable to their peer and social groups, teenagers are particularly susceptible, simply because consciousness of social *persona* intensifies at puberty. This is why they become keenly sensitive to bodily appearance and image, believing that they are constantly being observed. To offset this preoccupation with self-image, they invent trenchant forms of speech to describe how others act, behave, and appear: as *nerds, geeks, dorks, losers.* Adolescents are, in effect, using language as a catapult for hurling evaluative judgments onto others, so as to deflect attention from the self.

Pubilect also provides young people with speech patterns to gain access to peer-group settings and to reinforce gender identity. A teen, for instance, will typically use swear words to assert a position of dominance, to attract and maintain an audience, or to assert himself or herself when other speakers have the floor. Both males and females often test the verbal skills of one another in staged "verbal duels" in order to gain the upper hand. In many teen cliques, those with ineffectual verbal skills will either become outcasts or be compelled to accept lower status within the clique hierarchy; those with the greatest ability to "out-talk"—or more accurately to "out-insult"—the others are the ones who assert their leadership within their cliques. The goal during such duels is to "keep your cool" by not letting the opponent realize that you are wavering. The peer audience participating in the verbal battle acts as a kind of critic. If the contest ends with someone verbally destroying the other, the audience will typically proceed to ridicule and mock the loser.

The study of slang makes it obvious that language is both a tool and a weapon. As we saw above, during infancy language allows the child to model and reflect upon the world in abstract, sensory-independent ways, but, as the child discovers at puberty, it can also be used as a powerful weapon for inflicting harm on others and for protecting one's self.

GESTURE

As we saw in the opening chapter, the success of the smoking performance was entirely dependent on the ability of Cheryl and Ted to use the right kinds of gestures to emphasize their sexual *personae*. But *gesture* has many more functions. It is a "language" involving hand, arm, and head movement which can be used independently of, or in tandem with, speech. *Gesture languages* include the sign languages used by hearing-impaired individuals, the alternate sign languages used by religious groups during periods of imposed silence or during ritualistic practices, the hand signals used by police officers to control traffic, and the hand and arm movements used by conductors to lead an orchestra.

At an intuitive level, we feel that gesture is probably the default form of communication. One need not be a linguist to understand this. When people do not speak the language of the country they are visiting, they resort instinctively to gesture in order to get a message across or to negotiate a meaning. For example, to describe an automobile, a person might use the hands to portray a steering wheel and the motion used to steer a car, accompanying this gesture perhaps with an imitative sound of a motor. The *iconic* nature of gesture is what makes it a universal, less culture-dependent, mode of communication.

The ability to use the hands—the dominant limbs in the human species, given their physiological structure for grasping and pointing—was achieved by the first hominids who had the capacity to walk upright. The liberation of the hands from the requirements of locomotion not only allowed these early humans to make tools and to deliberately use fire, but also to use their hands for signaling. The capacity to point out and locate beings, objects, and events, in the immediate environment, and to convey their existence and location to others, conferred upon the human species a new and powerful control over the environment.

The first inscriptions and cave etchings were, no doubt, realized through gesture. For instance, the *iconic* hand movements used to portray shapes were probably transferred to a cave wall or some other surface with a sharp cutting tool. These "gesture-to-drawing" portrayals were humanity's first genuine works of art. Children, too, pass through an initial stage of gesture before they develop vocal language, and constantly point to things they recognize. Although speech eventually becomes the dominant form of communication, around the age of two, gesture does not vanish. It remains a functional subsystem of human communication that can always be enlisted as an alternate and more understandable form of message transmission.

The intriguing work of the linguist David McNeill has revealed that oral discourse is typically accompanied by gestures that depict the imagery implicit in the content of a message.[16] For example, when someone says, "Where did you get that idea?" he or she tends to use an accompanying gesture of the hand curved, up high in front of the face, with the fingers and thumb forward and apart, giving the appearance of holding onto something. With sentences such as "I gave him that idea," and "It's hard to get that idea across," the accompanying gesture is both hands extended, moving downward, making the speaker appear to be presenting an object to the other person along a conduit. With utterances such as "Your words are full of meaning" and "I can't get these ideas into words," the accompanying gesture is both hands forming a cup, with the fingers curled and palms up, to show two containers. Such gestures suggest an evolutionary link between gesture and vocal speech. On a beach, for example, we can hardly resist drawing on the smooth surface of the sand with our fingers, as a means of clarifying what we are talking about. This link has been the cause of much debate over the centuries. The French philosopher Jean Jacques Rousseau (1712–78), for instance, claimed that the "cries of nature" that our early ancestors must have emitted and shared with the animals, together with the gestures that accompanied them, led to the invention of vocal language. He explained the evolutionary transition as follows: when the accompanying gestures proved to be too cumbersome, the accompanying cries were there to replace them.

In the case of hearing-impaired individuals, the primary means of communication is through *sign language,* that is, language based on gesture signs. These signs are word-like units with both concrete and abstract meanings, made by either one or both hands, which assume distinctive shapes and movements. Spatial relations, directions, and orientation of the hand movements, as well as facial expressions and bodily movements, make up the grammar of sign languages.

Sign languages are not only used by the hearing-impaired. The Plains peoples of North America use sign language as a means of communication between tribes that do not share the same oral language. The gesture signs represent things in nature, ideas, emotions, and sensations. The sign for a *white person,* for instance, is made by drawing the fingers across the forehead, indicating a hat. The sensation of *cold* is indicated by a shivering motion of the hands in front of the body. The same sign is used for *winter* and for *year,* because Native Americans traditionally count years in terms of winters. Slowly turning the hand, relaxed at the wrist, means indecision, doubt, or possibility; a modification of this sign, with quicker movement, is the question sign. Special signs also exist for each tribe to represent the rivers, mountains, and other natural features within their particular habitats.

The possibility that gesture is a kind of "prelude" to speech, led some twentieth century animal psychologists to teach gesture to primates, who lack the requisite anatomical organs for vocal speech, in order to determine if they are capable of human language and concepts. A female chimpanzee, who was named Washoe by the Gardner husband-and-wife team, was taught American Sign Language beginning in 1966 when she was almost one year of age.[17] Remarkably, Washoe learned to use 132 signs in just over four years. What appeared to be even more remarkable was that she began to put signs together to express a small set of concepts resembling the early sentences of children. Inspired by such results, intensive research was undertaken throughout the 1970s and the 1980s, aimed at expanding upon the Gardners' teaching procedures. The Premack husband-and-wife team, for example, whose work began as far back as 1954, went further than the Gardners, teaching a five-year-old chimpanzee, who they called Sarah, a form of written language.[18] They instructed Sarah to arrange and respond to vertical sequences of plastic tokens that represented individual words: a small pink square = banana; a small blue triangle = apple, and so on. Sarah eventually developed the ability to respond to combinations of such symbols that included references to abstract notions.

Although there was an initial wave of enthusiasm over results such as these, with the media reporting on them on a regular basis, there has emerged no solid evidence to suggest that chimpanzees and gorillas are capable of symbolic verbal behavior *in the same way* that humans are. Washoe and Sarah could indeed communicate emphatically with their human trainers, but in the human world, language is not indispensable for communication. Touching and looking will do the job quite nicely. It is highly unlikely that lower primates will ever be able to grasp the connotations inherent in human words and utterances, not to mention irony, satire, and the verbal nuances in poetic texts.

5

KISSES SWEETER THAN WINE

Metaphor and the Making of Meaning

Midway between the unintelligible and the commonplace, it is metaphor which most produces knowledge.

—Aristotle (384–322 B.C.)

L et's rewind Martha's tape to the kissing scene described in Chapter 3. There is something else in that scene that is especially interesting, but which escaped our attention the first time around. During the small talk that followed the "first kiss," Ted can be heard saying, "Your kisses are sweeter than wine, Cheryl." As you might surmise by now, a semiotician would not construe Ted's statement as merely a figure of speech chosen to embellish his compliment. Unlike most people, who hardly notice such expressions, having become so accustomed to hearing and using them, the semiotician would see Ted's *metaphor* as revealing something much more fundamental about human discourse than meets the eye (to use a metaphor). To the semiotician, metaphor is the semantic glue that binds all the meaning systems and codes in the system of everyday life. The code that most reveals how it works is *language*.

ARISTOTLE AND THE DISCOVERY OF METAPHOR

If a very young child were to ask a parent "What is love?" one thing the parent would not do is give the child an encyclopedic definition of love.

Rather, he or she would relate the *meaning* of love to an *experience* of it that is familiar to the child: "Well, you know, love is like . . . when mummy or daddy kisses or hugs you . . . and that makes you feel warm and cozy inside, right?" Adults say things like this all the time because they intuitively know that children can relate an abstract concept like love to an emotional event or feeling connected with it. This is exactly what metaphor allows people to do—to link an abstraction to something concrete, familiar, and experienced. People the world over use similar *metaphorical stories* to explain morals, ideas, values, and other abstractions, to children. Metaphor is the innate faculty that allows the unknowing mind to grasp abstractions on the basis of previous experience. It is *the* faculty that makes *Homo sapiens* sapient, yet it is still largely the popular view that metaphor is a device of poets—a matter of extraordinary rather than ordinary language.

The term metaphor, itself a metaphor (*meta* "beyond" and *pherein* "to carry"), was coined by the Greek philosopher Aristotle (384–322 B.C.), who saw it as much more than poetic license. To understand what Aristotle meant take, as an example, the notion of *life*. How would one answer the question "What is life?" As Aristotle knew, there really is no literal way to answer this question satisfactorily. Aware of this, the poet would probably write a poem about it, the dramatist a play. The "common person," too, would come up with something just as inventive (albeit on a much smaller scale). He or she might say something like "life is a stage." Incredibly, that would be the end of the matter, for such an answer invariably seems to satisfy the questioner! Why? The word *life* refers to something that we know exists, but when asked to describe it, Aristotle explained, there is virtually no way of conveying its meaning in common words. This is because the *notion* of life is something abstract, and thus produces no concrete images to which we can put words. A *stage,* on the other hand, is something we can visualize, and thus describe easily in words—it is a raised platform on which theatrical performances are presented, where actors perform actions according to their roles, and so on. Now, the use of *stage* to describe *life* makes this notion *intelligible.* No further explanations are needed.

The "cognitive story" of metaphor does not end there, Aristotle insisted. Remarkably, in having described life as a stage, we now have a different understanding or view of what life means. Indeed, if one were asked "How would you change your life?" the metaphor itself would suggest the vocabulary required to formulate a viable answer. For example, one could say that a change in *role* or *setting* (whatever the case may be) would be appropriate to change one's life. In other words, the original metaphor, by its very nature, teaches and guides us by the new information it produces, as if by *magic*. Metaphor is, in fact, *word magic* in its most common, albeit largely unrecognized, form. People use metaphor, Aristotle suggested, not only to render intelligible what is abstract, but also to create new meanings, to seek new insights, to discover new concepts, and, remarkably, no special intellectual powers are required. The ability to coin and use metaphors is an innate skill of all humans, no matter how unintelligent or uneducated they may be.

Given its apparent open-endedness—one could have related *life* to many other visualizable things (to a river, to the seasons, etc.)—the question that comes to mind is how do we go about deducing the meaning of a given metaphor? Aristotle answered this question rather cleverly. He suggested that a metaphor is like a logical *proportion* that people must figure out in the same way, namely, in terms of the logical formula A is to B as C is to D. For example, consider the meaning of "old age is the evening of life." If *old age* is the A in the proportion, *life* the B, and *evening* the C, then a successful interpretation of the metaphor lies in figuring out the D in this formula: *old age* (A) is to *life* (B) as *evening* (C) is to ? (= D). The answer to this logical puzzle is *day: old age* is to *life* as *evening* is to *day*. Often, Aristotle continued, this type of reasoning provides the only way to describe something. In English, we use an agrarian term in the sentence "The ship *plowed* through the ocean," not as a mere stylistic convention, but because it is the only way we can talk about that action. So, too, with many other concepts. The notion of "mental depth," for instance, is a product of metaphorical reasoning. That is why in English we talk about thoughts as being *deep, profound* (a word that contains the Latin *fundus* "bottom"), or *shallow,* even though we do not consciously experience actual physical depth when using such words.

GIAMBATTISTA VICO

The Aristotelian account of metaphor goes counter to what became, after his death, the mainstream view in Western philosophy and rhetoric, namely, that meaning has a literal base and metaphor is added to this base so that discourse can be embellished—hence the use of the term *figure of speech* to describe how metaphor functions like a visual *figure* achieving an aesthetic effect beyond the range of literal language. Paradoxically, the person most responsible for entrenching this view was Aristotle himself. Although the Greek philosopher certainly saw the importance of metaphor to abstract thought, he ultimately relegated it to secondary status, affirming that it was, in practice, an ornamental strategy that people used to supplement their more basic, literal ways of speaking. Over two millennia went by before someone was perceptive enough to grasp fully the relevance of metaphor to human cognition—the eighteenth century Italian philosopher Giambattista Vico (1668–1744).

Like Aristotle, Vico saw metaphor as *the* strategy by which humans make abstract knowledge. However, he went further than Aristotle, attributing the ability to use metaphors to the workings of the human imagination, the *fantasia*. The first symbols of humanity, Vico claimed, were *sensory models* of experience. These reveal a strategy of knowing that he called *poetic*[1] because, like poets, people reflect on what they have sensed by inventing words that sound like things they have heard, that imitate natural rhythms they have felt, that enact feelings they have experienced, and so on. Then, through the *fantasia*, humans explore the world further, beyond their senses, beyond their *poetic* symbols. This results in metaphorical thinking and, ultimately, in systems of abstract thought. These systems, from language and art to science, are all interconnected metaphorically, existing *as we have imagined them*. To understand what Vico meant, recall the metaphor, life is a stage. The thought pattern that this embodies suggests specific ways of thinking and acting. These lead to real-life consequences. This simple metaphor lies, in fact, at the root of a whole series of concepts and rituals, such as wearing make-up and the common notion that people play *roles* in society (like actors on a stage). Metaphor underlies our entire systems of everyday life.

Vico's account would explain why human systems are ever-changing. Possessing, by nature, the *fantasia*, human beings feel impelled to constantly search for new meanings. They have little choice in the matter. Indeed, humanity is restless, never appeased, unless and until it is inventing something new. Humanity's greatest invention, Vico remarked, was culture. In the earliest stage of *culture-making*—which he called the age of the gods—human groups created religion, marriage rites, the family, burial rites, and other basic institutions. These are based on *common sense*, which Vico defined as "judgment without reflection, shared by an entire class, an entire nation, or the entire human race."[2] Since these institutions originated "among entire peoples unknown to each other" they must have a "common ground of truth."[3] Vico called this primordial phase of culture, the age of the gods, because it was founded by humans filled with an intense fear of gods, to whom they ascribed frightful events like thunder and lightning. In the succeeding age of heroes, a dominant class of humans— the heroes of the evolving culture—emerged, typically to subjugate the common people. These were men with great physical prowess who inspired fear and admiration in the common people, shaping cultural institutions to satisfy their goals and aspirations. After a period of domination, a third stage—the age of equals—is brought about by the common people rising up and winning equality. However, in the process, society gradually starts to disintegrate by force of "the misbegotten subtleties of malicious wits" that turn ordinary people "into beasts made inhuman by the barbarism of reflection."[4] At this point, Vico claimed, a culture has run its course, expiring "under soft words and embraces."[5]

The third age is an age of decline, of subtle irony and wit. Language is shallow, dispassionate, devoid of the poetic. But all is not lost. On the contrary, because of the *fantasia,* common folk start once again to seek new meanings to life, becoming once more "religious, truthful, and faithful."[6] In this renewal, or *ricorso* as Vico called it, new metaphors are invented fostering new thoughts, new forms of expression. The lesson of history, Vico concludes, is that human beings are constantly *reinventing* themselves, but in so doing are unwittingly following a larger goal: "It is true that men themselves made this world of nations . . . but this world without doubt has issued from a mind often diverse, at times quite contrary, and always superior to the particular ends that men had proposed to themselves."[7]

I. A. RICHARDS

Over a century after Vico, another philosopher, the German Friedrich Nietzsche (1844–1900), became both intrigued and disconcerted by the power of metaphor, identifying the capacity to use metaphors as humanity's greatest flaw because it allowed people to create an illusory reality in their minds and then to believe it as true. The growing interest in metaphor shifted away from philosophy towards the scientific domain with the founding of experimental psychology in Leipzig, Germany in 1879 by the German physicist Gustav Theodor Fechner (1801–87) and the German physiologist Wilhelm Wundt (1832–1920). However, the scholar who kindled serious interest in metaphor as something much more than a rhetorical technique was a British literary critic—I. A. Richards (1893–1979). In his ground-breaking 1936 book, *The Philosophy of Rhetoric*, Richards expanded upon Aristotle's basic idea that the function of metaphor was to create new meaning, by proposing, for the first time ever, a viable psychological theory of how this unfolded.[8] The new meaning that a metaphor produces, Richards suggested, was due to an *interaction* that is perceived to exist between the abstract *topic* of the metaphor (the *life* in "life is a stage") and its concrete *vehicle* (the *stage* in "life is a stage"). By this he meant that explaining an abstract notion (*life*) in terms of something concrete (a *stage*) is hardly a random process. Rather, it implies that people feel that the two share similar properties within the realm of their particular experiences. Richards called this perceived experiential *interaction* of properties the *ground* of the metaphor—the common area of meaning shared by the topic and the vehicle *in the mind* of the speaker. Metaphor generates meaning by providing a particular *mental perspective* from which to view something abstract. So, the metaphor "life is a stage," was forged in the first place, not through a pure flight of poetic fancy, but because the maker of the metaphor saw *life* and *stages* as existing on the same *ground* in his or her mind. The *mental perspective* provided by metaphor is, in effect, a counterpart to physical perception; in English we say that *ideas* (an abstract *topic*) can be *approached, looked at, touched, taken apart, seen* from different *angles,* as if *ideas* had location in space and thus visible properties.

Richards' theory provides insight into the uncanny power of metaphor to *create reality* within the mind, as Vico also claimed. Consider a common metaphor such as "John is a gorilla." The topic in this case is a person named John and the vehicle the animal known as a gorilla. Describing John in terms of a gorilla implies that an interaction of physical and personality properties is perceived to exist between John and a gorilla. Now, even if we do not know the John alluded to in the metaphor, the metaphor forces us to think of John in terms of gorilla-like, simian traits. In our mind, we cannot help but see John looking and acting like a gorilla. Changing the vehicle shows this even more sharply. If one were to call John a snake, a pig, or a puppy, then our image of John changes in kind—the person named John becomes serpentine, swine-like, and puppy-like in our mental view. John is, in short, what our metaphors say he is.

Following Richards' ground-breaking work, the psychologist Solomon Asch investigated metaphors in the 1950s based on words for sensations (hot, cold, heavy, etc.) in several unrelated languages.[9] Asch discovered something truly interesting, namely, that the same metaphorical pattern was used in all the languages, even though the meanings were different. For example, he found that *hot* stood for *rage* in Hebrew, *enthusiasm* in Chinese, *sexual arousal* in Thai, and *energy* in Hausa (the language of a people living in northern Nigeria, Niger, and adjacent areas). Intrigued by Asch's findings, psychologists in the 1950s and 1960s undertook similar studies, signaling a turning point in the study of metaphor. Indeed, since then, the amount of research on this phenomenon has been mind-boggling. In 1979, the literary scholar W. Booth calculated that given the number of books on metaphor published in the year 1977 alone, by the year 2039 there would be "more students of metaphor on Earth than people!"[10]

LAKOFF AND JOHNSON

By the end of the 1970s, psychologists were fairly confident in claiming that metaphor did indeed involve a special kind of *mental imagery*, just as Richards had suggested. The psychologist John M. Kennedy found this to be true even of visually impaired people who are, despite their handicap, capable of making line drawings of concepts such as wind, pain, and shouting if they are prompted by suitable contexts and appropriate metaphorical vehicles.[11] The kind of mental imagery to which psychologists allude is not limited to visualizable properties. For instance, mental images of sounds (the sound of laughter, the sound of thunder), touch (the feel of wet grass, the feel of a runny nose), smells (the smell of fish, the smell of a skunk), and tastes (the taste of toothpaste, the taste of ginger bread) can easily be elicited.

Several key studies in the late 1970s entrenched metaphor as a primary area of scientific interest for psychology. In one classic 1977 study, a series of verbal metaphors was presented to brain-damaged subjects who were asked to select one of four response pictures that best portrayed the meaning of each metaphor.[12] For the sentence "A heavy heart can really make a difference" the subjects were shown four pictures from which to choose: a person crying (= metaphorical meaning); a person staggering under the weight of a huge red heart (= literal meaning); a 500-pound weight (= a representation emphasizing the adjective *heavy*); a red heart (= a representation emphasizing the noun phrase *red heart*). The subjects were divided into those with damage to their left hemisphere (LH), those with right hemisphere (RH) damage, and a normal control group. Normals and LH subjects gave up to five times as many metaphorical responses; but the RH group showed great difficulty in coming up with the appropriate metaphorical answers. The researchers, Ellen Winner and Howard Gardner, thus established a link between the meaning of a metaphor and the RH of the brain. This was not an inconsequential finding, because the RH is the cerebral area responsible for producing most of our mental images. So, the idea that metaphor and mental imagery are intertwined turned out to be more than just speculation. Indeed, it was given an empirical basis by this key experiment. In the same year, 1977, the psychologist Howard Pollio and his associates found that metaphor was a statistically pervasive force in everyday discourse.[13] They found that speakers of English uttered, on average, 3000 novel metaphors and 7000 idiomatic expressions per week.

This kind of research laid the groundwork for the study that finally established metaphor as a fundamental area of concern for psychology and linguistics—George Lakoff and Mark Johnson's 1980 book, *Metaphors We Live By*.[14] The innovative claim of the book was that metaphor is the cornerstone of language because it is part of a conceptual system established by the community in which a language is spoken.

First, Lakoff and Johnson assert what Aristotle claimed two millennia before, namely, that there are two types of concepts—*concrete* and *abstract*. The two scholars add a remarkable twist to this Aristotelian notion—that *abstract concepts* are built up systematically from *concrete* ones through metaphor. They refer to abstract concepts as *conceptual metaphors*. These are generalized metaphorical formulas that define specific abstractions. Recall the example above of John and the animals to which he was associated metaphorically (gorilla, snake, pig, puppy). Each specific metaphor ("John is a gorilla," "John is a snake," etc.) is not an isolated example of poetic fancy. Moreover, since John can be replaced by any other person (Mary, Edward, etc.), each conceivable metaphorical combination ("John is a gorilla," "Mary is a snake," and so on) is really an example of a more general metaphorical formula: *people are animals*. Such formulas are what Lakoff and Johnson call *conceptual metaphors*, as shown in Figure 5.1.

Each of the two parts of the *conceptual metaphor* is called a *domain: people* is called the *target domain* because it is the abstract topic (the "target" of the conceptual metaphor); *animals* is called the *source domain* because it is

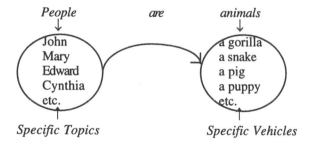

Figure 5.1: The Conceptual Metaphor *people are animals*

the class of vehicles that delivers the metaphor (the "source" of the metaphorical concept). An *abstract concept* can now be defined simply as a "mapping" of one domain onto the other. This model suggests that abstract concepts are formed systematically through such mappings and that specific metaphors are traces to the target and source domains. So, when we hear people talking, for instance, of *ideas* in terms of *geometrical figures and relations*—"Those ideas are *circular*," "I don't see the *point* of your idea," "Her ideas are *central* to the discussion," "Their ideas are *diametrically opposite*," etc.—we can now easily identify the two domains as *ideas* (target domain) and *geometrical figures/relations* (source domain) and, therefore, the conceptual metaphor as: *ideas are geometrical figures and relations.*

Conceptual metaphors pervade common discourse. A few examples will suffice to make this evident.

Happiness is up/Sadness is down
I'm feeling *up.*
She's feeling *down.*
That comment *boosted* my spirits.
My mood *sank* after I heard him speak.
Your joke gave me a *lift.*

Health and life are up/Sickness and death are down
I'm at the *peak* of my health.
He *fell* ill.
Life is an *uphill* struggle.
Lazarus *rose* from the dead.
He's *sinking* fast.

Light is knowledge/Dark is ignorance
I was *illuminated* by that professor.
I was left in the *dark* about what happened.
That idea is very *clear.*
Their theory is *obscure.*
His example *shed light* on several matters.

Theories are buildings
That is a *well-constructed* theory.
His theory is on *solid ground.*
That theory needs *support.*
Their theory *collapsed* under criticism.
She put together the *framework* of a very interesting theory.

Ideas and theories are plants
Her ideas have come to *fruition.*
That's a *budding* theory.
Aristotle's ideas have contemporary *offshoots.*
That idea has become a *branch* of mathematics.

Ideas are commodities
He certainly knows how to *package* his ideas.
That idea just won't *sell.*
There's no *market* for that idea.
That's a *worthless* idea.

As Lakoff and Johnson emphasize, we do not detect the presence of metaphor in such common expressions because of repeated usage. We no longer interpret the word *see* in metaphorical terms in sentences such as "I don't see what you mean," "Do you see what I'm saying?" because its use in such expressions has become so familiar to us. However, the association between the biological act of seeing outside the body with the imaginary act of seeing within the mind was originally the source of the conceptual metaphor, *seeing is understanding/believing/thinking,* which now permeates common discourse:

There is more to this than *meets the eye.*
I have a different *point of view.*
It all depends on how you *look* at it.
I take a *dim view* of the whole matter.
I never *see eye to eye* on things with you.
You have a different *world-view* than I do.
Your ideas have given me great *insight* into life.

In the inner world of abstract thought, ideas, like objects, can be seen, looked into, scanned, moved, arranged. This is why we have expressions such as *broad-minded, far-sighted, far-reaching, far-fetched, narrow-minded, short-sighted, world-view, insight, foresight,* and *hindsight.* As Walter Ong has pointed out, the universality of such words suggests that "we would be incapacitated for dealing with knowledge and intellection without massive visualist conceptualization, that is, without conceiving of intelligence through models applying initially to vision."[15]

The next important point made by Lakoff and Johnson in *Metaphors We Live By* is that there are three general kinds of psychological processes involved in conceptualization. The first one involves mental *orientation.* This produces concepts that are derived from our physical experiences of *up* versus *down, back* versus *front, near* versus *far,* etc. For example, the experience of *up* versus *down* underlies such conceptual metaphors as:

Happiness is up	=	I'm feeling *up*
Sadness is down	=	She's feeling *down* today
More is up	=	My income rose (went *up*) last year
Less is down	=	Her salary went *down* after her change of job

This *up versus down* schema derives from the accumulated experiences of such things as standing upright, climbing stairs, looking up. Let us assume, as a hypothetical scenario, that this image spontaneously appeared in the mind of an individual during a conversation in association with a topic that involved the notion of quantity (for example, *prices*). That individual might have said something like "Prices keep going *up.*" Caught by the force of this metaphorical image, a listener might have imitated the model, answering with something like "Yes, and my earnings have fallen." Continued associations between *up* and *more* and *down* and *less*—that is, between orientation and quantity—in routine communicative exchanges are what led over time to the establishment of the abstract concept: *more is up/less is down.*

In later work, Lakoff and Johnson referred to orientational patterns such as *up* versus *down, near* versus *far* as *image schemas.*[16] These are defined as largely unconscious mental outlines of recurrent shapes, actions, and dimensions that derive from perception and sensation. Image schemas are so deeply rooted that we are hardly ever aware of their control over conceptualization, but they can always be conjured up easily.[17] If someone were to ask you to explain an idiom such as *spill the beans,* you would not likely have a conscious image schema involving beans and the action of spilling them. However, if that same person were to ask you the following questions—"Where were the beans before they were spilled?" "How big was the container?" "Was the spilling on purpose or accidental?"—then you would no doubt start to visualize the appropriate schema. You would see the beans as kept in a container and the container as being about the size of the human head.

The second type of conceptualization process, according to Lakoff and Johnson, involves *ontological* thinking. This produces conceptual metaphors in which activities, emotions, and ideas are associated with entities and substances:

Time is a valuable commodity	=	That is not *worth* my time
The mind is a container	=	I'm *full* of memories
Anger is fluid in a container	=	You make my blood *boil*

The third type of process is an *elaboration* of the other two. This produces *structural metaphors* that distend orientational and ontological concepts. A structural metaphor is a conceptual metaphor built from existing conceptual metaphors of an orientational or ontological nature; as can be seen in the following examples:

Argument is war	=	I *demolished* his argument
Labor is a resource	=	He was *consumed* by his job
Time is a resource	=	Time is *money*

To get a firmer sense of how such abstract concepts shape discourse, consider the *argument is war* metaphor. The target domain of *argument* is conceptualized in terms of *warlike activities* (the source domain), and thus in terms of battles that can be won or lost, of positions that can be attacked or guarded, of ground that can be gained or lost, of lines of attack that can be abandoned or defended, and so on. These warlike images are so embedded in our mind that we do not normally realize that they guide our perception of arguments. They are nonetheless there, surfacing regularly in such common expressions as the following:

Your claims are *indefensible.*
You *attacked* all my *weak points.*
Your criticisms were *right on target.*
I *demolished* his argument.
I've never *won* an argument.

She *shot down* all my points.
If you use that *strategy,* I'll *wipe you out.*

The last relevant point made by Lakoff and Johnson in their truly fascinating book is that culture is built on metaphor, since conceptual metaphors coalesce into of a system of meaning that holds together the entire network of associated meanings in the system of everyday life. This is accomplished by a kind of "higher-order" metaphorizing—that is, as target domains are associated with many kinds of source domains (orientational, ontological, structural), the concepts they underlie become increasingly more complex, leading to what Lakoff and Johnson call *cultural* or *cognitive models.* To understand what this means, consider the target domain of *ideas* again.

The following three conceptual metaphors, among many others, deliver the meaning of this concept in three separate ways:

Ideas are food
Those ideas left a *sour taste* in my mouth.
It's hard to *digest* all those ideas at once.
Even though he is a *voracious* reader; he can't *chew* all those ideas.
That teacher is always *spoon-feeding* her students.

Ideas are people
Darwin is the *father* of modern biology.
Those medieval ideas continue to *live on* even today.
Cognitive linguistics is still in its *infancy.*
Maybe we should *resurrect* that ancient idea.
She *breathed* new life into that idea.

Ideas are fashion
That idea went out of *style* several years ago.
Those scientists are the *avant-garde* of their field.
Those revolutionary ideas are no longer in *vogue.*
Semiotics has become truly *chic.*
That idea is an old *hat.*

Recall from examples of everyday discourse, cited above, that there are many other ways of conceptualizing ideas—for example, in terms of *buildings, plants, commodities, geometry,* and *seeing.* The constant juxtaposition of such conceptual formulas in common discourse produces, cumulatively, a *cultural model* of ideas, as shown in Figure 5.2.

In summary, the gist of Lakoff and Johnson's 1980 work is that metaphor is at the basis of abstract thought and common discourse, although we are

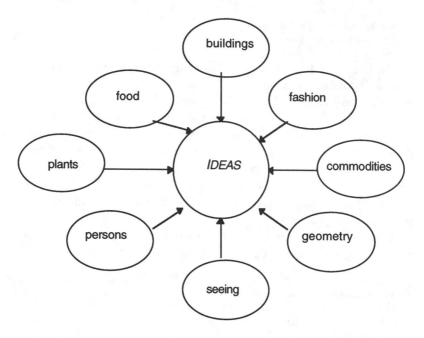

Figure 5.2: Cultural Model of *ideas*

largely unaware of its presence.[18] Everything that I have written in this book, too, has been structured by metaphorical cultural models. These have served me well in exposing the subject matter of semiotics; so, too, with every verbal text. Listen to a news broadcast, a sermon, a political speech, or read any textbook or newspaper article, and you will soon realize how each text has been woven together with the handiwork of metaphor. When a preacher talks about the need for being "cleansed" or "purified" he or she is utilizing the concrete force of the *sex is dirty* conceptual metaphor to impart a moral feeling of "uncleanliness" to believers.

Paradoxically, while metaphor is the *semantic glue* that holds conceptual systems together, it is also the source of innovation in such systems. As Vico argued convincingly, the metaphorical capacity is tied to the *fantasia* which predisposes human beings to search out or forge new meanings. This is why *novel metaphors* are being created all the time. If someone were to say "Life is a cup of coffee," it is unlikely that you would have heard this expression before. But its novelty forces you to reflect upon its meaning. The vehicle used, a cup of coffee, is a common object of everyday life and therefore easily perceivable as a source for thinking about that life. The metaphor compels you to start thinking of life in terms of the kinds of physical, gustatory, social, and other attributes that are associated with a cup of coffee. For this metaphor to gain currency, however, it must capture the fancy of many other people for a period of time. Then and only then will its novelty have become worn out and will it become the basis for a new conceptual metaphor: *life is a drinking substance*. After that, expressions such as "life is a cup of tea, life is a bottle of beer, life is a glass of milk," will become similarly understandable as offering different perspectives on life.

The ability to coin metaphors allows people not only to produce new concepts, but also to fill-in "knowledge gaps" in a creative, yet intellectually effortless, fashion. Recall from the previous chapter the story of my grandson at 15 months of age who, not possessing the appropriate term to describe the orange color of our household cat, Pumpkin, referred to it as *juice,* in obvious reference to the color of the orange juice that he drank on a regular basis. The child had obviously extracted the quality of "orangeness" from the liquid (the source domain) and applied it to a new referent—the cat's hair (the target domain). This is a perfect example of how children employ metaphor as a "conceptual gap-filler."

There are, of course, other figures of speech that occur in everyday discourse, but following Lakoff and Johnson's discovery of conceptual metaphors, these are now considered subcategories of the general process of metaphor. Nevertheless, there are two that are regularly studied separately—*metonymy* and *irony*—because of their particular semantic characteristics.

Metonymy is the use of an entity to refer to another that is related to it:[19]

She likes to read *Emily Dickinson* (= *the writings of Emily Dickinson*).
He's in *dance* (= *the dancing profession*).
My mom frowns on *blue jeans* (= *the wearing of blue jeans*).
New *windshield wipers* will satisfy him (= *the state of having new wipers*).

Synecdoche is a particular type of metonymy. It is the use of the part to represent the whole:

The *automobile* is destroying our health (= *the collection of automobiles*).
We need a couple of *strong bodies* for our teams (= *strong people*).

I've got a new *set of wheels* (= *car*).
We need *new blood* in this organization (= *new people*).

A conceptual formula of this type that requires special mention is *the face is the person.*

He's just another *pretty face.*
There are an awful lot of *faces* in the audience.
We need some new *faces* around here.

As we saw in Chapter 3, this concept also crystallizes in the nonverbal domain, especially in the art of portraiture. Expressions such as *saving face, face the music, putting on a happy/sad face* reveal our fascination with the face as a sign of character and personality.

Irony is the use of words to convey a meaning contrary to their literal sense: "I love being tortured"; "That stupid plan is clever." This is a truly remarkable form of discourse, based on exploiting the incongruities and complexities of an experience or a situation. As such, it is both a protective strategy, deflecting attention away from the self toward others, by which one can make value judgments without commitment, and a verbal weapon that can be used brutally against others.[20]

LOVE IS INDEED SWEET, METAPHORICALLY SPEAKING

We are now in a better position to provide an appropriate semiotic explanation to Ted's metaphorical statement: "Your kisses are sweeter than wine." First let's consider a few of the ways in which we conceptualize *love* in our culture:[21]

Love is a physical force
There were *sparks* between us.
We are *attracted* to each other.
My life *revolves* around her.
I am *magnetically drawn* toward her.

Love is a health/patient relationship
Theirs is a *sick* relationship.
Their romance is *dead;* it can't be *revived.*
Their relationship is *in good shape.*

Love is madness
I'm *crazy* about her.
I'm constantly *raving* about him.

He's gone *mad* over her.
I've *lost my head* over him.

Love is a magical force
She *cast* a spell over me.
The *magic* is gone.
She has *bewitched* me.
I'm *in a trance* over him.

Love is a sweet taste
You're so *sweet*.
She's my *sweetheart*.
He's my *honey*.

As these examples illustrate, *love* is indeed a stack of metaphors, as the poets have always known. Ted's statement is really no more than a particular use of the conceptual metaphor *love is a sweet taste*, which commonly surfaces in courtship and romance situations. This formula is a special manifestation of a broader one: *love is a taste in one's mouth*. This is why we say that *love* that is no longer *sweet* can leave a *bad, sour, rotten* taste in one's mouth. Like wine, love can both please and displease. So, as poetic as Ted might have appeared to his partner, he really was using a time-tested and time-worn formula to give a romantic verbal touch to his courtship performance.

Particularly productive as a source domain for *love* concepts is the perception of physical appearance and of its effects on the viewer. A few years ago, I collected data on this topic, by asking several teenage females in a Toronto high school how they would describe males in their school who they found to be *cool* or attractive by completing the sentence "He's . . ." Here's a sampling of the responses I got:[22]

Ironic insinuations of the "negative effect" the male teen is perceived to make on females
He's nasty
He's bad
He's down
He's heavy
He's dope

Perception of the male teen as an animal
He's a stag
He's fly
He's wild
He's a catch

Perception of the male teen as a rare or admirable object, entity, or place
He's a Ferrari

He's Park Avenue
He's divine
He's a god
He's an Adonis
He's a diamond

Perception of the male teen in terms of sexually stimulating bodily states
He's hot
He's a burning hunk of love
He sizzles
He's cool

Perception of the male teen as an edible food (implying a desire to eat him sexually)
He's full of beef
He's a stud muffin
He's a burger
He's sweet
He's yummy
He's got great buns

Perception of the male teen as a perfect work of art (thus imbuing him with a rare aesthetic quality)
He's a work of art
He's chiseled
He's a fine piece
He's a centerfold
He's picture-perfect
He's an 8 by 10

As Alice Deignan has recently argued, the use of such metaphorical strategies is not restricted to adolescent language; these are general strategies that allow people to encode subjective judgments in a way that conceals their subjectivity: "Speakers use a metaphorical expression to encode their approval, or—far more frequently—their disapproval, of a manifestation of desire. . . . The evaluation, thereby, takes on the appearance of objectivity."[23] Nor are such strategies peculiar to speakers of English. There are, in fact, many cross-cultural similarities in the ways in which sexual attractiveness and desire are modeled metaphorically. In the Chagga tribe of Tanzania, for example, the perception of *sex* and *love* as things that can be tasted manifests itself constantly in discourse about sex. In that society, the man is perceived to be the "eater" and the woman his "sweet food," as can be inferred from everyday expressions that mean, in translated form, "Does she taste sweet?" "She tastes sweet as sugar honey." Such a remarkable correspondence to the *love is a sweet taste* formula deployed by Ted suggests that this particular conceptual metaphor probably cuts across cultures.

METAPHOR IN EVERYDAY LIFE

Conceptual metaphors surface not only in common discourse, but in non-verbal codes, rituals, and behaviors as well. The metaphor *justice is blind,* for instance, crops up not only in conversations, but also in pictorial representations. This is why there are statues of blindfolded women inside courtrooms to symbolize justice. The metaphorical expression *the scales of justice* is evident in the sculptures of scales near or inside justice buildings. Similarly, Ted's *love is a sweet taste* concept finds expression not only in discourse, but in rituals of love-making in Western culture. This is why sweets are given to a loved one at St. Valentine's day, why matrimonial love is symbolized at a wedding ceremony by the eating of a cake, why lovers sweeten their breath with candy before kissing, and so on. Any ritualistic display of *love* will depend on what concept people infer to be more representative of a specific situation. For example, at weddings the concept of *sweetness* would probably be seen to fit the situation, whereas that of *physical attraction* would most likely be considered pertinent during other kinds of courtship situations.

More often than not, conceptual metaphors are also traces to a culture's historical past. A common expression such as "He has fallen from grace" would have been recognized instantly in a previous era as referring to the Adam and Eve story in the Bible. Today we continue to use it with only a dim awareness (if any) of its Biblical origins. Expressions that portray life as a journey—"I'm still a long way from my goal," "There is no end in sight"—are similarly rooted in Biblical stories. As the Canadian literary critic Northrop Frye aptly pointed out, one cannot penetrate such expressions, and indeed most of Western literature or art, without having been exposed, directly or indirectly, to the original Biblical stories.[24] These are the source domains for many of the conceptual metaphors we use today for talking about and judging human actions which bestow a kind of implicit metaphysical meaning and value to everyday life.

All *mythical* (from the Greek *mythos* "word," "speech," "tale of the gods") stories are, in effect, extended conceptual metaphors. These allow people to depict divine entities in terms of human images, with human bodily forms and emotions. It is extremely difficult to think of a divinity in any other way. In the Bible, for example, God is described as having physical characteristics and human emotions, but at the same time is understood to be a transcendent being.

The link to the past is also evident in proverbial language. Proverbs, like myths, are extended metaphors that provide sound practical advice:

You've got too many fires burning
(= advice to not do so many things at once)

Rome wasn't built in a day
(= advice to have patience)

Don't count your chickens before they're hatched
(= advice to be cautious)

An eye for an eye and a tooth for a tooth
(= equal treatment is required in love and war)

Early to bed and early to rise, makes a man healthy, wealthy, and wise
(= this was Benjamin Franklin's adaptation of Aesop's proverb "The gods help them that help themselves")

Every culture has its proverbs, aphorisms, and sayings. These constitute a remarkable code of ethics and of practical knowledge that anthropologists call "folk wisdom." Indeed, the very concept of *wisdom* implies the ability to apply proverbial language insightfully to a situation. As the American writer Maya Angelou (1928–) has put it, in proverbial language is "couched the collective wisdom of generations."

Homilies and sermons, too, dispense their own kind of advice and counsel through metaphor. Rarely does a preacher not use metaphorical discourse in a cohesive and persuasive way. The art of preaching lies in the ability to apply metaphorical concepts effectively to a topic—*sex is dirty, sin is punishable by fire,* etc.

The use of metaphor extends to scientific reasoning. Science often involves things that cannot be seen such as atoms, waves, gravitational forces, and magnetic fields. So, scientists use their metaphorical know-how to get a look, so to speak, at this hidden matter. That is why waves are said to *undulate* through empty space as water waves ripple through a still pond, atoms to *leap* from one quantum state to another, electrons to *travel in circles* around an atomic nucleus, and so on. The physicist K. C. Cole has put it into perspective as follows:[25]

The words we use are metaphors; they are models fashioned from familiar ingredients and nurtured with the help of fertile imaginations. "When a physicist says an electron is like a particle," writes physics professor Douglas Giancoli, "he is making a metaphorical comparison like the poet who says love is like a rose." In both images a concrete object, a rose or a particle, is used to illuminate an abstract idea, love or electron.

The poet and the scientist alike use metaphor to extrapolate a suspected inner connection among things. Metaphors are slices of truth; they are evidence of the human ability to see the universe as a coherent organism. When a metaphor is accepted as fact, it enters human life, taking on an independent conceptual existence in the real world, and thus it can suggest ways in which to bring about changes in and to the world. Euclidean geometry, for instance, gave the world a certain kind of visual metaphorical structure for millennia—a world of relations among points, lines, circles, and so on. This structure was, however, changed to suit new conditions and ideas. This is precisely what happened when the Russian mathematician Nicholai Lobachevski (1793–1856) imagined that Euclid's parallel lines would "meet" in some context, such as at the poles of a globe, thus giving the visual world a different structure.

6

NOW, YOU TELL ME ABOUT YOURSELF

Why Do We Tell Stories?

> Myth is an attempt to narrate a whole human experience, of which
> the purpose is too deep, going too deep in the blood and soul, for
> mental explanation or description.
>
> —D. H. Lawrence (1885–1930)

L et's rewind Martha's tape to the scene discussed in Chapter 4,
namely, when Ted asks Cheryl to tell him something about herself.
This time we note that after reciting her brief autobiography,
Cheryl turns to her partner and says, "Now, you tell me something about
yourself," obviously wanting to know a little about his life story.

To the semiotician, the telling of life stories is not simply a way to make
idle conversation. On the contrary, in such courtship performances the
semiotician would see it as yet another way of presenting an attractive *persona* to a sexual partner. However, that is not the primary reason why people tell their life stories to each other. They do so mainly to make sense of
who they are by weaving the various episodes and events of their life into
a story with a plot, with characters, with setting. This imparts structure,
purpose, and meaning (or lack thereof) to one's life in the overall scheme
of things.

Stories of all kinds give coherence and continuity to the thoughts and
experiences that people find meaningful. It would be no exaggeration, in
fact, to claim that human consciousness itself has a narrative structure.

This would explain why, early in life, children learn most of their concepts through the stories they are told. This would also explain why, throughout history, humans have produced narrative accounts—factual and fictional—to explain who they are, why they are here, and to make sense of otherwise random and chaotic events.

Interest in the origin and nature of storytelling is as old as civilization itself. In ancient Greece, the philosophers Xenophanes, Plato, and Aristotle criticized stories, especially myths, as artful and deceitful in explaining reality, and exalted reason instead as the only trustworthy form of intellect to gain access to reality. However, the exaltation of reason and its use in science has not eliminated the need for myth in Western civilization. On the contrary, we are constantly seeking stories (in the movies, on television programs, in novels) not only to be entertained, but also to gain insights into the mysteries of life.

NARRATIVE

The term *narrative* refers to something told, written, related (as in cinema), or exposed (as in scientific description). The narrative may be construed as *factual*, as in a newspaper report or a psychoanalytic session, or *fictional*, as in a novel, a comic strip, or a film. It is often difficult to determine the boundary line between fact and fiction, given the interplay of many psychological and social factors that coalesce in the production and interpretation of narratives. Whatever the case, in all cultures the narrative creations of story-tellers have always had a great impact on how people come to view human nature and the cosmos. This is why story-tellers enjoy an important status in all societies, be they soothsayers or writers of fiction (in the modern sense of the word). Even in an era of science, fictional works are felt by people as somehow revealing more about the human condition than do the piles of research papers written by so-called experts of the mind. As the writer David Lodge has phrased it, creating narratives "is one of the fundamental sense-making operations of the mind, and would appear to be both peculiar to and universal throughout humanity."[1]

The narrative mode of representing the world gives structure and logical coherence to a series of what would otherwise be perceived to be random actions. Animal programs on American television exemplify anecdotally how this mode accomplishes this. These are perceived by viewers as documenting animal behavior in scientific terms. Unedited, the actions of the animals caught on film—eating, hunting, mating—would hardly make up a meaningful story line. However, with the intervention of film editors, script writers, and ethological consultants, such programs always produce an intriguing account of the actions depicted on the film. The result is a scientific narrative of animal behavior that has been put together on the basis of ideas from genuine ethological sources. The narrative is compelling to the viewer because it "explains" the animals' actions in human terms, thus endowing them with human meaning and purpose.

Semiotically speaking, narratives are interpreted as signs. This is why we understand a novel or a movie, for example, not in terms of its parts but in terms of what it means overall (just as we do any individual sign). However, narratives are put together as texts, that is, according to a *code* which some semioticians prefer to call a *plot* or *narrative grammar*.[2] This provides the categories that allow people to talk coherently about characters and their actions. According to the late French semiotician Algirdas Julien Greimas (1917–92), these include such common themes as "hero," "opponent," "journey," "battle," which surface not only in novels, but also in a wide range of narrative texts from philosophical treatises to film plots and advertisements.[3] Indeed, life without heroes, opponents, journeys, and battles would be inconceivable, regardless of one's culture. Greimas claimed that differences in detail, and especially in how the final resolution or clarification of a plot unfolds, are due to the specific ways in which these categories are projected into the actual narratives of a culture. In a mystery novel, for instance, the hero may have several enemies, all of whom are the "opponent"; in a love story, a lover may be both a "hero" and an "opponent"; the dénouement of a love plot may end in a "battle;" and so on.

This would explain why the plots, characters, and settings that are found in stories across the world are remarkably similar. While one may lose some of the semantic nuances in translating stories from one language to another, one can easily transfer the basic narrative categories across languages with little or no loss of meaning. A story told in India is as understandable as a story told in Arkansas because their narrative grammars are virtually the same, Greimas would claim, even though their linguistic ones are vastly different.

Narrative grammar also provides the categories for sketching the autobiographies that people draw of themselves in situations such as our restaurant scene. In these, too, there are heroes, opponents, journeys, battles, just as there are in novels and movies. Biography is as old as recorded history. The rulers and nobles of ancient Egypt, Assyria, and Babylon had their deeds incised in stone and clay. The Old Testament tells of the lives of many patriarchs and prophets, and the four Gospels of the New Testament are essentially parallel biographies of Jesus Christ. Until about the middle of the seventeenth century, biography was generally commemorative, dealing with the exemplary lives of heroes and heroines, especially saints and martyrs, as well as with the cautionary lives of malefactors and tyrants—all of whom were depicted less as individuals than as actors in a stylized drama of salvation. The publication in 1791 of *The Life of Samuel Johnson, LL.D.* by James Boswell is generally thought to be the first biography in the modern sense of the word. During the nineteenth century, biographical writings proliferated, with the source materials—personal letters, journals, diaries—being preserved as if they were precious artifacts. In the twentieth century, the Austrian psychoanalyst Sigmund Freud (1856–1939) and other scientific observers of the individual and society, provided a further impetus for the exploration of personality through oral autobiographical narrative. This trend might explain why today it is felt that we can *know* a famous personage only if we *know* his or her biography. Programs on television, such as A & E's *Biography* series, play precisely on this widely held belief.

MYTH

The desire to know the biography of interesting people (artists, scientists, actors, etc.) is a modern-day phenomenon. In early cultures, people were hardly interested in each other's life stories, especially since they interacted with each other on a routine basis. Rather, the biographies that early peoples sought to know were those of the gods, of the supernatural beings who ran the world behind the scenes.

The stories that the early peoples told are known as *myths*. These poetic narratives provided reassuring information on the reason for things—on how the world came into being, who the gods were, how humans and animals were created, and how customs, gestures, and other human symbolic activities originated. Myths bespeak the spiritual nature of *Homo sapiens*. Spirit is a feeling rather than an idea, so the language most appropriate for talking about this feeling is not that of propositions or hypotheses, but of poetic images. Myths produced our first images of the spiritual world, images which to this day are felt in some undefined way to represent meaningful ideas. They persist, even in societies where they are not perceived to represent literal truths. The great mythical themes of all cultures are felt to be parables of a timeless logic, symbols of an intuitive knowledge of human nature and destiny which we feel must be present in our lives. Myths do not distinguish between spirit and nature, religion and life; neither do they separate symbolic truth or fantasy from literal truth or fact.

From the beginnings of Western culture, myth has presented a problem of meaning and interpretation, and a history of controversy has accumulated about both the value and the status of mythic traditions. In ancient Greece, myth (*mythos*) was seen to be in tension with reason (*logos*), which implied a rational and analytic mode of explaining reality, although Aristotle concluded that in some of the early Greek creation myths, *logos* and *mythos* often overlapped. Plato saw myths simply as allegories, as literary devices for persuasively developing an argument. In the Judeo-Christian tradition the notion of *history* has frequently been opposed to *myth*. Complicating this opposition was the concept that God, although existing outside of ordinary time and space, was revealed to humanity within human history and society. *Mythos, logos,* and history overlap in the prologue to the Gospel of John in the *New Testament;* there, Jesus Christ is portrayed as the *Logos,* who came from eternity into historical time. No wonder then that early Christian theologians, attempting to understand the Christian revelation, argued incessantly about the roles of *mythos, logos,* and history in the Biblical account.

In the eighteenth and nineteenth centuries, myth caught the interest of the emerging academic disciplines of cultural anthropology and the history of religions. A new cadre of scholars tried to make sense of the world's seemingly irrational and fantastic mythic stories, putting forth theories of how human cultures must have evolved from an early state of ignorance and irrationality to one of rationality. The hypothesis that gained a foothold in these new disciplines was that the earliest myths were genuine "theories" of the world, explaining natural events in a nonscientific way, in the same fashion that we impart knowledge of the world to children. The mythic tales we tell children are universally understandable as nonscientific stories about the world. The mythic imagination, these scholars claimed, ascribed lightning, thunder, and other natural phenomena to awesome and frightful gods. Only in succeeding stages did societies look for more scientific ways to explain natural phenomena.

In his *New Science* of 1725, Giambattista Vico saw the birth of culture in the mythic imagination (or *fantasia* as he called it). Recall from the previous chapter that Vico viewed the "life cycle" of cultures as unfolding according to three stages, the age of the gods, the age of heroes, and the age of equals. During the first age, the mythic *fantasia* created "poetic images" of the world that gave it a spiritual *raison d'être*. If there was thunder in the sky, then the mythic fantasia would hear it as the angry voice of a god; if there was rain, then it would see it as the weeping of a sorrowful god. During the second age (of heroes), the mythic fantasia gave way to a more heroic imagination. The tales that it impelled were no longer of gods and supernatural exploits, but of the culture's human heroes. These are known as *legends*—stories that document the deeds and accomplishments of real human beings, of their lives, and of their journeys. The mythic fantasia is still operative during this age, Vico affirmed, but less so than previously. For this reason legends are still highly imaginative, but at the same time also refer to actual events in the hero's life. Legends are, in fact, a blend of fact and fantasy. Among the most famous legends of all time are the *Iliad* and the *Odyssey* of ancient Greece and the *Aeneid* of ancient Rome. It is during the third age (of equals) that the fantasia becomes dim, and that the stories that people tell are no longer about gods or legendary heroes, but about society as a whole, about the roles that all people, from leaders to common folk, play in the social arena. The third age is an age of rational history, of objective facts and knowledge (dates, treaties, social movements, political ideologies, etc.) behind which the "tellers of history" can hide their personal perspectives. Indeed, the reason why histories are constantly being revised is not only because they are by their nature incomplete, but also because they can never be totally free of the historian's perspective. On the other hand, myth and legend, like all works of the fantasia, are perceived to enfold eternal truths about the human condition. For this reason they are handed down and preserved unrevised for posterity.

The primary function of myth is to relate how the world came into being. In some cultures, the creation of the world is said to proceed from a state of nothingness. The deity who made it is portrayed as all-powerful, and may come to the forefront to become the center of social life, or else may withdraw and become a distant or peripheral deity. In other cultures, the deity is seen as giving order to a universe in a state of chaos, separating light from darkness, and assigning the sun, moon, stars, plants, animals, and human beings to their proper roles in life.

There are several other types of creation themes detectable in the world's mythic traditions. Among the Navajo and Hopi tribes of North America, for example, creation is thought to be a progression upward from the underground. The emergence of the human world is said to be the final progression. A Polynesian myth places the various layers of human emergence in a coconut shell. In many African and oriental mythic traditions, creation is imagined as breaking forth from a fertile egg. The egg is the potential for all life and, sometimes, as in the myth of the Dogon people of West Africa, it is referred to as the "placenta" of the world.

A common theme of other mythical traditions is that of the "first parents." In the Babylonian creation story, for instance, the first parents, Apsu and Tiamat, bear offspring who later defeat their parents in a battle. From the immolated body of Tiamat the earth is created. In other world-parent myths, such as those of the Egyptians and Polynesians, the parents beget offspring but remain in close embrace; the offspring live in darkness, and in their desire for light they shove the parents apart, creating a space for the deities to create the human world. In other mythic traditions, such as those found throughout Romania and India, creation comes about not through parents, but through the agency of a bird who dives into the primordial waters to bring up a small piece of earth which later expands into the world.

Related to such *cosmogonic* myths, but at the other extreme, are myths describing the end of the world (so-called *eschatological* myths). These are usually products of urban traditions. They also presuppose the creation of the world by a moral deity, but one who in the end destroys the world he or she created, having become angry with the very creatures he or she made. Meanwhile human beings are supposed to prepare for an afterlife existence of happiness or of eternal anguish, according to how they have lived their lives on earth. A universal conflagration and a final battle of the gods are envisioned as part of this mythic tradition. In an Aztec myth, for instance, several worlds are created and destroyed by the gods before the creation of the human world. In other myths, death is not present in the world for a long period of time, but enters it through an accident or because human beings have overstepped the proper limits of their knowledge.

Myths that describe the actions and character of beings who are responsible for the discovery of a particular cultural artifact or technological process are called myths of the *culture hero*. Prometheus (in Greek mythology), who stole fire from the gods, is a prototype of this kind of figure. In the Dogon culture of West Africa, the blacksmith who steals seeds for the human community from the granary of the gods is similar to Prometheus. In Ceram, in Indonesia, Hainuwele is yet another such figure; from the orifices of her body she provides the community with essential and indulgent goods.

Usually related to initiation rituals, myths of *birth* and *rebirth* tell how life can be renewed, time reversed, or humans transmuted into new beings. Such myths are found in several tribal cultures of Africa, South America, and Melanesia, as well as in many of the founding myths of Western culture. These myths typically describe the coming of an ideal society or of a savior who will bestow new life among the people.

Since the beginnings of cities, sometime in the fourth and third millennia B.C., some creation myths have recounted the founding of cities. *Foundation* myths, as they are called, thus tell of how cities developed out of ceremonial centers that were seen to possess sacred power that could be summoned in a specific sacred place. The myth of Gilgamesh in Babylon and that of Romulus and Remus in Rome are typical foundation myths.

As mentioned above, narratives are put together on the basis of a *plot grammar*. This applies as well to myth. A German scholar who spent most of his academic life in England in the nineteenth century, Friedrich Max Müller, claimed that the categories of myth were, in fact, embryonic grammatical forms, constituting the blueprint from which language grammar evolved. Following an in-depth study of the religions and myths of India, Müller posited, for example, that the gods and their actions did not represent beings or events, but rather incipient nouns and verbs representing visual images of natural phenomena (such as thunder or the sea).[4] The French anthropologist Claude Lévi-Strauss (1908–) pursued this line of reasoning further in the twentieth century, pointing out that there are certain clusters of relationships in myth that, although expressed in the narrative and dramatic content of the story, conform to the structure of the language in which they are framed. Later, he contended that the same mythological form is at work in all languages and cultures, in scientific works and tribal myths alike.[5]

If such scholars are correct, then myth, language, and culture came into being at the same time. This would explain why ancient mythic rituals continue to be performed to this day (in contemporary versions, of course, as we shall see below). Indeed, there are remarkable points of contact between the kind of structure a society's system of everyday life reveals and the cosmic order that myths describe. For instance, in Indo-European cultures the form that a myth takes reflects a tripartite structure that mirrors the tripartite nature of Indo-European social structure, with a priest or ruler at the top of a hierarchy, warriors in the middle, and farmers, herdsmen, and craftsmen at the base. This tripartite structure of myth operates as a primordial kind of language for the formulation of fundamental meanings within Indo-European cultures.

This is also why many psychoanalysts nowadays view the dynamics of individual psychic life and the "collective unconscious" of society as images of each other. Sigmund Freud, for instance, framed his theory of personality conflicts in terms of the Oedipus and Electra stories of ancient Greece. Carl Jung (1875–1961), too, developed his theory of *archetypes* from the simple observation that people living all over the world possess remarkably similar mythic rituals and symbols. Jung saw the unconscious part of the mind as a "receptacle" of primordial images, memories, fantasies, wishes, fears, and feelings that are too weak to become conscious. So, he claimed, they manifest themselves instead by their influence on conscious processes and, most strikingly, by the symbolic forms they take in dreams, art works, and rituals. For instance, the genital symbols and themes that cultures incorporate into their rites of passage, that they represent in their varied works of art, and that find their way into the stories that are communicated in cultural context, are understandable in approximately the same ways by all humans because they evoke universal sexual imagery at the level of the mythic unconscious. This level of mind continues to influence patterns of perception and meaning-making in the modern-day human species.

As an illustration of the Jungian notion of archetype, consider his example of the "trickster." In every person there lies a certain instinct for childlike mischief. This may be expressed as a playful desire for capriciousness or by the need to play devil's advocate in a conversation. On the other hand, it may manifest itself as a malicious urge to mock or ridicule someone else's achievements. It might cause us to contemplate stealing something for the sheer thrill of it or to torment someone by hiding his or her belongings. At such times, the "trickster archetype" is directing our behavior. Jung looked at the ways these archetypes gain expression not only through such everyday behaviors, but also through images and symbols contained in dreams, fairy tales, myths, legends, poetry, and painting. In Western culture, the trickster archetype surfaces, for instance, as

Dickens' Artful Dodger, as the fabled character known as *Rumpelstiltsken,* as Shakespeare's Puck in *A Midsummer Night's Dream,* and in the art of many contemporary comedians. Archetypes can take any form according to Jung; they can crystallize, for instance, as an object or an animal in stories and in works of pictorial art.

The gist of the psychoanalytic work on myth is that the images of mythic tales have become embedded in human consciousness. This would explain why there is a constant need in the human species to think transcendentally and to search for meaning beyond earthly life. No culture can be understood without an understanding of its myths. Rituals are explicit enactments of myths. They are attempts to harmonize the human condition with the patterns of nature by dramatizing such fundamental phenomena as the daily rising and setting of the sun, the alternation of the seasons, the changing phases of the moon, and the annual planting and harvesting of crops. Ritual, as found in primitive religions, is a mythic art form expressing and celebrating humanity's meaningful participation in the affairs of the universe.

In some contemporary cultures, the mythological perspective continues to be so intertwined with the system of everyday life that it is impossible to distinguish it from the other components of the system. Only greater and lesser degrees of the mythic or sacred exist. In such cultures, religion as a separate domain does not exist and members of such societies would have the greatest difficulty in talking about their religion as such. They would have no way of distinguishing their rituals for, say, successful hunting from what Western culture would call the pure technique of hunting. Symbolic forms on spears, boats, and household utensils are not unessential decorations in these cultures but functional symbols imbued with mythic meanings for their effective use.

FAIRY TALES

The mythic imagination has spawned its own progeny of narrative genres in all cultures. Folktales, legends, fairy tales, and fables are the narrative descendants of myth. Like myth, these do not mirror what happens: they explore and predict what can happen. They not only recount states and events; they interpret them.

Take, for example, the kind of story told commonly to children known as the fairy tale. Taking place in a wonderland filled with magic and unusual characters, fairy tales (which rarely have to do with fairies) hold a strange magical appeal over every child, no matter what age. The persistence of stories such as *Cinderella, Snow White,* or *Little Red Riding Hood* attests to this enduring fascination. These tales tell of an underdog hero or heroine who is put through great trials or must perform seemingly impossible tasks, and who, with magical assistance, secures his or her birthright or a suitable marriage partner. Frequently, such stories begin with "Once upon a time" and end with "And they lived happily ever after," formulas that imbue them with a sense of eternity and transcendental meaning.

A fairy, in folklore, is a diminutive supernatural creature who typically has a human form and lives in an imaginary region called a fairyland. Stories abound of its magical interventions in mortal affairs, from ancient legendary tales to Disney's modern-day cinematic portrayals. The mythic imagination not only conceives of fairyland as a distinct domain, but also visualizes fairies as living in everyday surroundings such as hills, trees, and streams. The belief in fairy-like creatures is an almost universal attribute of early cultures. In ancient Greek literature the sirens in Homer's *Odyssey* are fairies, and a number of the heroes in the *Iliad* have fairy lovers in the form of nymphs. The *Gandharvas* (celestial singers and musicians), who figure in Sanskrit poetry, were fairies, as were the *Hathors,* or female genies, of ancient Egypt, who appeared at the birth of a child and predicted the child's future. The belief in fairies seems to point to an unconscious *animism—* the deeply embedded feeling that natural objects have a form of consciousness that can assume a separate, spiritual, phantom-like form outside of the object. It can move from person to person, from the dead to the living, and from and into plants, animals, and lifeless objects.

Fairies are depicted in European literature in such works as Shakespeare's *A Midsummer Night's Dream* and *Romeo and Juliet* (in Mercutio's "Queen Mab" speech), *The Faerie Queene* by Edmund Spenser, *L'Allegro* and *Comus* by John Milton, *Tales of Mother Goose* by Charles Perrault, *Grimm's Fairy Tales,* by the brothers Jacob and Wilhelm Grimm, and *Irish Fairy Tales* by William Butler Yeats. In these stories, fairies are generally considered beneficent towards humans—like the "tooth fairy" that we describe to our children today. They are sensitive and capricious, however, and often inclined to play pranks; so if their resentment is not to be aroused, they must be spoken well of and always treated with obedience. Bad fairies are portrayed instead as being responsible for such misfortunes as the bewitching of children, the substitution of ugly fairy babies, known as changelings, for human infants, and the sudden death of animals.

One of my own favorite collections of fairy tales is the *Brer Rabbit* set of stories which were recited as part of the mythology of West Africans before Africans were brought as slaves to the American South. In America, however, West African religion was almost obliterated by Christianity, and although African-Americans continued to tell *Brer Rabbit* stories, these tales no longer functioned mythologically, until Walt Disney revived a version of them for the silver screen. In the *Brer Rabbit* tales, animals are portrayed as having the power of speech and the ability to conduct themselves as humans. Although the point is sometimes disputed, the *Brer Rabbit* stories may have served the function of indirect social satire, being filled with criticism of society which would have been dangerous to express directly.

THE PERSISTENCE OF MYTH

Mythic thinking is now largely unconscious, but it shows up nevertheless in social rituals, performances, and spectacles that are shaped by its themes. Even if we live in a culture that is based largely on rational thinking—for example, we plan our days around a series of socially fixed events, we mark time precisely, we live by the principles of science and technology—the mythic form of thinking and communicating has not disappeared from our system of everyday life. Its remnants are everywhere: we give cards with poetic, mythic messages on them, we tell nursery rhymes and fairy tales to our children, we read the horoscope daily, and so on. From our mythological heritage, we have inherited the names of the days of the week and months of the year. Tuesday is the day dedicated to the Germanic war god Tir, Wednesday to the Germanic chief god Wotan, Thursday to Thor, Friday to the goddess of beauty Frigga, Saturday to the god Saturn, January to the Roman god Janus, and so on. Our planets bear a nomenclature similarly derived from myth: Mars is named after the Roman god of war, Venus after the Greek goddess of beauty. Mythic themes, like that of the earth as a mother, of life as a journey, of an eternal battle between the forces of good and evil, reverberate in our feasts and spectacles. As the semiotician Roland Barthes showed, the presence of myth can be detected even in such an apparently idiotic spectacle as commercial wrestling. This spectacle is emotionally involving for many people because it represents a mythic fight between good and evil.[6] This is why some people become excited and even aggressive at wrestling matches: they perceive them as a battle between the forces of good and evil. The good is symbolized in the persona of a handsome and muscular wrestler, the bad in that of a depraved, ugly wrestler.

If Barthes is right, then mythic thinking, which originally had a cosmological function allowing the early peoples to understand how they fit into the natural scheme of things, has now taken on sociological and pedagogical functions, supporting and validating a certain social order and instructing individuals of that order how to live their lives. In early Hollywood westerns, for instance, the mythic good versus evil theme was often symbolized by having heroes wear white, and villains black. So, too, in sports events this theme transforms the game into a mythic battle between the forces of good (the home side) and those of evil (the intruder or visiting team). The fanfare associated with preparing for the "big event," like the World Series of baseball or the Superbowl of American football, has a ritualistic quality to it similar to the pomp and circumstance that ancient armies engaged in before going out to battle. The symbolism of the home team's (army) uniform, the valor and strength of star players (the heroic warriors), and the tactical leadership abilities of the coach (the army general) all have a profound emotional effect on the home fans (one of the two warring nations). The game (the battle) is perceived to unfold in moral terms—as a struggle of righteousness and beauty against the forces of ugliness and baseness. The players are exalted as heroes or condemned as villains. Victory is interpreted in moral terms as a victory of good over evil, or as a crushing defeat from a conquering army. The game is, as television and radio announcers were wont to say a few years back, "real life, real drama!"

FOOD AS MYTH

Barthes suggested that virtually anything that we consume or take part in communally continues to have mythic connotations that recall the kinds of beliefs that ancient people had. To grasp what he meant, consider the kinds of attitudes people show towards food. In our culture, we tend not to eat rabbits, keeping them instead as pets. Why? The reason, Barthes would no doubt suggest, is that rabbits have a mythic status in our unconscious mind—think of all the stories we tell our children with rabbits in them as heroic figures (for example, the Easter Bunny). For this reason we do not think of rabbit meat as edible in the same way as we do other kinds of animal meats that we routinely ingest, such as lamb meat, poultry meat, and especially bovine meat (beef steaks, hamburgers, etc.). In India, on the other hand, a cow is classified as sacred and, therefore, is not perceived to be a source of food. It is something unassailable and revered, a veritable *sacred cow*. In North American culture, not only rabbits, but also foxes and dogs are not eaten because they resonate with mythological meanings by way of our tales, legends, and traditions; but foxes are reckoned a culinary delicacy in Russia, and dogs a special treat in China. This is why differences in cuisine tend consistently to be perceived as fundamental differences in world-view and lifestyle. Consider this example. Those living in an Anglo-American culture eat fish willingly, but not the eyes of fish; in other cultures, fish eyes are eaten along with the rest of the fish. Those not accustomed to eating the eyes of fish generally experience discomfort or queasiness upon seeing someone else eat them. It is a small step from such an unpleasant sensation to a conception of the eaters as "barbaric" and the food as "unnatural." It is instructive to note, by the way, that when someone eventually comes to accept the food tastes of others as appetizing, the previously "unnatural" food is reclassified as an "exotic" delicacy. Indeed, such reclassifications manifest themselves routinely in the desire North Americans have to eat Italian, Mexican, and Japanese cuisine.

Claude Lévi-Strauss referred to the meanings associated with food as falling into two domains—"the raw" and "the cooked."[7] Cooking is concrete evidence of the human ability to transform nature. According to Lévi-Strauss, this transformation was accomplished by two processes, roasting and boiling, both of which were a result of the first technological advances made by human beings. Roasting implies a direct contact between the food and a fire and, thus, is technologically primitive. It is associated with "the raw." Boiling reveals an advanced form of technological thinking, since the cooking process is mediated by a pot and a cooking medium. Boiling is thus associated with "the cooked." Interestingly, this opposition is the source of various social traditions. In the Hindu caste system, for instance, the higher castes may receive only raw food from the lower castes, whereas the lower castes are allowed to accept any kind of cooked food from any caste.

To get a firmer sense of the interconnection between culture and food, imagine being in a "Robinson Crusoe" situation. Robinson Crusoe, the hero of Daniel Defoe's 1719 novel of the same name, was a shipwrecked

English sailor who survived for years on a small tropical island. Let's suppose that you have somehow been abandoned alone on an isolated island in the middle of nowhere, cut off from the rest of the world, to fend for yourself. Without the support and protection systems of society, your instincts will urge you to survive in any way that you can. Clearly, your need for food and water will at first take precedence over all else. In a basic sense, your cognitive state will "descend" to a purely biological level of existence. When your hunger becomes extreme, your tastes in food will hardly be guided by cultural perceptions of "naturalness" or lack thereof. You will consume any flora or hunt any fauna that will satisfy your hunger. Eating food in such a drastic situation has only one function—to ensure survival.

Now, let's suppose that you discover other similarly abandoned people on a remote part of the same island. Since there is strength in numbers, you all decide to stay together as a group. To reduce the risk of not finding food and of not eating, the group decides to assign specific roles to each person for hunting food and for its preparation. After a period of time, what will emerge from these agreements is a "proto-culture," based on a shared survival strategy. As time passes, other "social contracts" and arrangements will undoubtedly be made, and the cooking of food will become more and more routine and subject to communal taste preferences.

The purpose of this vignette has been to exemplify how the preparation of food was probably the event that led to the creation of culture. No wonder then that in early cultures, food—the source of survival—was offered to the gods. The sacredness of food continues to be felt to this day. Virtually all of the world's religious ceremonies are centered on food. The *raison d'être* of the Catholic mass, for instance, is to partake symbolically of the consecrated body and blood of Christ. Specific types of food are served and eaten traditionally at Thanksgiving, Easter, Christmas. Food, invariably, is a primary constituent of communal rituals and feasts like weddings. We plan our days around meals. Even going out on a date would be unthinkable without some eating component associated with this event (from the popcorn eaten at movie theaters to the elaborate restaurant meal that our two protagonists consumed in our imaginary vignette).

The act of eating in a public setting typically reflects ritualistic structure. We do not devour food when others are around, we do it according to an *eating code.* The predictable routines leading up to the eating event at a high-class restaurant, for instance, are suggestive of an intrinsic need for ritual. There is no motive for eating at such places, really, other than to engage with our eating partner or partners in an act of symbolic acknowledgment that eating is basic to our existence, both biologically and symbolically.

The symbolic value of food can be seen in most of the world's mythic and religious accounts of human origins. The story of Adam and Eve in the Bible revolves around the eating of an apple. In the Garden of Eden, the apple is described by the Biblical account as a "forbidden" fruit. The apple's latent religious symbolism is the probable reason why Apple Computers chose this fruit as its logo, thus imbuing the use of its computers with connotations of "forbidden" knowledge.

The discovery and cultivation of the apple date back to 6500 B.C. in Asia Minor. Ramses II of Egypt cultivated apples in orchards along the Nile in the thirteenth century B.C. The ancient Greeks also cultivated apple trees from the seventh century B.C. onwards. They designated the apple "the golden fruit," since Greek mythology, like Christian doctrine, assigned a primordial significance to the apple. An apple from the Garden of the Hesperides was given to Hera as a wedding present when she married Zeus. The mention of the apple in the Bible is of unknown origin. In its original version, there is no mention of an apple in the Book of Genesis, just of a "forbidden fruit." It was only much later, when painters and sculptors became interested in the story artistically, that they assigned to the forbidden fruit an identity, namely, that of the apple.

The point of this mythic excursus on the apple is to underscore the point that food is imbued with mythic meaning across all cultures. Foods like bread and lamb, for instance, invariably evoke latent mythic symbolism in our culture. This is why we talk of the *bread of life*, of *earning your bread*, of *sacrificial lambs*. Indeed, in many western European languages the words for bread are often synonymous with life. Many Christians say grace before starting a meal together; many Jews say special prayers before partaking of wine and bread.

So, what about fast food? How does it fit in with the theme of myth? In a society where "fast living" and "the fast lane" are appropriate metaphors for the system of everyday life, everything seems indeed to be "moving too fast," leaving little time for mythic rituals. However, this is not the case. Since the middle part of the twentieth century, the fast-food industry has become a multi-billion dollar business. Why do people go to fast-food restaurants, the semiotician would ask. Is it because of the food?

Is it to be with friends and family? Is it because the food is affordable and the service fast? Is it because the atmosphere is congenial? Most people would answer these questions affirmatively. The fast-food restaurant seems to provide an opportunity to stay a while with family or friends, and most people would acknowledge that the food at a McDonald's or a Wendy's is affordable and that the service is fast and polite. Indeed, many people today probably feel more at home at a McDonald's restaurant than in their own households. This is, in fact, the semiotic key to unlocking the meaning of fast-food restaurants.

Consider the case of McDonald's. As of 1973, one new McDonald's outlet was being opened every day. Today, billions of McDonald's hamburgers are sold every month. Ronald McDonald is as much a cultural icon and childhood mythological figure as is Santa Claus. The McDonald's "golden arches" logo is now one of the more recognized ones in the world. The mythology of eating has, clearly, not disappeared. It has been revamped by marketers and advertisers to meet new demands, new social realities.

The message underlying the McDonald's symbolism is one basically of puritan values: law and order, cleanliness, friendliness, hospitality, hard work, self-discipline, and family values. In a society that is on the verge of shedding its traditional puritanical heritage and value systems, McDonald's comes forward as a savior which claims to "do it all for you." Eating at McDonald's is, like any religious ceremony, imbued with ritual and symbolism. The golden arches, like the arches of ancient cities, herald a new age, one based on traditional values. By satisfying a "Big Mac attack," you are, in effect, satisfying a deep metaphorical need to eat symbolically. From the menu to the uniforms, McDonald's imposes standardization, just as do the world's organized religions. As with any ritualistic experience, the eating event at McDonald's is designed to be cathartic and redeeming.

The success of McDonald's is tied, of course, to changes in society. The socioeconomic need to have a two-person, working household led to radical changes in the traditional family structure in the late 1960s. Fewer and fewer North American families had the time to eat meals together within the household, let alone the energy to prepare elaborate dinners. In modern-day households, meals are routinely consumed in front of television sets and, given the increasing number of such sets in the house, family members may not even be in the same space at dinner. The home, ironically, has become a place where very busy people now tend to eat apart. Enter McDonald's (or Wendy's, or Burger King) to the rescue! Eating out at such fast-food places—which are affordable, quick, and cheery—brings the family together, at the same table, under the same roof.

It is interesting to note that in the 1950s food eaten at such "joints" was perceived to be "junk": injurious to one's health and only to be consumed by adolescents because their youthful metabolism could break it down more quickly and because they could eventually "recover" from its negative health effects. In no time whatsoever junk food, promoted by effective ad campaigns, became an indulgence permissible to anyone of any age, from very young children to seniors. The compulsion to consume junk food has now even led to descriptions such as "junk-food addict," "junk-food mania," and the like, which reflect the "insanity" of eating such food. Yet, we continue to do so and with great zeal. "I'm going to give myself a treat," is the expression we use to rationalize our self-indulgences into the "junk heap" of food items that are replete with a concoction of chemicals that are dangerous to health. As we shall see in Chapter 10, the very fact that fast food has become part of our system of everyday life attests, rather conspicuously, to the persuasive power of media advertising.

7

AT ARM'S LENGTH

The Meanings of Spaces

We shape our buildings: thereafter they shape us.

—Winston Churchill (1874–1965)

Martha's videotape contains much more footage that is of interest to semioticians. Let's pick another segment to view randomly—the part where a third person, Mark, enters the scene. He is one of Ted's friends, who happened to be at the same restaurant. Seeing Ted and his companion, he decides to go over to their table and say hello. A typical greeting encounter ensues, whereby Ted introduces Mark to Cheryl. Now, before proceeding to view the introduction let's pause the tape for a second to ponder a few relevant questions. During the greeting ritual, how close do you think the two strangers, Cheryl and Mark, will stand to each other? Will they shake hands delicately or with force? For a relatively short or for a drawn-out period of time? Will they touch any other parts of each other's bodies?

As we allow the tape to go forward, we see that they stood, predictably, at arm's length from each other, that they did not touch any part of each other's bodies other than the hands. To the semiotician, the predictability of these behaviors suggests the existence of a *proemic code* regulating the zones Cheryl and Mark maintained between each other and a *tactile code* governing touch. Executing the greeting protocol at a close distance would have been perceived by both Cheryl and Mark to constitute a breach of "personal space." It would, in effect, have been interpreted as a transgression of an imaginary boundary line around the body which can only be traversed by those with whom a person is intimate. This is also why they did not touch any other body part, other than the hands. Now, since Cheryl's and Mark's behavior is coded, it should come as no surprise to find that it is not universal. Indeed, people in other cultures touch much more upon meeting one another and stand closer to each other than we do in North America.

Proxemic codes pervade the entire system of everyday life. Consider the following typical scenario, as a case in point. Imagine entering an elevator on the fifth floor of a multi-floor skyscraper. There are three people already in the elevator, obvious strangers to each other, near or leaning against the walls of the elevator, facing the door or looking down at the ground, and silent. Where will you stand? Near one of the others? Or will you go to the remaining corner? In what direction will you orient your body? Will you face the other passengers or will you face the door? Without going into a detailed analysis of the situation, if you have been living in American society for a period of time, you will know exactly what proxemic code is applicable to the socially structured space known as the elevator. The code informs you to face the door or look down at the floor to avoid eye contact with the others, and, of course, to maintain silence. So critical is this code in maintaining social harmony that if you decide to act in some other way—that is, to face the others, to look directly at them, to sing—the others would become uneasy or angry at you, because they would interpret your behavior as being either conflictual or disturbed. To cope with your breach of conduct, they might ignore your actions completely, as if they had not occurred.

INTERPERSONAL SPACE

To execute the greeting ritual, Mark and Cheryl extended their right hands, but kept their bodies at arm's length from each other. The anthropologist Edward T. Hall, fascinated by the invisible boundaries people keep when interacting in such situations, decided to measure them in the early 1960s.[1] Remarkably, he found that these could be measured very accurately, allowing for predictable statistical variation, and that they varied systematically from culture to culture. In North American culture, he found that a distance of under six inches between two people was reserved for intimates. Within this zone the senses of people are activated and their physical presence is unmistakable. It is a space reserved for love-making, comforting, and protecting. A 6 to 12 inch zone between individuals is the space where interactions between family members and close friends unfold. A distance of 1.5 to 4 feet is the minimal comfort zone between nonintimate individuals. This is the space where handshaking and other forms of tactile communication are carried out. A distance of 4 to 6 feet is considered non-involving and non-threatening by most individuals. This is the space in which people carry out casual social discourse. Formal discourse, on the other hand, occurs within a 7 to 12 foot zone. Finally, Hall found that a distance of 12 feet and beyond is the zone people tend to keep between themselves and public figures. Discourse at this distance is highly structured and formalized (for example, lectures, speeches, etc.). Parenthetically, it is interesting to note that the connotations associated with interpersonal spaces are reflected in language. This is why we use such expressions as *Keep your distance, They're very close, We've drifted far apart, You're trespassing into my personal space, I can't quite get to him, Please keep in touch.*

Follow-up research has shown that such distances are modified by various factors. For example, younger people maintain closer zones when interacting than do older people; similarly, those of the opposite sex stay farther apart than do those of the same sex. Also influencing interpersonal zones are such factors as: the topic of discourse (pleasant topics attract, unpleasant ones detract), the setting (lighting, noise, available space, etc.), the physical appearance of an interlocutor (those perceived to be more attractive draw in the person more), the interlocutor's personality (people tend to stay closer to a friendly person), and the status of the interlocutor (those with higher social status are given more space than those of less).

Proxemic codes not only regulate interpersonal zones, but also the orientation of the body and the social meanings ascribed to its relative location (above or below a platform, behind or in front of a desk). When someone is standing on a stage at the front of an audience, for example, he or she is perceived to be more important than those sitting down. Speeches, lectures, classes, and musical performances are coded in this way. Officials, managers, directors, and the like sit behind a desk to convey importance and superiority. Only their superiors can walk behind it to talk to them. To show friendliness, the person behind the desk would have to come out and sit with the other person in a different part of the room.

TOUCH

Like proxemic codes, tactile codes also regulate social interaction. When people shake hands, for instance, the length and dynamics of the handshake will communicate much more than greeting—the longer a handshake lasts, for instance, the more it entails an emotional response. Holding hands with a child presupposes a different dynamic (variation in force or intensity) than holding hands with a lover. Patting a superior to convey approval or appreciation also involves a different dynamic than touching a friend. These codes vary significantly from culture to culture.[2] In San Juan, Puerto Rico the rate at which people touch each other during social discourse is 180 times per hour, in Paris it is 110, and in London and New York it is 0. In Japanese society, during infancy and childhood a close tactile relationship among family members is encouraged, but at adolescence and beyond, touch in general is discouraged. Some clinical psychologists attribute many of the depressive syndromes that afflict people living in North American urban centers to a culturally-conditioned fear and abhorrence of touch. Opportunistically, "touch therapy" clinics have sprung up all over North America to combat these syndromes.

Whatever the truth, there is no doubt that touch still occurs in all cultures, but that its manifestations vary from culture to culture because it is *coded* differently. For this reason, it is shaped by the class, status, and social roles of the interlocutors. Tactile codes inform individuals who they are allowed to touch and who not to touch, where it is permissible to touch another person, and so on. For example, a doctor or nurse may touch a patient, but the reverse is normally perceived as a trespass. An adult may pat a child on the head to designate approval, but a child patting an adult on the head has no specifiable social meaning. Touching oneself in certain parts, like the head and the face, is generally acceptable, but touching oneself in the genital area is construed as either offensive or, in some places, illegal. Linking arms normally indicates companionship, putting one's arm around someone's shoulder typically indicates friendship or intimacy, and holding hands conveys intimacy. In North American culture, male friends touch each other more on the shoulders, chest, and legs than do female friends. Female friends, on the other hand, touch each other on the hair, face, neck, and forearms more than do male friends.

The most common form of tactile communication is handshaking. The zoologist Desmond Morris claims that the Western form of this ritual may have started as a way to show that neither person was holding a weapon.[3] It thus became a "tie sign," because of the bond it was designed to create. Throughout the centuries, this sign became a symbol of equality among individuals, being used to seal agreements of all kinds. Indeed, refusing to shake someone's outstretched hand will invariably be interpreted, even today, as the opposite—a sign of aggressiveness or a challenge. Predictably, handshaking reveals a high degree of cross-cultural variation. People can give a handshake by squeezing the hand (as Europeans and North Americans do), shaking the other's hand with both hands, shaking the hand and then patting the other's back or hugging him or her, leaning forward or standing straight while shaking hands, and so on. Handshaking is not a universal social protocol. Southeast Asians, for instance, press their palms together in a praying motion to carry out the greeting ritual. Handshaking can be accompanied by the action of patting someone on the arm, shoulder, or back, hugging to indicate happiness at seeing a friend or a family member, and kissing on the cheeks among friends to execute the greeting ritual.

Anthropologists are unclear as to why touching patterns vary so much across cultures. In some societies, people think of themselves as literally "contained" in their skin. The privacy zones that define "self-space" in such cultures, therefore, include the clothes that cover the skin. On the other hand, in other cultures—as, for example, in Arabic ones—the self is perceived as being located down within the body shell. This results in a totally different patterning and perception of proxemic relations. As a consequence, Arabs are in general more tolerant of crowds, of noise levels, of touch, of eye contact, and of body odors than are most North Americans.

Some psychologists claim that, in evolutionary terms, one of the original functions of touch was to initiate a mating encounter. Remnants of this mechanism can still be seen in the fact that lovers hold hands, touch each other on the hair and face, pat each other to convey affection, and so on. Sexual touching is universal, although its specific *coding* varies widely. In her book, *The Gift of Touch*, Helen Colton poses the following embarrassing situation to illustrate how culturally diverse the sexual coding of touch is.[4] Let us say that someone comes upon a strange woman in her bath. Which part of her body would the woman touch in order to conceal it? According to Colton, it depends on which culture she belongs to. An Islamic woman would probably conceal her face, a Laotian woman her breasts, a Chinese woman her feet, a Sumatran woman her knees, a

Samoan woman her navel, a Western woman her breasts with one arm and her genital area with the other hand. Clearly, as Colton's scenario reveals, the specific bodily parts that are perceived to be sexually connotative differ widely from culture to culture. As Foucault argued, "sins of the flesh" are associated with both the viewing and the touching of sexual organs. The Puritans of England saw touch during sex as a kind of necessary evil. "Temptation" continues to be interpreted by many people primarily in terms of which bodily parts can be viewed and/or touched. Interestingly, what is erotic or obscene touching behavior in some cultures, is considered natural or desirable behavior in others.

TERRITORIALITY

According to some biologists and psychologists, interpersonal zones and touch patterns are remnants of an innate *territoriality* instinct. Biologists define territoriality as a mechanism that allows an animal to gain access to, and defend control of, critical resources such as food and nesting sites found in certain habitats. This is why animals compete for territories, either fighting actual battles or performing ritual combats as tests of strength, with the defeated animal being excluded from holding a territory or forced to occupy a less desirable locale. The victor then typically marks the boundaries of its conquered territory in a species-specific way. A cat, for instance, will urinate along the boundary that marks the territory it claims as its own. This sends out a scent to potential competitors signaling possession of a certain tract of land.

The Austrian zoologist Konrad Lorenz (1903–89) was among the first scientists to identify and document territoriality patterns. Such patterns, he proposed, were an important part of an animal's repertoire of survival strategies, as critical, in evolutionary terms, as its physiological characteristics. Lorenz also suggested that human aggression and warfare were explainable as residual territoriality impulses. Lorenz's controversial theory gained widespread popularity through a best-selling book by R. Ardrey published in 1966, *Territorial Imperative*. The book subsequently generated a heated debate in academia and society at large on the nature and origin of human aggression.[5] The notion of "human territoriality" has an intuitive appeal: intrusions into one's home or car are perceived as signals of aggression, in the same way that a cat would react to another cat which intruded upon its territory by urinating. Incidentally, humans also mark off their territories. They do so with such props as landmarks, boundary lines, and fences, which would seem to have similar functions to the territoriality mechanisms of other species.

The instinct for securing territories as "survival spaces" became the target of psychological experiments with rats in the 1950s and 1960s. These received broad media coverage because of the implications for the quality of life in crowded urban areas they seemed to have. When experimenters enclosed two laboratory rats in the same cage, they found that each would instinctively secure an area for itself and that the two areas were of approximately equal dimensions. When the researchers introduced a third rat into the cage, a tripartite arrangement of equally subdivided areas would seem to be negotiated by the three rats, after some initial reluctance to do so on the part of the rats already in the cage. Minor altercations among the three rats at the beginning of the negotiations were typical. As additional rats were introduced into the cage, the level of aggression would increase proportionately until a critical mass was reached whereby the rats would either fight to the death for more space or demonstrate some form of aberrant behavior. The objective of these experiments was to show how aggression and behavioral deviance were linked to an instinctual territoriality mechanism, but the implications that they had for life in overcrowded urban centers were not missed by media reporters. It was suggested that humans, too, have an inborn "territorial critical mass" mechanism that determines what population thresholds in modern cities should be. When this critical mass is surpassed the consequences can be seen throughout the urbanized world in the form of increased criminal, violent, and aberrant behaviors.

The territorial mechanism does indeed endow an animal species with the ability to secure a survival space within the habitat to which it has become adapted. Many animals also have the ability to construct appropriate shelters within their habitats to protect themselves from the elements and to procure a safeguard against intruding enemies. For example, beavers build dams to widen the area and increase the depth of water around their habitats; groundhogs make burrows in the ground where they can hibernate safely during the winter. In the human species the story does not stop there. Human territoriality and shelter-making presuppose more than survival; they also constitute signifying systems.

MAPS

A *map* is the signifying system by which cultures represent territories and boundaries. A map has *indexical* properties because it indicates to a viewer where places are. It also has *iconic* features, since it represents places in spatial relation to each other. However, it is overall a *symbolic* system of representation because the user must have knowledge of the notational system with which the map is constructed, known as a legend, in order to use it. It is mind-boggling to think that this signifying system has made it possible to travel and explore the world with ease, as well as to classify the *terra firma* in efficient ways. To say "I am here, but I want to get to there," using a map, involves understanding: (1) that *here* and *there* are points in map space standing for points in real space, and (2) that the movement from *here* to *there* on a map stands for the corresponding movement between two points in real space. In this way, maps make it possible to plan a journey through real space with amazing accuracy, all within the imagination.

Maps are hardly objective. They allow the members of a culture to understand and locate themselves and their environment in relation to the surrounding space. Like all signs they produce a world-view. Consider the technique in Western map-making of *cylindrical projection*—a method for making two-dimensional maps by projecting the globe onto a flat surface. Developed by the Flemish geographer Gerardus Mercator (1512–94), this technique consists of wrapping a cylinder around the globe, making it touch the equator, and then projecting: (1) the lines of latitude outward from the globe onto the cylinder as lines parallel to the equator, and (2) the lines of longitude outward onto the cylinder as lines parallel to the prime meridian (the line that is designated 0° longitude passing through the original site of the Royal Greenwich Observatory in England). The resulting two-dimensional map represents the world's surface as a rectangle with parallel lines of latitude and parallel lines of longitude (which are perpendicular to those of latitude). Because of the curvature of the globe, the latitude lines on the map nearest the poles appear closer together. This distortion makes the sizes of certain land masses appear smaller than that of other land masses. This, in turn, influences perception—larger or more prominent is interpreted as superior; smaller or less prominent as inferior. Indeed, the very phrase world-view is a synonym for map-view—view of the world as it is shown on a map.

Inspired by Mercator's projection maps, Western map-makers began devising their projections according to the principles of Cartesian coordinate
geometry, because of its mathematical applicability to the two-dimensional
plane. In a coordinate system, a pair of lines on a flat surface are made to
intersect at right angles. Each line is called an *axis,* and the point where they
intersect is called the *origin.* The axes are referred to as the *x* and *y* axes. In
this way, points in the plane (a map) can be accurately defined, making
them correspond to real points on the earth. Projection maps thus allow for
the representation of "real spaces" in terms of "map spaces" with higher or
lesser degrees of fidelity. The *x axis* of modern maps is the 0° latitude line
around the equator and the *y axis* the 0° longitude line going through
Greenwich, England. It was at an international conference held in Washington in 1884 that many countries agreed, through negotiation, that 0° of
longitude would be assumed to pass through Greenwich. This meridian is
now widely, though not universally, used for map-making. As this shows,
map systems require real conventions, negotiations, and agreements.

The first known maps date back to the Babylonians around 2300 B.C.
Carved on clay tablets, they were largely land surveys made for the purposes of taxation. More extensive regional maps, drawn on silk and dating
from the second century B.C., have been found in China. The precursor of
the modern map, however, is believed to have been devised by the Greek
philosopher Anaximander (ca. 611–ca. 547 B.C.). His map was circular
and showed the known lands of the world grouped around the Aegean Sea
at the center and surrounded by the ocean. Anaximander's map constituted one of the first attempts to think beyond the immediate territorial
boundaries of a particular society—Greece—even though he located the
"center" of the universe in the Aegean Sea. Then, around 200 B.C., the
Greek geographer Eratosthenes (ca. 276–ca. 196 B.C.) introduced the technique of using parallel lines to indicate latitude and longitude, although
the lines were not evenly and accurately spaced. Eratosthenes' map represented the known world from present-day England in the northwest to the
mouth of the Ganges River in the east and to Libya in the south. About
150 A.D., the Egyptian scholar Ptolemy (ca. 100–ca. 170 A.D.) published
the first textbook in cartographic methodology, entitled *Geographia.* Even
though they contained a number of errors, his maps of the world were
among the first to be made with an early, crude technique of projection.
At about the same time in China, map-makers were also beginning to use
mathematically accurate grids for making maps.

The next step forward in map-making came in the medieval era when Arab seamen showed the world how to make highly accurate navigation charts, with lines indicating the bearings between ports. Then, in the fifteenth century, influenced by the publication of Ptolemy's maps, European map-makers laid the foundations for the modern science of cartography. In 1507 the German cartographer Martin Waldseemüller (ca. 1470–ca. 1522), became the first to apply the name America to the newly identified transatlantic lands, separating it into North and South—a cartographic tradition that continues to this day—and differentiating the Americas from Asia. In 1570 the first modern atlas was put together by the Flemish cartographer Abraham Ortelius (1527–98). The atlas, titled *Orbis Terrarum*, contained 70 maps.

Undoubtedly, the most important development in the sixteenth century came when Mercator developed the technique of cylindrical projection in 1569. As mentioned above, this allowed cartographers to portray land masses on a surface, at the expense, however, of accuracy of relative size. This technique led, in the first half of the seventeenth century, to the development of more precise methods of determining latitude and longitude. By the eighteenth century, the modern-day scientific principles of map-making were well established. With the rise of nationalism in the nineteenth century a number of European countries started to conduct topographic surveys to determine political boundaries. In 1891, the International Geographical Congress proposed the political mapping of the world on a scale of 1:1,000,000. Throughout the twentieth century, advances in aerial and satellite photography, and in computer modeling of topographic surfaces, greatly enhanced the accuracy and fidelity of map-making.

Despite genuine attempts to make maps as "objective" as possible, a map is nonetheless a sign, and thus constitutes a *representation* of the world. This involves giving the map an *orientation* (from *orient* meaning the East, the direction of the rising sun). A map has no *up* or *down*. So, up and down must be assigned to the map. The common practice of making North the up dimension gives that area visual prominence, reinforcing *by representation* the global rise and economic dominance of northern Europe.

Maps of American aboriginal cultures provide a completely different view of spaces and territories. Whereas Western map-making is based on the principles of Cartesian geometry, which segments the map space into determinable points and calculable distances, aboriginal map-making is based instead on portraying the interconnectedness among the parts within the map space through a distortion of distance, angulation, and shape. This produces a more holistic view of the land.

SIGNIFYING SPACES

The discussion of territoriality and maps brings us logically to the topic of space as a signifying system. All societies build and design streets, marketplaces, abodes, and public edifices of villages, towns, and cities in characteristic ways. These are felt throughout the world to have culture-specific meanings and functions. Indeed, a building is hardly ever perceived by the members of a society as simply a pile of bricks, wood, or straw put together to provide shelter. Rather, its shape, size, features, and location are perceived to be signifiers that refer to a broad range of meanings. The rules that govern private and public spaces are the outcome of these meanings: in Western culture one knocks on the door of private dwellings, but not on the door of retail stores, to seek permission to enter (because a store is perceived to be a building that is literally open for business); one sits and waits for someone in a public foyer, atrium, or lobby, but not normally in a public bathroom (because the latter is a secretive or personal space); one walks on a public sidewalk, but not on someone's porch without permission (because the porch is a private space).

Because it is a signifying space, people perceive their social community as a *communal body*. This is why we refer to societies as being healthy, sick, vibrant, beautiful, or ugly. Indeed, visitors habitually judge a society instinctively as they would a human person, namely, on how the public spaces appear to the eye—neat, dirty, organized, chaotic, and so on. This is also why a community feels violated "as a single body" if someone defaces its public or sacred places. Conflicts among tribes or nations are often triggered by such transgressive acts against the communal body.

The experience of one's society as a communal body also explains why we talk of a city's roads as its arteries, of its downtown areas as its heart, of its design as being warm or cold. In ancient Greece religious and civic structures in cities were designed to give a sense of aesthetic balance; streets were arranged in a grid pattern and housing was integrated with commercial and defense structures to give a feeling of organization and security. Renaissance city planners built radial streets leading to a central point, like spokes of a wheel, so as to promote social interaction. To this day, the downtown core is known as *centro* in Italy, reflecting the Renaissance design of cities as circles. The city of Siena is a classic example of this kind of design; so, too, is the city plan of seventeenth century London and the streets of Mannheim and Karlrushe in Germany.

After the industrial revolution the concept of the Cartesian grid started to gain a foothold on city designs. This is evident in New York City's plan of 1811 which divided Manhattan into identical rectangular blocks which were named in coordinate terms—for example, 52nd and 4th refer to the intersection point of two perpendicular lines in the city grid. In a fundamental semiotic sense, modern cities are the "structural byproducts" of the world-view that has been produced by the widespread use of Cartesian maps since the early sixteenth century. Since the 1960s, with the rise of the automobile as the primary means of transportation, new city structures have increasingly been designed with an infrastructure of roads to allow the automobile access to the larger city cores and escape into the suburbs.

The gist of the semiotic story is that cities, shelters, buildings, communal sites invariably constitute *codes*. Many become symbolic. This is why the buildings of a particular university stand for that institution visually, why St. Peter's basilica or the Taj Mahal symbolize specific religions, and so on. Market squares, sacred sites, and other kinds of communal places are invariably perceived as signifying systems by the members of a tribe or society. Like all such systems, therefore, they cohere into *spatial codes* that mediate the meanings and uses of *public, private,* and *sacred* spaces. *Public* spaces are those sites where communal or social interactions of various kinds take place; *private* spaces are those places that individuals have appropriated or designated as their own; and *sacred* spaces are those locales that are purported to have metaphysical, mythical, or spiritual attributes and meanings. Spatial codes inform people how to act and behave in such places: the way one dresses for church is different from the way one dresses for work; the way one behaves in a restaurant is different from the way one behaves at home. As mentioned throughout this book, this interconnectedness among the various codes is what gives coherence and meaning to cultural activities and routines in the system of everyday life.

A concrete example of this interconnectedness can be seen in the phenomenon of the modern-day shopping mall. In all societies, certain spaces are set aside for community interaction. In villages, for instance, the market square is a locus for people to enact certain rituals, to exchange goods and services, and to socialize. These same kinds of functions are served, in modern urban societies, by the shopping mall. The mall, however, has become much more than just a locus for shopping. The modern mall satisfies several psychic and social needs at once. It is a safe and "purified" space for human social activities, a haven for combating loneliness and boredom. With its theatrical atmosphere proclaiming the virtues of a consumerist utopia, it imparts a feeling of security and protection against the outside world of cars, mechanical noises, and air pollution; it shields against rain, snow, heat, cold; it conveys a feeling of control and organization.

Increasingly, cinemas, high-class restaurants, and even amusement parks are being built within malls. The Mall of America in Bloomington, Minnesota, for instance, has more than 400 stores, 50 restaurants, 9 night clubs, and a giant roller coaster, drawing an average of 40 million visitors per year, more than Walt Disney World, the Grand Canyon, and Graceland (the home of rock legend Elvis Presley) combined. Malls are, indeed, fast becoming self-contained "fantasylands," where one can leave the problems, dirt, and hassles of ordinary urban life literally outside. In the controlled environment inside the mall everything is clean, shiny, cheery, and ever so optimistic. The mall is thus experienced as a nirvana of endless shopping, cosmeticized and simplified to keep grisly reality out of sight and out of mind. Like a remote-controlled television set, one can "switch" from scene to scene—from clothing store, to coffee stand, to pinball parlor, to lottery outlet.

The mall is a sign standing for our system of everyday life. The meaning of this sign is essentially *shopping = paradise on earth;* but this is ultimately an empty, vacuous meaning. Very few people will claim that their experiences at shopping malls are memorable, rewarding, or meaningful. Indeed, they do not remember them for very long past the last time they were there.

BUILDINGS

Buildings are not just shelters. They evoke feelings. We typically react to our home as if it were an extension of self-space. At a denotative level, a home, whether a crude hut or an elaborate mansion, has a straightforward meaning: it is a shelter providing protection from weather and intruders. Many animal species also have the capacity to build shelters—bees make hives, beavers dams, moles holes, and so on.

Homes also demarcate territory, constituting a privately-bounded space that ensures safety and preserves sanity. When one steps inside, one feels as if one has retreated into the safety of one's own body. Intrusion into a home is felt as a violation of the self.

Within the home, each room elicits a specific type of feeling and meaning. Concealing a bedroom has a biological basis: we are extremely vulnerable when we are sleeping, and so it is judicious to keep sleeping areas concealed or secret. The ancient Egyptians concealed their bedrooms at the back or the sides of their homes. North American families also prefer to keep their bedrooms away from the line of sight, perceiving them as havens for protecting and sheltering the self. This is why only "intimates" are allowed to share that space literally and symbolically.

Conceptions of "clean" and "dirty" in a home can only have relevance in relation to space. Dirt is really no more than displaced matter. An object "out of its proper place" must be put back or reallocated, otherwise it might be perceived as litter or debris. This is particularly true with regard to our kitchens, because we think of them as "dirt-free" or "dirt-removal" spaces. We can tolerate "dirty" bedrooms much more because food is not involved and because they are out of the line of sight.

The experience of the *home* space contrasts with the experience of other kinds of spaces, especially those defined as *sacred*. When one enters a church, a chapel, a synagogue, a temple, or a mosque, one tends to speak with a lower voice, to walk more quietly, to feel a sense of respect and reverence. The configuration and set-up of the sacred space is also laden with meanings. In a Catholic church, for example, the altar is more sacred and therefore less traversable than the area containing the pews. A confessional is a very intimate enclosure. It cannot be lit or made overly amenable. It imparts a feeling of intimate reflection, providing a physical space within which one can look into the dark depths of the soul to reveal to God one's weaknesses.

The way the altar faces is also highly connotative. As a table for eating spiritually along with Christ, it was once put against the wall of the church with the priest's back to the people, removing him and the mass symbolically from the people. The language spoken was Latin, which further imbued the ceremony with a detached, abstract, and yet, seemingly spiritual, quality. Nowadays, the altar and the priest are oriented towards the faithful. This new configuration conveys a feeling of "communion with and among the people," not just of "communion with God through the priest." The change in orientation of the altar reflects, clearly, a change in emphasis on the part of the Church and its members.

All sacred buildings make individuals feel that they have entered a special place, a place where contact with the deities is real and meaningful. Indeed, the word church comes from Greek *ekklesia,* meaning "those called out," that is, those called by God away from their communities to form a new and spiritually deeper community. New Testament metaphors for the church bear this out. Christians refer to the *body of Christ,* to Christ as the *head,* and to the faithful as *members* (originally meaning "limbs"). This feeling that the congregation is part of a communal body has spawned its own architectural traditions. In some modern-day designs of churches the altar is placed in the center of a circular arrangement, because this allows people to face each other and thus to feel more united as a body in the ongoing ceremony.

Churches and temples stand out clearly from their surroundings and have a pronounced architectural character. Tribal people sought to establish their relationship to the forces of nature by building substantial structures commanding attention, in places where the divinities could be reached, and where miracles and supernatural events were thought to take place. Around these, the ceremonies of worship were elaborated, and the attendant shamans became very powerful. In early cities, temples were often positioned in relation to some natural feature, such as a holy mountain, and they were often tall or placed on an elevated spot, lessening the distance between mortals and the heavens.

In ancient Egypt these structures were built to confer symbolic power on rulers and priests. Egyptian rulers were obsessed with the afterlife. They built elaborate tombs in the form of *mastabas,* rectangular masses of masonry which were transformed into the great pyramids around 1500 B.C. These immense buildings testify symbolically to the vast social control that Egyptian pharaohs exerted over the populace and also the fascination of Egyptian architects with geometrical perfection. All cultures have similar monuments. In India, the commemorative monument takes the form of a large hemispherical mound, called a *stupa;* in Southeast Asia it is called a *wat*—a richly sculptured stone complex which is approached by a ceremonial bridge. In the Mayan and Inca cultures, ceremonial monuments resembled the Egyptian pyramids, in that they used the same kinds of monolithic design. In Islamic cultures, a typical tomb consists of a high central dome surrounded by smaller chambers arranged around two intersecting axes, so that all four sides of the structure are alike.

Churches were the tallest buildings of medieval European cities and towns. The spires on those churches rose majestically upwards to the sky, imparting a sense of awe as people looked up. There was no doubt as to which group had political and social power in medieval Europe. The churches were, literally and symbolically, places of power and wealth. As the churches started to lose their clout and wealth after the Renaissance, other kinds of buildings emerged to reflect architecturally the new cultural order.

Today, the tallest buildings in sprawling urban centers are certainly not churches. In cities like New York, Toronto, Chicago, and Los Angeles, the tallest buildings belong to large corporations and banks. Wealth and power now reside in these institutions. Inside these monolithic structures, the symbolism follows a hierarchical arrangement—the jobs and positions with the lowest value are at the bottom of the building; the more important ones are at the top. The company's executives reside, like the gods on Mount Olympus, on the top floor. The atmosphere on this level is perceived to be rarefied and other-worldly. This why we use such expression as *working one's way up, making it to the top, climbing the ladder of success, setting one's goals high*. These conceptual metaphors reflect the symbolism of power as represented in architectural forms.

In addition to size and shape, a building's location is also meaningful. An office building in the downtown core connotes, in general, more prestige than a building on the outskirts of town. Head offices are normally located downtown. Since the late 1960s, the design of such buildings in urban centers has been influenced by the movement known as postmodernism, which values individuality, intimacy, complexity, and above all else, the ironical and the trivial. The American architect Robert Venturi (1925–) became one of the first proponents of the postmodern trend in architecture. The AT&T building in New York City, built in 1984, is a classic example of this style. With its allusions to Renaissance architectural forms and its pediment evoking Chippendale furniture, it combines the elegant with the ironic and satirical, the old with the new, the important with the trivial. Postmodernists strive for individuality, mocking those who seek communal, standardized ways of gleaning meaning from human artifacts and buildings. Using vivid color and various decorative elements in their building designs, postmodern architects attempt to break with history, with cultural evolution, hoping, somehow, that their buildings will stimulate an ironic perspective on human life and, thus, a reflective one. Their architecture evokes and repudiates tradition at the same time.

8

WHAT A BEAUTIFUL RING!

The Meaning of Clothes and Objects

I believe in the total depravity of inanimate things, the elusiveness of soap, the knottiness of strings, the transitory nature of buttons, the inclination of suspenders to twist and of hooks to forsake their lawful eyes, and cleave only unto the hairs of their hapless owner's head.

—Katharine Walker (1840–1916)

M artha's videotape has still much more to offer the semiotician. We can see, for instance, that Cheryl wore an enticing red skirt and matching black lace blouse, Ted a dark-blue suit, white shirt, and matching blue tie. Near the middle of the tape, moreover, something that Ted said merits our attention: "Oh, what a beautiful ring, Cheryl! Who gave it to you?" "It's a friendship ring," Cheryl replies. "I've worn it since I was 14."

Why is it, a semiotician would ask, that we are so attached to, and meticulous about, our clothes and our trinkets of jewelry? More generally, why is it that people find such significance in the objects they make? What role do objects play in culture? What do they reveal about the human species? Do clothes *make* the person, as the expression goes? Why do we associate clothing with ritual behaviors, such as the courtship ritual unfolding between Cheryl and Ted?

CLOTHES AND DRESS

Let's start our semiotic discussion of these questions with the topic of clothing. Imagine the following situation. Suppose you have a 20-something-year-old brother who has an important job interview at the head office of a bank. During his adolescent years, your brother became accustomed to dressing like a punk rocker. So, he has decided to ask you to help him get dressed appropriately for the occasion. To put it in semiotic terms, your task is to acquaint him with the *dress code* that will allow him to put together an appropriate *clothing text* through which he can present an acceptable *persona* to a potential employer. As you know, the code suggests that he must be well-groomed, that he should wear a white or blue, long-sleeved shirt, with no designs on it, with a suitable tie. It also suggests that he should wear a gray or blue jacket with matching pants, and, finally, that he should wear black shoes, preferably with shoelaces. Like any code, there is some latitude in the choices and combinations of *signifiers* (clothing items) your brother has in constructing his apparel text, but not very much. He certainly cannot ignore the basic *structure* of the dress code, for if he does—if he decides not to wear a tie, or if he decides to put on sneakers, for instance—the chances are that he would not even get past the door of the job interviewer. Deploying the appropriate dress code will not guarantee him a job, but it will at least get him past that door. Dressing for the occasion is indeed a social requirement.

Now, let's switch the situation from the standpoint of gender. Suppose that this time your sister is the one with an important job interview at the head office of a bank. Once again, as an adolescent she had become accustomed to dressing in a youthful style with nose rings, jeans, etc. Like your brother, she comes to you for help. In her case, the *code* suggests that she set her hair in an appropriate way; that she wear a blouse with soft colors, preferably white; that she wear a gray or blue jacket with a matching skirt; and that she put on shoes, preferably, with high or semi-high heels. Although there are some *paradigmatic* (selectional) differences in the female dress code with respect to the male one, there are also many similarities. This suggests that the type of job both are seeking cuts across gender categories. In such cases dress codes tend to be more flexible or "unisexual."

Clothes supplement the body's biological resources (bodily hair, skin thickness) for counteracting environmental fluctuations, such as weather changes. At this rudimentary denotative level, they are "additions" to these resources, as the variation of clothing in relation to different climates testifies. In the system of everyday life clothes also function as signs, and therefore are organized into the various dress codes (from Old French *dresser* "to arrange, set up") that are interconnected meaningfully with the other codes of this system.

Predictably, dress codes vary across cultures. Their *raison d'être* is the same one the world over: to convey *persona* (identity, gender, age, status, etc.) and to regulate social interaction. To someone who knows nothing about Amish culture, the blue or charcoal *Mutze* of the Amish male is just a jacket, but within the Amish culture the blue *Mutze* indicates that the wearer is between 16 and 35 years of age, the charcoal one that he is over 35. Similarly, to an outsider the Russian *kalbak* appears to be a brimless red hat; to a Russian living in rural areas, it means that the wearer is a medical doctor.

The dress code, like any of the codes within the system of everyday life, can also be used to beguile, seduce, mock, lie, and deceive. Criminals can dress in three-piece suits to look trustworthy; con artists can dress like police officers to gain the trust of their victims; and so on. To avoid the possibility of deceiving via clothes, some societies have even enacted laws that strictly define dress codes. In ancient Rome, for instance, only aristocrats were allowed to wear purple-colored clothes; in religiously oriented cultures, differentiated dress codes for males and females are regularly enforced to ensure modesty; and the list could go on and on. When people put clothes on their bodies, they are not only engaged in making images of themselves to suit their own eyes, but also to conform to ideological and lifestyle models. Before the middle part of the twentieth century, females in Western culture did not wear pants. The one who *wore the pants* in a family meant, denotatively and connotatively, that the wearer was a male. With the change in social-role structures during the 1960s, women too began to wear pants regularly in acknowledgment of this change. The reverse situation has never transpired (so far). Except in special ritualistic circumstances—for example, the wearing of a Scottish kilt—men have never, openly, worn skirts in modern Western cultures. If they do, then we label it an act of "transvestitism," with the particular kinds of negative connotations that this entails.

The identification of gender through clothes is a characteristic of cultures across the world. Psychological research has shown that as the child develops a sense of gender, he or she often wants to experiment with the dress code of the other gender. In so doing, the child is apparently trying to cull from cross-dressing episodes a better understanding of his or her own sexual persona; by assuming the gender of the other sex *through* the dress code, the child is attempting to unravel what it is like *to be* the other sex, contrasting it with his or her own sense of sexual identity, and thus coming to a better grasp of its meaning.

The power of dress as conveyor of sexual *persona* becomes particularly noticeable at puberty. In tribal cultures, the clothes that individuals are expected to wear at sexual maturity are dictated by the elders or leaders of the collectivity. In modern industrialized cultures, pubescent youth are left alone to develop their own *sui generis* dress codes to mark the coming of age. Indeed, the history of youth dress styles since the mid-1950s is the history of contemporary adolescence. In the 1950s, tight slacks, push-up bras, bobby socks, and bikinis characterized the female's rite-of-passage dress code, while motorcycle jackets, blousey shirts, and pencil-thin slacks marked the corresponding male code. The unisexual coming-of-age styles of the hippie 1960s—ripped, tattered, but colorful clothing items, long hair, sandals—emphasized rebellion against the establishment, free love, sexual equality, and ecological harmony. In the 1970s, two adolescent dress codes emerged. One was known as "disco style," epitomized in John Badham's movie, *Saturday Night Fever,* of 1977; the other was associated with the *punk* movement of the late 1970s. The disco scene was an unabashed celebration of sexuality, evocative of a hedonistic coming-of-age rite softened only by the glitter of high fashion. Many other teens, however, rejected the disco scene as superficial. The counter-disco trend that emerged came to be known as punk. The difference was dramatic—the punk dress code was raw, desperate, vulgar, dangerous. Punks dyed their hair with bizarre colors and cut it in unconventional ways; they wore clothes emphasizing degradation and depravity; they used various kinds of props (for example, safety pins stuck through their nostrils) to send out their counter-cultural messages. They wore chains, dog collars, black clothes, army boots, and hairstyles that ranged from shaved heads to the wild-looking "Mohican" hairdos of every color imaginable.

Although the punk movement started as an ideological statement from working class youths in England, by the time its symbolism was acquired by the larger teen culture, it ended up being all things to all classes. The swastika insignia, for instance, lost its ideological overtones becoming a "put on" aimed at provoking those of a middle-class, bourgeois mentality.

The 1980s and 1990s saw the emergence of eclectic dress codes among adolescents, reflecting the increasing diversity of modern society. The refined, clean-cut look of *preppie* teens clashed on the one side with the more menacing appearance of *hard rockers* (with their ripped jeans, leather boots, jackets, and T-shirts), and on the other side with the "gangster look" of *rappers* (with their hooded jackets, earrings for males, multiple earrings for girls, oversized baggy jeans, and unlaced sneakers). Without belaboring the topic further, suffice it to say that such dress codes are part of the coming of age in modern-day societies. They constitute the signifying means by which adolescents define themselves socially, identify with peers, and fashion a sexual *persona*.

NUDITY

The association between clothing and sexuality is an ancient one. As anthropologist Helen Fisher aptly observes, even in the jungle of Amazonia, Yanomamo men and women wear clothes for sexual modesty.[1] A Yanomamo woman would feel as much discomfort and agony at removing her vaginal string belt as would a North American woman if she were asked to remove her underwear. Similarly, a Yanomamo man would feel just as much embarrassment at his penis accidentally falling out of its encasement as would a North American male if he were to be caught literally "with his pants down."

This association explains why the counterpart of dress, nudity, has great meaning in the system of everyday life. We are the only animal that does not "go nude," without triggering some form of social repercussion (unless, of course, the social ambiance is that of a nudist camp, strip joint, or doctor's room). Nudity is defined culturally. We are all born nude, but we learn in childhood that nudity has special connotations. That part of the body which is considered acceptable to expose will vary widely from culture to culture, even though the covering of genitalia seems, for the most part, to cross cultural boundaries. The instinctual act of concealing sexual organs suggests, in fact, that a primary social function of clothing is to cover these organs. Nudity, too, is a *code*.

To see how powerful the symbolism associated with nudity is, consider the "art" of strip-teasing (male and female). A semiotician would ask: Why do we attend (or desire to attend) performances whose sole purpose is the removal of clothing to reveal the genitals and, in the case of female strip-teasing, also the breasts? The semiotician would, of course, seek an answer to this question in the domain of the signifying order.

The act of "suggestive clothing-removal" in an audience setting has, first and foremost, something of a ritualistic quality to it. The dark atmosphere, the routines leading up to the act, the predictability of the performance with its bodily gyrations imitating sexual activities, and the cathartic effects that it has on spectators are all suggestive of a rite worshipping carnality and sexuality. There is no motive for being at such performances other than to indulge in a fascination with forbidden sexuality. This is, as Freud claimed, a propensity in people living in repressive social systems. Freud suggested that, by denying sexual urges, society has guaranteed, paradoxically, that such urges will constantly seek an outlet not only through artistic representations, but also in the form of spectacles such as strip-teases. Covering the body is an act of modesty. Curiously, by covering the sexual organs they have in effect become imbued with a kind of "secret" desirability below the covered surface, if Freud is correct. So, at a strip-tease performance, the shedding of clothes does several symbolic things at once: it removes culturally imposed moral repressions of sexuality; it exposes those bodily parts that have taken on such great significance by virtue of being covered; and it allows people to indulge in more carnal ways of feeling and of expressing themselves.

This perspective of nudity might also explain why visual artists have an age-old fascination for the nude figure and for erotic representation generally. The ancient Greek and Roman nude statues of male warriors, Michelangelo's powerful *David* sculpture (1501–04), Rodin's *The Thinker* (ca. 1886) are all suggestive of the brutal power of male sexuality. It is this suggestiveness that enhances male sexuality, not the size of the penis. On a "weakling" body, male genitals are hardly ever perceived as sexual, no matter what size they are. On the other side of this paradigm, the female body has historically been portrayed as soft, sumptuous, and submissive, although this has changed in tandem with changing definitions of gender in the West.

The modern-day fascination with erotic materials is a contemporary testament to our fascination with nudity as a code in our system of everyday life. Those who see exploitation in such materials, and seem prepared to become everyone else's moral guardian by censoring them, are probably more overwhelmed by the connotative power of this code than are most people. Depicting the human body in sexual poses or activities reveals, to the semiotician, a fascination with sexuality—no more, no less. Only when such depictions are repressed does this fascination become perilous, as Freud argued.

FASHION

The above discussion leads logically to a consideration of fashion. What is fashion? Why are fashion shows so popular the world over? The answer is to be found, again, in the meanings of dress codes. Until relatively recently, fashion trends were primarily the concern of the aristocracy, while the dress codes of ordinary people changed far less regularly and radically. Even among the upper classes of Medieval and Renaissance Europe, clothing was costly enough to be cared for, altered, reused, and passed from one generation to the next, more so than it is today. Indeed, radical changes to this pattern occurred infrequently until the Industrial Revolution of the nineteenth century made the production of both cloth and clothing far easier and less expensive.

Let us return briefly to the dress code with which we started this discussion—the business suit—to see how fashion trends are formed and institutionalized. The message underlying this apparel text is, of course, *dress for success*. How did this message crystallize in our culture? As you might know by now, the semiotician would look at the history of the business suit to seek an answer.

In seventeenth-century England there existed a bitter conflict to gain political, religious, and cultural control of English society between the Royalist Cavaliers, who were faithful to King Charles I, and the Puritans, who were followers of Oliver Cromwell and controlled the House of Commons in the English Parliament. The Cavaliers were aristocrats who only superficially followed the teachings of the Anglican Church. Their main penchant was for flair and the good life. They dressed flamboyantly and ornately, donning colorful clothes and feathered hats, and favoring beards and long flowing hair. The romantic figure of the cavalier aristocrat has been immortalized by such novels as *The Three Musketeers* (Alexandre Dumas, 1844) and *Cyrano de Bergerac* (Edmond Rostand, 1897). The Puritans, on the other hand, frowned on ostentation and pomp. Known as the Roundheads, Cromwell's Calvinist followers cropped their hair very closely, forbade all carnal pleasures, and prohibited the wearing of frivolous clothing. They wore dark suits and dresses with white shirts and collars. Through their clothes they hoped to convey the sobriety, plainness, and rigid moralism of their lifestyles.

The Cavaliers were in power throughout the 1620s and the 1630s. During this period the Puritans fled from England and emigrated to America, bringing with them their moralistic lifestyle and rigid codes of conduct and dress. Then in 1649, the Puritans, led by Cromwell, defeated the Royalist forces and executed the king. The king's son, Charles II, escaped to France to set up a court in exile. For a decade, England was ruled by the Puritans. Frowning upon all pleasurable recreations, they closed down theaters, censored books, stringently enforced moralistic laws. Unable to tolerate such a strict way of life, many Cavaliers also emigrated to America. The Puritans had set up colonies in the northeast; the Cavaliers settled in the south. With Cromwell's death in 1658, the Puritans were eventually thrown out of power and England welcomed Charles II back. Known as the Restoration, the subsequent 25-year period in England saw a return to the lifestyle and fashion trends of the Cavaliers. For two centuries the Puritans had to bide their time once again. They were excluded from holding political office, from attending university, and from engaging in any socially significant enterprise. Throughout those years, however, they never strayed from their severe moral philosophy and lifestyle.

By the time of the Industrial Revolution, the Puritans had their final revenge. Their thrift, diligence, temperance, and industriousness—character traits that define the "Protestant work ethic"—allowed Cromwell's descendants to become rich and thus take over the economic reigns of power. Ever since, Anglo-American culture has been influenced by Puritan ethics in the work force, especially after the defeat of the Cavalier south in the American Civil War. The origins of modern corporate capitalism are to be found in those ethics. The belief that hard work, clean living, and economic prosperity are intrinsically interrelated became widespread by the turn of the twentieth century.

The business suit is a contemporary version of the Puritan dress code. The toned-down colors (blues, browns, grays) that the business world demands are the contemporary reflexes of the Calvinist's fear and dislike of color and ornament. The wearing of neckties, jackets, and short hair are all Puritan signifiers of solemnity and self-denial. During the hippie era of the late 1960s and early 1970s, the office scene came briefly under the influence of a new form of Cavalierism. Colorful suits, turtle-neck sweaters, longer hair, sideburns, Nehru jackets, medallions, and beards constituted, for a time, an emerging dress code that threatened to enliven the world of corporate capitalism. However, this fashion experiment failed, as the Cavalier 1960s were overtaken by neo-puritanical forces in the late 1970s and 1980s. The Puritan dress code became once again prevalent in the business world, with only minor variations in detail.

The story of the business suit makes it obvious that fashion is *statement* and, thus, like any form of discourse, can be used rhetorically. Military dress, for instance, connotes patriotism and communal values; but outside the military world it can convey a counter-cultural statement, a parody of nationalistic tendencies. It also shows that fashion trends correlate with social trends. Consider the case of blue jeans. In the 1930s and 1940s, blue jeans were cheap, strong, and mass-produced blue-collar working clothes. High fashion articles, on the other hand, were manufactured with expensive fancy materials and fabrics, and aimed at those with discriminating tastes. As early as the mid-1950s, the emerging youth culture adopted blue jeans as part of its dress code. By the 1960s and 1970s, blue jeans were worn by all young people to proclaim equality between the sexes and among social classes, but by the 1980s they became fashion statement. This is why blue jeans became much more expensive, much more exclusive, often personalized, and available at chic boutiques.

In a sense, the contemporary mania for fashion is symptomatic of an era of history marked by a constant thirst for innovation. Fashion is predicated on producing ever new tastes. It thus perpetuates a restless psyche, always seeking what is new, exciting, and "in," as the expression goes, while avoiding what is old and passé. More and more individuals in industrialized cultures seek their identities in constantly new and trendy clothes, looks, attitudes, and lifestyle, fearful of being out-of-date or unfashionable.

OBJECTS

Recall Cheryl's friendship ring. It is indeed remarkable that a simple object can have such meaning. To the semiotician, however, this comes as no surprise. Any human-made object is perceived as a sign and is thus imbued with meaning. Marshall McLuhan claimed that objects are extensions of the human species which evolve by themselves and, in turn, influence the evolution of the species.[2] From the invention of tools to the invention of computers, human evolution has indeed been shaped by the objects people make.

The perception of objects as meaningful things became peculiarly obvious across North American society in the 1950s and 1960s when contemporary artists started using everyday commercial items, like bottles, cans, and hygiene products as *objets d'art*, as symbols standing not for themselves but for consumerist values. The 1970s even witnessed a fad involving a "pet rock." Many social critics considered this a quick money-making ploy devised by shrewd marketers, who foisted this mania upon a gullible public spoiled by affluence and thus easily duped by an advertising campaign. Whatever the truth, one thing became clear even to the harshest critics—everyday objects are hardly neutral things. From the dawn of civilization, objects have had great personal and cultural significance for no apparent reason other than they appeal to people. Gold, for instance, became a "precious metal" from which all kinds of valuable artifacts continue to be made, from money to wedding rings. Some objects are even felt to have magical qualities, revealing a mythic dimension. If we find a "lucky object," like a penny, we somehow feel that the gods are looking favorably upon us. If, however, we lose some valued object, then we feel that our fate is insecure.

Archeologists reconstruct ancient cultures on the basis of the artifacts they uncover at a site. The reason why they are able to do this is because the objects humans make—jewelry, clothes, furniture, ornaments, tools, toys, etc.—reveal personal and social meanings and, thus, social organization. Archeologists can imagine the role that any object they find played in the society by stacking it up against the other objects at the site. This helps them reconstruct the system of everyday life of the ancient culture.

To see how intrinsic objects are to this system, consider the case of toys. Denotatively, toys are objects made for children to play with; but toys connote much more than this. This becomes obvious every Christmas. At no other time in North America did this become more apparent than during the 1983 Christmas shopping season. That season is now often described by cultural historians as the Christmas of the Cabbage Patch doll. Hordes of parents were prepared to pay almost anything to get one of these dolls for their daughters. Scalpers offered the suddenly and unexplainably out-of-stock dolls for hundreds (and even thousands) of dollars through classified ads. Adults fought each other in line-ups to get one of the few remaining dolls left in some toy store. How could a simple doll have caused such mass hysteria? Only something with great connotative power. The Cabbage Patch dolls came with "adoption papers." Each doll was given a name, taken at random from 1938 state of Georgia birth records. Like any act of naming, this conferred upon the doll a human personality. Thanks to computerization, no two dolls were manufactured alike, emphasizing their "human personality" even more. The doll became alive in the child's mind, as do all objects with names, providing the precious human contact that children living in nuclear families with both parents working desperately needed. The dolls were "people substitutes." No wonder they caused such hysteria.

North Americans are not unique in personifying dolls. In some societies, adults even believe that physical or psychological harm can be passed on to a person by damaging a doll constructed to resemble that person. The Cabbage Patch doll craze was, really, a modern version of this ancient belief, which anthropologists call *animism*, or the view that objects have an inner being. In 1871 the British anthropologist Sir Edward Burnett Tylor (1832–1917) described the origin of religion in terms of animism.[3] According to Tylor, primitive peoples believed that spirits or souls are the cause of life in both human beings and objects. The difference between a living body and an object, to such peoples, was one of degree of animism, not lack thereof.

Before the Industrial Revolution of the eighteenth and nineteenth centuries, most people lived in agricultural communities. Children barely out of infancy were expected to share the workload associated with tending to the farm. There was, consequently, little distinction between childhood and adult roles. Society perceived children to be adults with smaller and weaker bodies. Indeed, in the medieval and Renaissance periods the "babes" and "children" that appear in portraits look more like midgets than they do children. During the Industrial Revolution the center of economic activity shifted from the farm to the city. This led to a new social order in which children were left with few of their previous responsibilities, and a new conceptualization, or more accurately *mythology,* emerged, proclaiming children as vastly different from adults, needing time for school and play. Child-labor laws were passed and the public education of children became compulsory. Protected from the harsh reality of industrial work, children came to have much more time at their disposal. As a result, toys were manufactured on a massive scale so that children could play constructively in the absence of parental tutelage.

Since then, toys have become inseparable from childhood, and thus reveal how adults relate to children and what kinds of values they want to instill in them. Toys, as the logo for a major toy chain states, "are us" *(Toys 'R Us)*. Aware of the signifying power of toys, manufacturers make them primarily with parents in mind. Toys symbolize what the parent wishes to impart to the child: educational toy-makers cater to parents who emphasize learning, musical toy-makers to those who stress music, doll-makers to those who give emphasis to nurturing values, and so on. Children, on the other hand, often seem to prefer playing with objects they find around the house than with the toys that are bought for them. The adult fascination with toys is also a clear sign that the distinction between *young* and *old* is being blurred more and more in our culture. Toys are being designed with layers of meanings aimed at adults. Today, grown-ups enjoy children's music, comic books, and motion picture heroes like Batman and Superman—all once considered strictly kid stuff! Toys are still for children, but childhood isn't as childish as it used to be, and adulthood tends to be a lot less adult than it once was.

TECHNOLOGY

The methods and techniques that a society employs to make its objects is known as its *technology*. The term is derived from the Greek words *tekhne,* which refers to an "art" or "craft," and *logia,* meaning an "area of study." Although it is a product of a culture, technology eventually becomes a contributing factor to the culture's development, transforming traditional signifying systems, frequently with unexpected social consequences. Technology is both a creative and a destructive force.

The earliest known human artifacts are hand-ax flints found in Africa, western Asia, and Europe. They date from about 250,000 B.C., signaling the beginning of the Stone Age. The first toolmakers were nomadic groups of hunters who used the sharp edges of stone to cut their food and to make their clothing and shelters. By about 100,000 B.C. the graves of hominids show pear-shaped axes, scrapers, knives, and other stone instruments, indicating that the original hand ax had become a tool for making tools. This is the chief characteristic of human technology. The use of tools is not specific to the human species; it can be observed in other animal species. However, the capacity for creating tools to make other tools distinguishes human technology from that of all other animals.

Perhaps the biggest step forward in the history of technology was the control of fire. By striking flint against pyrites to produce sparks, early people could kindle fires at will, thereby freeing themselves from the necessity of perpetuating fires obtained from natural sources. Besides the obvious benefits of light and heat, fire was also used to bake clay pots, producing heat-resistant vessels which were then used for cooking, brewing, and fermenting. Fired pottery later provided the crucibles in which metals could be refined.

Early technologies were not centered only on practical tools. Colorful minerals were pulverized to make pigments which were then applied to the human body as cosmetics, and to other objects as decoration. Early people also learned that if certain materials were repeatedly hammered and put into a fire, they would not split or crack. The discovery of how to relieve metal stress eventually brought human societies out of the Stone Age. About 3000 B.C., people also found that alloying tin with copper produced bronze. Bronze is not only more malleable than copper but also holds a better edge, a quality necessary for making such objects as swords and sickles. Although copper deposits existed in the foothills of Syria and Turkey, at the headwaters of the Tigris and Euphrates rivers, the largest deposits of copper in the ancient world were found on the island of Crete. With the development of ships that could reach this extremely valuable resource, Knossos on Crete became a wealthy mining center during the Bronze Age.

By the time of the Bronze Age, the human societies that dotted every continent had long since made a number of other technological advances. They had developed barbed spears, the bow and arrow, animal-oil lamps, and bone needles for making containers and clothing. They had also embarked on a major cultural revolution—a shift from a nomadic hunting culture to a more settled one based on agriculture.

Farming communities first emerged near the end of the most recent ice age, about 10,000 B.C. Their traces can be found in widely scattered areas, from southeastern Asia to Mexico. The most famous ones emerged in Mesopotamia (modern Iraq) near the temperate and fertile river valleys of the Tigris and Euphrates. The loose soil in this fertile crescent was easily scratched for planting, and an abundance of trees was available for firewood.

By 5000 B.C., farming communities were established in areas known today as Syria, Turkey, Lebanon, Israel, Jordan, Greece, and the islands of Crete and Cyprus. The people living in these new social systems constructed stone buildings, used the sickle to harvest grain, developed a primitive plowstick, and advanced their skills in metalworking. By 4000

B.C., farming had spread westward from these centers to the Danube River in central Europe, southward to the Mediterranean shores of Africa (including the Nile River), and eastward to the Indus Valley.

Clearly, technology shapes cultural evolution. Take as a simple example the invention of the clock in 1286 and of the printing press in the fifteenth century. The invention of the clock meant that, from that moment on, people would no longer live in a social world based primarily on the daily course of the sun and the yearly change of the seasons. The precise measurement of time made it possible for people to plan their day and their lives much more rationally. The clock also became essential for the growth of modern science. The invention of the printing press set off a social revolution that is only now being eclipsed by an electronic revolution. The Chinese had developed both paper and printing before the second century A.D., but these innovations did not become generally known to the Western world until the German printing pioneer Johannes Gutenberg solved the problem of molding movable type around 1450. Once developed, printing spread rapidly and began to replace hand-printed texts for a wider audience. As a consequence, intellectual life was no longer the exclusive domain of church and court, and literacy became a necessity of urban existence.

Perhaps the most important period of technological development was the Industrial Revolution, which started in England because that nation had the technological means, political system, and varied trade networks already in place. The Industrial Revolution brought a new pattern to the division of labor and reconfigured the nature and social roles of the family, religion, and government. It did this by creating the modern factory, a technological system of production wherein workers were not required to be artisans, nor necessarily to possess skills. Because of this, the factory introduced an impersonal remuneration process based on a wage system. This division of labor into integrated tasks and operations that were more and more narrowly described became the determining feature of work in the new industrial society. The factory became a basic institution of modern culture, with the work of people becoming just another commodity in the production process.

Such nineteenth and twentieth-century inventions as the telephone, the phonograph, the wireless radio, motion pictures, the automobile, television, the airplane, and the computer have added to the nearly universal respect that society in general has come to feel for technology. With the advent of mass-production technology, not only has the availability of objects for mass consumption become a fact of everyday life, but mass consumption has itself become a way of life. Not everyone thinks that technology is a blessing. Since the middle part of the twentieth century, many people have reacted against the very consumerist lifestyle and worldview that it has engendered, believing that the overwhelming nature of modern technology threatens the quality of life. Supporters of this viewpoint propose a value system in which all people must come to recognize that the earth's resources are limited and that human life must be structured around a commitment to control the growth of industry, the size of cities, and the use of energy.

"BABBAGE'S GALAXY"

No other invention since the printing press has changed society more radically than the computer. The computer has started the process of transferring the human archive of knowledge from paper to electronic storage. It is a social and economic process that is probably irreversible. Today, information storage is measured not in page numbers but in gigabytes. Common desktop computers can now store the equivalent of hundreds of books. They can retrieve any page within milliseconds. If a disk becomes full, data can be archived to some other small device (a disk of some kind). Within seconds, anyone with a modem and a personal computer can access any item from the a vast store of human information.

According to some culture analysts, the computer may have already replaced the book, in the same way that alphabetic writing came to replace the oral transmission of knowledge. Different types and sizes of computers are used throughout society in the storage and handling of data, from government files to banking transactions to private household accounts. Computers have opened up a new era in manufacturing through electronic automation, and they have considerably enhanced modern communication systems. They have become essential tools in almost every field of research and applied technology, from constructing models of the universe to producing weather forecasts. Their use has in itself opened up new areas of conjecture. Database services and computer networks make available a great variety of information sources. The World Wide Web system of resources available to computer users who are connected to the Internet enables them to view and interact with a variety of information systems

and codes, including magazine archives, public and university library resources, current world and business news, and programs of all types. These
resources are organized to allow users to move easily from one to another.
The same advanced techniques, however, also make possible invasions of
privacy and of restricted information sources, and computer crime has become a new risk. In effect, we no longer live in "Gutenberg's Galaxy," as
McLuhan called the age of the book, but in "Babbage's Galaxy," to coin a
parallel phrase in reference to the nineteenth century British mathematician who worked out the principles of the modern digital computer,
Charles Babbage (1792–1871).

The computer has radically revised the way in which information and
knowledge are being coded in the world. Living in Babbage's Galaxy, the
modern human being is now more inclined to learn from the screen than
from the book. The mystique associated with the author of a published
work is starting to fade as the world's texts become available literally at
one's fingertips. The whole notion of authorship and narrative art is being
drastically transformed by the computer.

Living in a technological society, one cannot but admire and take delight
in the staggering achievements made possible by the computer revolution.
But our naive faith in the computer is really no different from other forms
of animism. The computer is one of *Homo sapiens'* greatest technological
achievements. As a maker of objects and artifacts, the human species has finally come up with an object that is felt more and more to have human-
like qualities. This, too, reflects an ancient aspiration of our species. In
Sumerian and Babylonian myths there were accounts of the creation of life
through the animation of clay. The ancient Romans were fascinated by au-
tomata that could mimic human patterns. By the time Mary Shelley's
grotesque and macabre novel, *Frankenstein,* was published in 1818, the idea
that robots could be brought to life horrified the modern imagination.
Since the first decades of the twentieth century the quest to animate machines has been relentless. It has captured the imagination of many image-
makers. Movie robots and humanoid machines like HAL, in *2001: A Space
Odyssey, Robocop,* and *Terminator* have attributes of larger-than-life humans.
Modern human beings are experiencing a feeling of astonishment at finding themselves for the first time ever at the center of everything. But, there
is a risk here. It is easy to forget that we are much more than machines, possessing a consciousness imbued with *fantasia,* sensitivity, intuition, and
pathos, which comes with having human flesh and blood.

9

ART IS INDISTINGUISHABLE FROM LIFE

The Artistic Nature of the Human Species

> Art is not to be taught in Academies. It is what one looks at, not what one listens to, that makes the artist. The real schools should be the streets.
>
> —Oscar Wilde (1854–1900)

Martha's videotape contains other episodes that are of direct interest to the semiotician. There is one scene, for instance, where Cheryl takes out a photograph of a sculpture that she had made, showing it proudly to her amorous partner. Ted looks at it with admiration, remarking, "How beautiful, Cheryl. I didn't know you were so talented." "I have always loved to draw and sculpt," she responds. "For me art is indistinguishable from life, as the saying goes." The semiotician would agree completely.

The making of art is unique to the human species. The capacity to draw and appreciate pictures, to make music, to dance, to put on stage performances, to write poetry, is a truly extraordinary and enigmatic endowment of our species. Art not only gives pleasure and delight, but also affords a truly profound perspective on the human condition.

WHAT IS ART?

Art comes so naturally to human beings that it is impossible to define it adequately as separate from human nature. There is no culture that does not have its own repertoire of art forms. Art expresses the entire range of human feelings and spiritual beliefs. It is indisputable evidence of the workings of what Vico called the *fantasia,* the human capacity for knowing from within. Art is everything to everyone. Art works can be seen, heard, touched, and experienced in different ways; art gives pleasure, excites the senses, "moves" the spirit, and appeases the gods. Art survives because it is valued as precious, because it is perceived as transcending time, because it is seen as saying something about human nature. Yet art is indefinable. It is something that everyone knows and recognizes, but which defies definition with words.

The word art is derived from the Latin *ars* (skill). Art is, at one level, skill at performing a set of specialized actions such as, for example, the skilled actions required to be a gardener or to play chess competently. In its broader sense, however, it implies creative imagination in the use of these actions—in singing, in drawing figures, in telling stories, and in many other ways. Art provides the person or people who produce it and the community that observes it with an experience that is both emotional and intellectual. In classical and medieval times, poets and other writers who used mental skills were usually ranked above actors, dancers, musicians, painters, and sculptors, who used physical skills. From the Renaissance on, as all aspects of human creativity came to be valued, those skilled in the visual and performing arts gradually gained greater recognition and social prestige. Today, art in all its categories is considered an essential part of human achievement, and all types of artists are ranked among the most prominent citizens of the world.

Traditionally, art has combined practical and aesthetic functions. In eighteenth century Western culture, however, a more sophisticated public began to distinguish between art that was purely aesthetic and art that was mainly practical. The *fine arts* (*beaux arts* in French)—literature, music, dance, painting, sculpture, and architecture—came to be distinguished from the *decorative* or *applied arts,* such as pottery, metalwork, furniture, tapestry, and enamel, which were demoted to the rank of *crafts.* Since the mid-twentieth century, however, greater appreciation of crafts and of non-Western and folk traditions has tended to blur this distinction. Both categories are valued as art once again.

Originally, art probably had ritualistic and mythological functions. The notion of artists as individualists and eccentric creators is a modern one. Only during the last few hundred years have artists of all kinds created art

for its own sake—to be put in galleries, to be played in public performances, to be read by anyone who is literate, and so on. In ancient cultures, art was part of ritual, of magic ceremonies, and thus a form of
creative behavior meant to please the gods. It was made and performed by
various members of the community, rather than by professionals alone. Art
was anonymous because it belonged to everyone. In aboriginal cultures of
North America, art continues to be perceived as one aspect of community
rituals that are designed to ensure a good harvest or to celebrate a significant life event such as a birth.

Even in modern technological cultures, art continues to reverberate
with ritualistic connotations. At a performance of a piece of classical
music, there is ritualistic silence and stillness in the audience. At a rock
concert, on the other hand, there is ritualistic shouting and movement.
Hanging a painting in an art gallery invites an individualistic interpretation; drawing something on a city wall, on the other hand, invites social
participation (graffiti, commentary, modifications, etc.). In the first cities,
art was meant to decorate the public square, to give communal life a sense
of purpose, to commemorate some meaningful event, and to invite opinions. Anonymous, participatory art is much more ancient than the "private" or "authored" art that has become the standard since the
Renaissance. In a public space, art is open to "contributions" from observers. In a gallery setting, on the other hand, interpretation focuses on
the intentions of the individual artist, and any "contribution" to the painting by an observer would constitute defacement.

Archeologists trace the origin of visual art to the Old Stone Age (20,000
to 15,000 B.C.). The well-known figure of a bison painted on the rock wall
of a cave in Altamira, Spain, is one of the first examples of art-making in
human history. What it means remains a mystery, but the features that
make it art are easily noticeable. It is not just a reproduction of a bison,
but of a bison in motion, seemingly scared, perhaps running away from
something or someone. It is, in a word, a reflective representation, an interpretation of an event which attempts to provide a particular perspective
of its broader meaning.

As the American philosopher Susanne Langer observantly pointed out,
art is powerful because it works on our perceptions and our feelings. We
experience a work of art not as an isolated event, but in its entirety as a
global whole, and as interconnected with larger life events.[1] Trying to understand what it means forces us, however, to analyze why the art work so

moved us. But, no matter how many times we try to explain the experience, it somehow remains beyond analysis. One can, of course, "explain" Beethoven's *Moonlight Sonata* as a series of harmonic progressions and melodic figures based on the key of C# minor. This tells us how Beethoven put his text together, with the *code* of early nineteenth-century harmony; but when one hears it played with passion, one hardly focuses on the harmonic and melodic details. Rather, one feels the sonata as a passionate whole, as an aesthetic experience, as a commentary on life.

The word *aesthetic* requires some commentary. It means, literally, "perceiving with all the senses." More generally, it refers to a sense of beauty or a feeling of *meaningfulness*. The first aesthetic theory of any scope was that of Plato, who believed that reality consists of ideal forms, beyond human sensation, and that works of art are imitations of those forms. However, fearing the power of art to move people, Plato wanted to banish some types of artists from his ideal society because he thought their work encouraged immorality, caused laziness, or incited people to immoderate actions. Aristotle also spoke of art as imitation, but not in the Platonic sense. For Aristotle, the role of art was to complete what nature did not finish by imitating it. The artist separates the form from the matter of objects, such as the human body or a plant, and then imposes that form on another material, such as canvas or marble. Thus, imitation is not just copying an object, nor is it devising a symbol for it; rather, it is a particular representation of an aspect of the object. Because Aristotle held that happiness was the aim of life, he believed that the major function of art is to provide satisfaction. In *Poetics*, his great work on the principles of dramatic art, Aristotle argued that tragedy so stimulates the emotions of pity and fear, which he considered morbid and unwholesome, that by the end of the play the spectator is purged of them. This *catharsis*, as he called it, makes the audience psychologically healthier and thus more capable of happiness.

Art in the Middle Ages was viewed as serving religious functions. It was during the Renaissance that art reacquired its more secular roles. The Renaissance also saw little difference between the artist and the scientist. Indeed, many were both: Leonardo da Vinci (1452–1519), for example, was a painter, writer, and scientist. It was only after the Enlightenment and Romantic movements in Western society that a division emerged, pitting artists against scientists. But this is a misguided view, the semiotician would remark, because both are "seekers of meaning," trying to represent the world and to convey their experience of the world to others in their own way.

The view of the artist as an eccentric genius impelled by his or her own creative energies, free of the yoke of culture, is very much a product of Romanticism. Traditionally, artists were considered employees of society. Sumerian priests and Renaissance princes, for instance, provided sufficient wealth to professional artists to enable them to work comfortably. Even the kind of art that artists created was dictated by social needs and conditions. In stoneless Mesopotamia, Sumerian architects built in brick. Nomadic Asian herders wove wool from their flocks into rugs. Medieval European painters worked on wood panels, plaster walls, stained-glass windows, and parchment books in an era before the use of paper in the West. The Romantic movement, which lasted from about 1800 to 1870, changed all this dramatically. The Romantics praised subjectivity and the passions. The individual artist's art was seen as intrinsic to his or her life. From this period we have inherited our modern assumptions about the primacy of artistic freedom, originality, and self-expression.

THE PERFORMING ARTS

Performance is, literally, the communication of an artistic form (from Latin *per* "through" and *forma* "form"), framed in a special way and put on display for an audience. Performances are given spatial prominence, through a raised stage or a platform; they generally involve using props and paraphernalia such as costumes, masks, props, and artifacts of various kinds; they occur within a socially defined situation (they are scheduled, set up and prepared in advance); they have a beginning and an end; they unfold through a structured sequence of parts (for example, acts in a play); and they are coordinated for public involvement.

From the very beginning of time performances have been mounted to serve ritualistic and social functions: to get people to reflect upon the values and goals of the culture, to critique them, to convey the "will of the gods," and so on. Great performances are indeed *reformative*, forcing observers to reflect upon who they are and what is truly of value to them. Performance art impels spectators to look within themselves through the roles and actions of the performers. These offer an opportunity for self-reflection "from a distance," so to speak.

The type of performance called *theater* extends right back to the origins of culture. Theatrical performances reenact some event in nature or in social life, involving actors and a spatial location, such as a raised stage, around which an audience can view and hear the performance. The term theater describes both the performance itself and the place where it takes place, because the stage setting is intrinsically intertwined with the dramatic text. The performance involves both words and actions, but it can also be based purely on bodily movement. The latter is referred to more precisely as *pantomime,* or the art of dramatic representation by means of facial expressions and body movements rather than words. Pantomime has always played a basic part in theater generally. In the open-air theaters of ancient Greece and Rome, where the audience could see more easily than it could hear, it was a critical element of acting. Ancient actors used stylized movements and masks to portray a character to the accompaniment of music and the singing of a chorus.

The most common form of theater in Western culture is the *drama,* which comes from the Greek word *dran* meaning "to do." Drama puts on view personages, actions, and events that allow us to reflect on matters of importance to our existence. The first great dramas of Western civilization—those of Aeschylus, Sophocles, and Euripides in ancient Greece, for example—tell as much, if not more, about the meaning of life as do any of the ponderous writings of philosophers. Indeed, in their dramatic representations of human thoughts, actions, aspirations, desires, pain, and suffering, these plays continue to give us insight into life's enigmas.

Most theories on the origin of drama point to ancient religious rites and practices. Residues of this function can still be seen in rites like the Catholic mass and the Easter reenactment of the *Via Crucis.* The first evidence that drama became what we now define as performance art was in ancient Greece in the sixth century B.C. where dramatic performances were scripted to enact tales of the gods. The plays of the first Greek dramatists were drawn from myth and legend, though their focus was not a simple reenactment of the mythic story but a portrayal of the tragedy of human actions. The oldest extant comedies are by the Greek satirist Aristophanes, who ridiculed public figures and the gods equally. The comedic approach to theater was continued in the Roman plays of Plautus and Terence. A few centuries later, the emerging Christian Church attacked this approach as too bawdy. So, with the fall of the Roman Empire in 476 A.D., all classical forms of theater were banished. These did not reemerge for more than 500 years, replaced by a new form called *liturgical drama.* The liturgical plays were based on Bible stories, evolving, by the fifteenth century, into *morality plays,* self-contained dramas performed by professional actors dealing with the theme of life as a journey.

The origin of the modern drama can be traced to the Renaissance when the Florentine statesman and writer Niccolò Machiavelli (1469–1527) wrote and staged *The Mandrake,* which revived the ancient world's penchant for farce, bawdiness, and satire. A little later, there emerged in Italy a form of theater, called the *Commedia dell'arte,* which brought about a different dimension to theatrical art—*improvisation.* Modern-day comedy routines, TV sitcoms, and the like are inheritors of this tradition. The *Commedia dell'arte* originated in northern Italy in the 1550s and flourished for 200 years. Troupes of actors relied on stock characters, masks, broad physical gestures, and clowning to entertain large, diverse crowds. The character types of the *Commedia* were instantly recognizable—lecherous, cunning *Arlecchino* (Harlequin) wore a black, snub-nosed mask; gullible *Pantalone* disguised his old age by wearing tight-fitting Turkish clothes, hoping to attract young women; the pot-bellied rascal *Pulcinella* (Punch) concocted outrageous schemes to satisfy his desires; and so on. Although some governments attempted to censor and regulate this popular form of theater, the characters of the *Commedia* were so popular they eventually were incorporated into conventional theater.

From the Renaissance on, theater reacquired its primary role as a social performance art. Names such as Shakespeare, Molière, Calderón, Goethe, Pirandello, Ibsen, Chekhov, Brecht, Beckett, to mention but a small handful, have become names recognizable to virtually everyone. Drama is studied in schools, and it is put on as a significant social event. Citations from Shakespeare, allusions to actions in the plays of Molière and Pirandello, references to dramatic characters for explaining certain aspects of human nature (Oedipus, Hamlet, Lear, etc.), are testaments to the all-pervasiveness of the dramatic text in our culture. Unlike Eastern forms of drama, where audience participation is encouraged, Western performance art has become increasingly a *reflective* form of art.

Reflective performances are psychologically powerful. Take, as a case in point, Samuel Beckett's (1906–89) late 1940s play, *Waiting for Godot,* a dramatic "countertext" to the religious text of the morality plays. The latter portrayed life as a spiritual journey, and the world as a place created by God for humans to earn their way back to the paradise lost by Adam and

Eve, who were expelled from the Garden of Eden because of their original sin. Within this moral framework, human actions are seen as centered on God's plan and desires; they are the guarantee that death is not extinction. The medieval morality plays made this the basic thematic element of their dramatic text.

Beckett's *Waiting for Godot* is a disturbing parody of this text. In Beckett's world there is only a void, no heaven or hell. Human beings fulfill no particular purpose in being alive. Life is a meaningless collage of actions, leading to death and a return to nothingness. The play revolves around two tramps stranded in an empty landscape, passing the time with banalities reminiscent of slapstick comedians or circus clowns. The tramps, Vladimir and Estragon, seem doomed to repeat forever their senseless actions and words. They call each other names, they ponder whether or not to commit suicide, they reminisce about a senseless past, they threaten to leave each other, but cannot, they perform silly exercises, and they are constantly waiting for a mysterious character named Godot, who never comes. A strange couple, Lucky and Pozzo, appears, disappears, reappears, and finally vanishes. Pozzo whips Lucky, as if he were a cart horse. Lucky kicks Estragon. The two tramps tackle Lucky to the ground to stop him from shrieking out a deranged parody of a philosophy lecture. Vladimir and Estragon talk endlessly about nothing in particular, and keep on waiting, pointlessly, for Godot. Allusions in their dialogue to the Bible are sardonic and acrimonious—there is a bare tree on stage in parody of the biblical tree of life, the tramps constantly engage in trivial theological discourse, satirizing the questions raised by the Bible. On and on it goes like this throughout the play, which ends with no resolution. "In the beginning was the Word," the Book of Genesis declares; "the word is hollow," Beckett's play retorts. Life is meaningless; a veritable circus farce. The God we are supposed to meet will not come.

Beckett's bleak portrait spurs us on, paradoxically, to search for the very meaning it denies. Like the six characters in Pirandello's 1921 play, *Six Characters in Search of an Author,* humans see themselves as characters in a life drama, searching for an author to write them into existence, as the play argues. Ironically, through desperate plays like Beckett's masterpiece, we are led to a profound reevaluation of our most fundamental beliefs. Beckett's text impels us to think "Please, let there be a God!" The greatness of Beckett's play rests not in its parody of the traditional religious search for meaning, but in stimulating a reexamination of who we are. We may be condemned to waiting for Godot, and the rational part of our mind might tell us that existence is absurd, but at a more profound level we seem to sense that there is a spiritual reality within ourselves, one that cannot be denied, no matter how nihilistic the culture we live in has become.

That is how drama works. The ancient tragedies portrayed life as a mythic struggle between humans and the gods. Medieval morality plays put on display actions and themes that informed the populace how to live according to a divine plan. Playwrights like Beckett capture the modern angst, the fear of nothingness, all the while stimulating in us a more desperate search for meaning.

THE MUSICAL ARTS

Another universal performance art is *music*. Music plays a role in all societies, existing in a large number of styles, each characteristic of a geographical region or a historical era. Like all art, music is not easy to define, and yet most people recognize what it is and generally agree on whether or not a given sound is musical. Musical art is yet more striking evidence that human beings are "meaning-seeking creatures." The great works of musical art of all cultures transcend time and are performed again and again, forcing listeners to extract meaning about themselves and the world they inhabit. In a fundamental sense, music is an international language, since its structures are not based on word meanings and combinations, but on melody, rhythm, and harmony. The latter seem to be universal in that they evoke feelings rooted in the human spirit.

Indefinite border areas exist, however, between music and other sound phenomena such as speech. Thus, a tribal chant, a half-spoken style of singing, or a composition created by a computer program may or may not be accepted as music by members of a given society. Muslims, for example, do not consider the chanting of the Koran to be music, although the structure of the chant is similar to that of secular singing. The social context in which sounds are made determines whether or not they are regarded as music. Industrial noises, for instance, are not considered music in our society, unless they are presented as part of a concert of experimental music in an auditorium. Opinions differ as to the origins and spiritual value of music. In some African cultures music is seen as *the* defining trait of human nature; among some Native American cultures it is thought to have originated as a way for spirits to communicate with humans; in Western culture it is regarded as one of the sublime arts. In some other cultures, however, it has low value, associated with sin and evil, and is thus prohibited.

In our society, three basic forms of music are distinguished: *classical* music, composed and performed by trained professionals originally under the patronage of aristocratic courts and religious establishments; *folk* music, shared by the population at large and transmitted orally; *popular* music, performed by professionals and disseminated through radio, television, records, film, etc., and consumed by a mass public. Although most of our musical performances are text-based (composed by someone in advance), some involve improvisation. The latter usually proceeds on the basis of some previously determined structure, such as a tone or a group of chords, as in jazz. In other cultures, however, improvisation schemes can be devised within a set of traditional rules, as in the *ragas* of India or the *maqams* of the Middle East.

Music is used in many societies to accompany other activities. For example, it is usually associated with dance and typically plays a substantial role in cultural rituals, in theater, and in entertainment. Music as art is a relatively recent phenomenon, dating back to the sixteenth and seventeenth century, and especially to the music of Johann Sebastian Bach (1685–1750). Since then, some music is perceived as something to be appreciated for its own sake. The most ubiquitous use of music, however, is as a part of religious ritual. In some tribal societies, music served as a special form of communication with supernatural beings. Its prominent use in religious services is a remnant of this function. Another, less obvious, function of music is social integration. For some social groups, music can serve as a powerful symbol of group structure and values: the hierarchy of performers in an ensemble symbolizes the caste system of India; the avoidance of voice blending in a singing group reflects the value placed on individualism by the Plains tribes of North America.

An interesting amalgam of music and theater is *opera*, which traces its origins ultimately to the chorus of Greek tragedy whose function was to provide commentary on the drama being performed. Similar genres exist throughout the world. The puppet drama, *wayang*, of Indonesia is a musical and dramatic reenactment of Hindu myth. Acting, singing, and instrumental music are mingled with dance and acrobatics in the many varieties of Chinese musical theater. In Japan, the theatrical genres of *No* and *kabuki* represent a union of drama, music, and dance.

In Western culture, the few secular medieval plays to survive, such as *Le jeu de Robin et Marion* (The Play of Robin and Marion, 1283), alternate spoken dialogue and songs. During the Renaissance, aristocratic courts staged performances that mixed pageant, recitation, and dance with instrumental, choral, and solo vocal music. Out of these, opera crystallized in Florence near the end of the sixteenth century, becoming shortly thereafter an autonomous art form. A group of musicians and scholars who called themselves *Camerata* (Italian for "salon") decided to revive the musical style used in ancient Greek drama and to develop an alternative to the highly contrapuntal music (the technique of combining two or more melody lines in a harmonic pattern) of the late Renaissance. Specifically, they wanted composers to pay close attention to the texts on which their music was based, to set these texts in a simple manner, and to make the music reflect, phrase by phrase, the meaning of the text.

The first composer of genius to apply himself to opera was the Italian Claudio Monteverdi (1567–1643). He molded songs, duets, choruses, and instrumental sections into a coherent text based on purely musical relationships. Monteverdi thus demonstrated that a wide variety of musical forms and styles could be used to enhance the drama. Opera spread quickly throughout Italy. In the eighteenth and nineteenth centuries, it had become popular in most parts of Europe. Wolfgang Amadeus Mozart, Ludwig van Beethoven, Richard Wagner, Giuseppe Verdi, to mention a few, infused the opera form with dramatic strength and musical profundity. In the twentieth century, Alban Berg introduced atonality (the absence of a tonal center) into opera with his 1925 masterpiece *Wozzeck,* a nightmarish portrayal of human degradation. In 1951, Gian Carlo Menotti (1911–) wrote the first opera specifically for the television medium, *Amahl and the Night Visitor.*

What is particularly interesting is that traditional opera—that of Mozart, Rossini, Verdi, Puccini, Wagner—has perhaps never achieved more favor with the general public than it has today. This is because technology has exposed new audiences to traditional opera, especially through the proliferation of recordings. By the last quarter of the twentieth century, opera as a spectacle had become a thriving enterprise.

THE VISUAL ARTS

Visual art predates civilization. Art works of remarkable expressiveness have been discovered by archeologists deep within caves of southern Europe that go back to the Paleolithic period, roughly between 40,000 and

10,000 B.C. The invention of sharpened flint blades by Paleolithic humans also made possible the earliest art objects—small carved or incised pieces of wood, ivory, and bone. These symbolized a dependence on hunting and a worship of fertility. Such art apparently played a part in early rituals, and many art objects were believed to possess great magical powers.

In the caves of Lascaux, France, and Altamira, Spain, highly sensitive, colored figures of horses, bulls, and other animals are portrayed with amazing accuracy. These representations were painted in bright colors composed of various minerals ground into powders and mixed with animal fat, egg whites, plant juices, fish glue, and even blood. The pictures may have been part of magic rituals, although their purpose is unclear. In a cave painting at Lascaux, for example, a man is depicted among the animals, and several dark dots are included. The purpose of the design remains obscure, but it shows the cave dwellers' ability to think in symbols. I would like to suggest that these primitive art works reveal a fascination with consciousness. The same fascination can be seen in young children who start to draw at about the same time they become reflective thinkers.

Every culture has developed its own particular way of representing the world through visual images. The aesthetic pleasure these give seems, by itself, to be a motivation for their creation. Paintings and sculptures betray an innate fascination in our species with what the eye sees and attempts to understand. The signifiers that make up the world's visual art codes include *value, color,* and *texture.* Value refers to the darkness or lightness of a line or shape. It plays an important role in portraying contrasts. Color covers a broad range of signification, evoking many feelings in paintings. This is why in English one speaks of "warm," "soft," "cold," "harsh" colors. Texture refers to any tactile sensation that is evoked when one looks at some surface. People react differently to a smooth round figure like a circle, than to a "jagged edge" figure.

In Western culture, painting became a sophisticated visual art form with the development of the principles of linear perspective by various Italian architects and painters early in the fifteenth century. This enabled painters to achieve, in two-dimensional representations, the illusion of three-dimensional space. Renaissance artists also introduced innovations in how to represent human anatomy, and new media and methods, such as oil painting and fresco (painting on fresh, moist plaster with pigments dissolved in water) techniques. Masters of the High Renaissance, such as Leonardo da Vinci, Raphael, Michelangelo, and Titian, developed these techniques to perfection. Paradoxically, Leonardo left but a handful of paintings, so occupied was he with the scientific observation of natural phenomena and with technological inventions. His surviving fresco paintings have badly deteriorated—notably, the *Last Supper.* Raphael perfected earlier Renaissance techniques involving color and composition, creating ideal types in his representations of the Virgin and Child and in his penetrating portrait studies of contemporaries. The Vatican's *Sistine Chapel,* with its ceiling frescoes of the *Creation,* the *Fall,* and the vast wall fresco of *The Last Judgment* attest to Michelangelo's genius as a painter. Titian's portraits include representations of Christian and mythological subjects, and his numerous renderings of the female nude are among the most celebrated of the genre.

Since the late nineteenth century, visual art has found a new medium of expression—*photography.* The Swedish photographer Oscar Rejlander (1813–75) and the English photographer Henry Peach Robinson (1834–1901) were the first true art photographers, emulating painting techniques with their cameras. Recording events and scenes, as well as capturing portraits of people on film, they showed how the photographic image provides the same kinds of aesthetic perspectives that painting affords.

Photographs capture a fleeting and irretrievable moment in time, extracting it from the irreversible flux of change that characterizes life. Such "encapsulated moments" have strong appeal because they allow us literally to freeze time on film and reflect upon a certain moment. Through the photographic image we can relive the moment or recall someone as he or she was at that point in time. The photographs that adorn tables and walls in homes, offices, and other buildings are visual testimonials of who we are, giving a visual form to human memory. Photographs provide visual proof that we do indeed exist or that we have lived. This signifying power of the photograph is brought out in Michelangelo Antonioni's (1912–) 1966 movie masterpiece, *Blow-Up.* The movie revolves around a search for clues to a murder in a blow-up of a photograph, evolving into a metaphor for the search for clues to the meaning of our own existence.

To conclude the discussion of visual art, one cannot ignore the power and influence of cinematic art. Cinema is perhaps the most influential visual art form of the contemporary world. Possessing the narrative and theatrical qualities that paintings, sculptures, and photographs do not, the cinema is similar to dramatic and literary art forms, while at the same time retaining the same sensory properties of the other visual arts. Indeed, it is the blend and juxtaposition of plot, character, dialogue, music, scenery, and action that makes cinema a particularly effective means of artistic expression. No wonder, then, that today movie actors and directors are better known, and certainly more popular, than writers and playwrights. Names such as Fellini, Spielberg, Polanski, Hitchcock, De Mille, Cocteau, to name but a few, are part of modern cultural lore. Cinema actors enjoy more fame and recognition than do scientists and philosophers. The giving of Oscar awards constitutes a spectacle of mythological proportions.

The most influential filmmaker of the early silent period was the American producer and director D. W. Griffith (1875–1948). His controversial film about the American Civil War, *The Birth of a Nation* (1915), marked the emergence of cinema as a full-fledged art form. Among the early silent classics, one can mention *The Cabinet of Dr. Caligari* (1919), *Nosferatu* (1922), and *Metropolis* (1926).

In 1927 the Warner Brothers studio released *The Jazz Singer,* the first talking picture, starring American entertainer Al Jolson. By 1931 sound films became an international phenomenon. At first, gangster films, musicals, and horror movies dominated the screen. Then in 1939 one of the most popular films in motion-picture history, the epic *Gone with the Wind* (1939), was made, changing the course of movie-making. In 1953 the Twentieth Century-Fox studio premiered its biblical epic, *The Robe,* in a new process called CinemaScope, which created a wide-screen revolution in the film industry.

In Italy during the late 1940s the cinematic movement called *neo-realism* captured worldwide attention. Launched by director Roberto Rossellini in *Open City* (1945), the movement was characterized by films of an intense realism, set against natural backgrounds and featuring non-professional actors. Other outstanding neo-realist directors were Vittorio de Sica (*The Bicycle Thief,* 1949), Federico Fellini (*La Strada,* 1954; *La Dolce Vita,* 1960; *8 1/2,* 1963), Pier Paolo Pasolini (*The Gospel According to Saint Matthew,* 1966), and Michelangelo Antonioni (*L'Avventura,* 1959; *Red Desert,* 1964).

Perhaps the most influential director of all time is Sweden's Ingmar Bergman (1918–), who brought an intense emotional and intellectual depth to the cinema genre by treating problems of human isolation, sexuality, and religion. His numerous films include *The Seventh Seal* (1956),

Wild Strawberries (1957), *Persona* (1966), *Cries and Whispers* (1972), *Scenes from a Marriage* (1973), and *Autumn Sonata* (1978). Interestingly, the cinema art form has produced a new view of authorship. Although there is a script-writer, the director is perceived as the primary "author" of a film, the one who gives the cinematic text the individual stamp of his or her personality. In theater, the director is still viewed as an interpreter of the playwright's text; but in cinema the director is viewed as the maker of the text.

THE VERBAL ARTS

As already discussed in Chapter 6, every culture has produced verbal accounts (tales, stories, etc.) to make sense of the world. The most ancient and universal verbal art is poetry—a form of expression that creates an aesthetic effect through the sounds, rhythms, and imagery produced by its language. These characteristics mark the difference between poetry and other kinds of verbal art.

Views on the nature and function of poetry in human societies have been varied. Plato asserted that poetry was divinely inspired, but that it was nonetheless a mere imitation of ideal forms in the world. Aristotle, on the other hand, argued that poetry was the most sublime of the creative arts, representing what is universal in human experience. The philosopher Vico saw poetry as the primordial form of language. Vico called the first speakers "poets," which etymologically means "makers," because their first words were true verbal inventions. The many poetic-like texts found by archeologists at ancient Sumerian, Babylonian, Hittite, Egyptian, and Hebrew sites suggest that poetry originated alongside music, song, and drama as a communal form of expression to seek favor from, or give praise to, the divinities. This ritualistic aspect of poetry is still functional in many societies. In the Navajo culture, for instance, poetic forms are used as incantations for rain. In our own culture, ritualistic and pedagogical uses of poetry abound. We use poetic form on greeting cards and on special kinds of invitations; we use poetry to impart knowledge of language to children (consider the widespread use of nursery rhymes and children's poetry books in our society).

Alongside poetry, the world's cultures have also developed prose forms of verbal art. The novel, for instance, has become a major form of literature in Western culture. The word novel, from Latin *novellus* "new," was first used by the great Italian writer Giovanni Boccaccio (1313–75) to refer to the anecdotal tales that he spun in his *Decameron* of 1353. This collection of 100 stories is set within a framework of ten friends telling stories to one another. To escape an outbreak of the plague, the friends have taken refuge in a country villa outside Florence, where they entertain one another over a period of ten days with a series of stories told by each one in turn. Boccaccio called the stories, more specifically, *novelle*, "new things." The novel is an outgrowth of the novella.

Many of the tales that subsequently became part of the European literary tradition originated in Egypt. Narrations also enjoyed considerable popularity among the Greeks in the early centuries of the Christian era. Worthy of mention are the *Æthiopica* (third century A.D.) by Heliodorus of Syria, the *Ephesiaca* (second century A.D.) by Xenophon of Ephesus, and *Daphnis and Chloë* (second century A.D.) one of the most exquisite of the pastoral romances, generally attributed to Longus. The chief examples of "proto-novels" written in Latin are the *Golden Ass* (second century A.D.) by Lucius Apuleius and the *Satyricon* (first century A.D.), which is generally considered the work of Petronius Arbiter. It must not be overlooked that in Japan, the Baroness Murasaki Shikibu (978?–1031?) wrote what many literary scholars now regard as the first real novel, *The Tale of Genji* in the eleventh century (translated 1935).

The long narrative verse tale, the equally voluminous prose romance, and the Old French *fabliau* flourished in Europe during the Middle Ages, contributing directly to the development of the modern novel. Advances in realism were made in Spain during the sixteenth century with the so-called picaresque or rogue story, in which the protagonist is a merry vagabond who goes through a series of realistic and exciting adventures. Between 1605 and 1612 the Spanish writer Miguel de Cervantes (1547–1616) wrote what is considered the first great novel of the Western world, *Don Quixote de la Mancha*. As the novel became increasingly popular during the eighteenth century, writers used it to examine society and the human condition with greater depth and breadth. They wrote revealingly about people living within, or escaping from, the pressures of society, criticizing society for failing to satisfy human aspirations.

From the nineteenth century onwards, novels have been widely read texts, ranging from trashy bestsellers to works of great import and substance. In the latter category, one thinks, for example, of the novels of Dostoyevsky, Tolstoy, Dickens, Hesse, Mann, Woolf, the Brontë sisters, Poe,

Hemingway, Camus, Sartre, Kafka, Twain, and Joyce. Such writers used the novel genre as a narrative framework for probing the human psyche.

To conclude the discussion of art, it is remarkable indeed that even in seemingly commonplace situations, such as a courtship performance, human beings are constantly attempting to transcend their biological urges and desires to reach for something elusive. Cheryl's pride in her artistic abilities reminds us that there is more to life than flesh and blood. For humans, art is indeed indistinguishable from life. Art is a guarantee that our weary search for meaning is itself meaningful. Life would be inconceivable without art, that is, without music, poetry, stories, and all the other forms of expression that allow us to become truly sapient creatures.

10

THERE'S MORE TO PERFUME THAN SMELL

Advertising, Pop Culture, and Television

Advertising is the greatest art form of the twentieth century.

—Marshall McLuhan (1911–80)

There is one other scene on Martha's videotape that is worth discussing from a semiotic standpoint. Near the end of the evening, Cheryl turns inquisitively to Ted and says: "Hmm, the cologne you're wearing, Ted, smells very nice. Is it *Drakkar Noir?*" "Yes," replies Ted. "Do you like it? I decided to try it on because of an ad I saw a few weeks ago in a magazine." "Oh, can you describe the ad to me?" retorts Cheryl. Ted's description of the ad follows. "Well, actually, I remember the bottle was a ghastly, frightful, black color. It was placed right in the center of the ad. I also remember that the dark background was shattered by a beam of white light that just missed the bottle but illuminated the platform on which it stood. That had a bizarre effect on me. I felt as if I were in awe of the bottle!"

The semiotician would find Ted's description of the ad text intriguing. Parenthetically, with the theme of advertising and pop culture, we have come full circle, back to the human fascination with such apparently trivial objects as cigarettes and high heels. Ted's reaction to the ad indicates that ours is a world beset by media images that stimulate an incessant need for new items of consumption—a craze that Roland Barthes called "neomania." Obsolescence is regularly built into a product, so that the same product can be sold again and again under new guises. The glitz and imagery of ads and TV commercials yell out one promise to all: Buy this or that and you will not be bored; you will be happy!

The sad truth is that happiness cannot be bought, as an old proverb warns us. We are living in a very unstable world psychologically, because it puts more of a premium on satisfying physical desires than it does on spirituality and wisdom. Advertisers rely on a handful of hedonistic themes—happiness, youth, success, status, luxury, fashion, and beauty—to promote their products, promising solutions to human problems in the form of deodorant soap, beer, expensive cars, and the like.

Let's start our final semiotic discussion by interpreting Ted's *Drakkar Noir* ad. Darkness connotes fear, evil, the unknown. This is why we talk of "black masses," why we often see "evil" characters in movies dressed in black; and why in stories forbidden, mysterious happenings occur in the dark. The dark background of the ad taps into these connotations. The perfume bottle's placement in the middle of the scene, as if on an altar, is suggestive of veneration, idolatry, of a dark ritual being performed secretively. This is reinforced by the sepulchral name of the cologne. Its guttural sound—obviously reminiscent of Dracula, the deadly vampire who mesmerized his sexual prey with a mere glance—arouses fear and desire at once. To complete the picture, the piercing beam of light (the paradigmatic opposite of dark) that just missed the bottle, illuminating the platform on which it stood, makes the bottle stand out as the "center of attention." Since perfume is worn to enhance one's sexual attractiveness and to entice a prospective mate, the ad elicits a web of sexual and macabre connotations: *darkness of the night = sexuality = forbidden pleasures = pagan rites = collusion with the devil = fear = desire = mystery = vampirism.* This lacework of meaning is reinforced by the vaginal shape of the bottle.

The *Drakkar Noir* ad illustrates rather strikingly how ingenious ad texts are in generating a chain of meanings that enlists various levels of interpretation. In a real sense, the ad is a small "work of art," which has, however, the specific commercial purpose of enhancing sales of a product. Deciphering such texts involves uncovering their connotations. Semiotic theorists call these *subtextual* and *intertextual* meanings.

The term subtext refers to any meaning that a given text connotes that is not immediately accessible to interpretation. It is the meaning *below the text.* The subtext in the *Drakkar Noir* ad is, as mentioned, *darkness of the night = sexuality = forbidden pleasures = pagan rites = collusion with the devil*

= *fear,* etc. The subtext thus plays on male fantasies and on a fear of women, a theme that surfaces in all kinds of narratives, from the Greek myth of Diana to contemporary movies (*Fatal Attraction, Basic Instinct, Disclosure,* etc.). What is emphasized in the subtext is not the actual act of sexual intercourse, but the mythical connotations that it entails in our culture. *Intertextuality* refers to the parts of a text that are understandable in terms of other texts or codes. The placement of the bottle in the center of the scene, with a dark background broken by a beam of light, recalls a sacrificial ritual or code wherein the vaginal bottle is worshipped and then conquered.

Subtexts in advertising can also be of a purely social nature. Take, for example, two beer brands, Budweiser and Heineken. Both beers taste about the same, but during the 1980s and early 1990s the social subtexts they entailed in advertising catered to vastly different "tastes" in lifestyle. Budweiser ads of that era spoke to a blue-collar working-class audience, while Heineken ads addressed an upscale white-collar one. Budweiser ads and TV commercials were set in working-class bars where country music was played, where the men looked rugged and tough, and where the women appeared highly "sexualized." Heineken ads, on the other hand, showed a much more sophisticated scene—nightclubs, country clubs, etc.—where the men looked suave and debonair, and the women chic, sophisticated, and charming. These images created a *personality* for each product that made it attractive to specific types of people. This is, in fact, the central notion of the modern-day science of marketing.

ADVERTISING

The term *advertising* derives from the medieval Latin verb *advertere* (to direct one's attention to). It designates any type or form of public announcement intended to direct attention to specific commodities or services. In consumerist societies, advertising has become a privileged discourse, which has more rhetorical force, by and large, than the traditional forms of rhetorical discourse such as sermons, political oratory, proverbs, and wise sayings. Advertising exalts and inculcates lifestyle values by playing on hidden fears—fear of poverty, sickness, loss of social standing, and unattractiveness. As Barthes claimed, in a society that relies on mass consumption for its economic survival, it is little wonder that the trivial has become artistic.[1]

The origins of advertising predate the Christian era by many centuries. One of the first known methods of advertising was the outdoor display, usually an eye-catching sign painted on the wall of a building. Archaeologists have uncovered many such signs. A poster found in Thebes in 1000 B.C. is thought to be one of the world's first ads. In large letters it offered a gold coin for the capture of a runaway slave. An outdoor placard found among the ruins of ancient Rome offered property for rent; another, found painted on a wall in Pompeii, called the attention of travelers to a tavern located in a different town. Similar kinds of posters have been found scattered throughout ancient societies.

Throughout history, advertising in marketplaces and temples has constituted an effective means of promoting the barter and sale of goods. In medieval times town "criers," employed by merchants, read public notices aloud to promote their wares. With the invention of the printing press in the fifteenth century, fliers and posters could be printed easily and posted in public places or inserted in books, pamphlets, newspapers, and magazines. By the latter part of the seventeenth century, when newspapers were beginning to circulate widely, print became the primary medium for the promotion of products and services. The *London Gazette* became the first newspaper to reserve a section exclusively for advertising. So successful was this venture that by the end of the century several agencies came into being for the specific purpose of creating newspaper ads for merchants and artisans.

Advertising spread rapidly throughout the eighteenth century, proliferating to the point whereby the writer and lexicographer Samuel Johnson (1709–84) felt impelled to make the following statement in the newspaper, *The Idler:* "Advertisements are now so numerous that they are very negligently perused, and it is [sic] therefore become necessary to gain attention by magnificence of promise and by eloquence sometimes sublime and sometimes pathetic."[2] Ad creators were starting to pay more attention to the design and layout of the ad text. The art of coining and inventing new language to fit the ad text was becoming widespread. Advertising was thus starting to change language and society radically. Everything, from clothes to beverages, was promoted with ingenious rhetorical methods— repetition of the firm's name or product, phrases set in eye-catching patterns, contrasting font styles and formats, the deployment of effective illustrations, and the creation of slogans.

Near the end of the nineteenth century the advertising agency came onto the scene. By the turn of the twentieth century, such agencies had themselves become large business enterprises, constantly developing new techniques and methods to get people to think of themselves as "market units" rather than as individuals or as a public. Throughout the twentieth century, advertising focused on promoting and ensconcing consumerism as a way of life, proposing marketplace solutions to virtually all psychological and social problems. No wonder, then, that the shopping malls are filled with thrill-seekers who would otherwise become stir-crazy. Perhaps, as many social critics warn, we do indeed live in a world conjured up by lifestyle ads and TV commercials.

The pervasiveness of advertising today raises a number of issues. Has it become a force molding cultural mores and individual behaviors or does it simply mirror the cultural tendencies of urbanized, industrialized societies? Is it a legitimate form of artistic expression, as the Cannes Film Festival clearly believes (awarding prizes to the best advertisements)? The starting point of the debate on advertising was probably Vance Packard's 1957 book *The Hidden Persuaders,* which inspired an outpouring of studies examining the purported hidden effects of advertising on individuals and on society at large.[3]

But to what extent are the warnings contained in research papers and monographs on the effects of advertising accurate or justified? Is advertising to be blamed for causing virtually every contemporary affliction, from obesity to street violence? Are media moguls the shapers of behavior that so many would claim they are? Are the victims of media, as Brian Wilson Key quips, people who "scream and shout hysterically at rock concerts and later in life at religious revival meetings?"[4] There is no doubt that media images play a role in shaping some behaviors in some individuals. But although people have become conditioned to mindlessly absorbing the images of advertisements, and although these may have some effects on behavior, people accept media images, by and large, only if they suit already established preferences. Advertisers are not innovators. They are more intent on reinforcing lifestyle behaviors already present in the system of everyday life than in spreading commercially risky innovations. Advertisements are not in themselves disruptive of the value systems of the cultural mainstream; rather, they reflect shifts already present in popular culture. If they are indeed psychologically effective, then it is primarily because they tap into the system of everyday life more successfully than do other forms of discourse.[5]

In our contemporary "ad-mediated society," as some critics describe it, business and aesthetics have joined forces, tapping into unconscious desires, urges, and mythic motifs embedded in the human psyche. The messages coming out of ads and commercials offer the kind of hope to which religions and social philosophies once held exclusive rights: security against the hazards of old age, better position in life, popularity and personal prestige, social advancement, better health, happiness, and eternal youth. The advertiser stresses not the product, but the benefits that may be expected from its purchase. The advertiser is becoming more and more successful at setting foot into the same subconscious regions of psychic experience that were once explored only by philosophers, artists, and religious thinkers.

Today, a large portion of our information, intellectual stimulation, entertainment, and lifestyle models are derived from media images and portrayals. As Marshall McLuhan cleverly put it, the *medium* has become the *message*.[6] However, blaming advertising for our social ills is like blaming the messenger for the message that is embedded in the materialistic ethos of consumerist societies. Unraveling the meanings of the ad's subtexts and intertexts is perhaps the only way to become truly immune to any effects advertising might have on human consciousness. That is the underlying principle of semiotic analysis and, essentially, the theme of this book.

POP CULTURE

Advertising is one of the forms of expression that characterize what has come to be known as pop culture. This term was coined in analogy to pop art, short for populist art, a post–World War II movement rejecting high art and traditional forms of art-making. Pop artists drew and sculpted beer bottles, soup cans, and comic book heroes. For many artists of that era, among them the renowned Andy Warhol (1928–87),[7] the supermarket became their art school. Traditional art critics panned the movement, but people loved it, no matter how trashy the "art." To the average person, it proclaimed that art was for mass consumption, not just for the *cognoscenti,* no matter what its message might be. This movement spread to the other arts, and to most of the other cultural forms of expression—hence the term pop culture.

Pop culture is a culture of youth. This is why the style and contents of many movies and television programs are anchored in the experiences of youth, why fashion styles of all kinds pass quickly from the adolescent culture to the mainstream culture. The very definitions of young and old are

blurred in pop culture. As Gail Sheehy has cogently argued, the prolonga-
tion of life expectancy by medical science has brought about an extended
period of social maturation which extends well beyond the adolescent
years.[8]

Following World War I young adults came to be viewed as a distinct
group by society. The term teenager was coined in the mid-1940s to acknowledge the emergence of a new social *persona,* requiring a special kind
of handling in the marketplace, in the media, at home, and at school. By
the mid-1950s, the culturally fashioned image of the "sweet sixteener" was
enshrined in books, songs, and cinema prototypes. Songs of that era, like
Sixteen Candles, Happy Birthday Sweet Sixteen, She Was Only Sixteen, bore
witness to the crystallization of the new social reality. The breakpoint of
"sixteen" was extended by a few years during the hippie 1960s and early
1970s to encompass the entire high school period. Since the 1980s, the period of adolescence has increased, from well before puberty to well beyond
the high school years. Human beings become sexually mature between the
ages of 11 and 16 (the pubescent period), but in our culture they do not
become adults legally until they approach 20 or so years of age. Socially
they are not looked upon as adults until they are well into their 20s and
have settled into the work world. This gap, in modern society, between the
advent of sexual maturation and expectations of social adulthood has had
behavioral consequences. The extension of the adolescent years, and a
youth-based mindset, has been carefully nurtured and vigorously reinforced by social institutions (the marketplace, the media). The modern
teenager is a convenient creation of our culture. Without teens, work related to schooling, to a large chunk of the music and cinema industries, to
the faddish clothing business, to the fast-food commercial empire, would
virtually disappear.

Pop culture took a stranglehold on our system of everyday life in the
mid-1950s, when the courtship of the teenage consumer by the media and
the entertainment industries began in full earnest. Songs, movies, television programs, and magazines, became progressively juvenilized in content, reflecting a new focus on the teenager as consumer.

The advent of rock 'n' roll—which is usually traced to the 1955 hit
song by Bill Haley and the Comets, *Rock Around the Clock*—gave the
emerging youth culture a musical voice. The first heroes of pop culture
were rock 'n' roll artists. Male singers like Elvis Presley and Jerry Lee
Lewis brought adolescent girls to tearful frenzy as they swung their hips

in rhythmic imitation of sexual movements. Female rock stars like Annette Funicello and Connie Francis made pubescent boys and girls swoon with feelings of infatuation. An incident that occurred in the winter of 1958 epitomized the emotional power that media-based heroes of rock 'n' roll had over teenagers. Three popular singers, Buddy Holly, Ritchie Valens, and the Big Bopper, were killed, in that year, in an airplane crash on the way to a rock concert. Their death was treated by the media as a tragedy of mythical proportions. Teenage girls and boys throughout North America cried as they heard the voices of their departed heroes live on through the magic of audio reproduction. Photographs and posters of the three were transformed into icons of veneration.

The figure who most epitomized the emotional power of pop culture was Elvis Presley (1935–77). At each of his live performances, teenage girls screamed, fainted, or attempted to reach and touch the star on stage. After appearing on *The Ed Sullivan Show* in 1956, he became an instant teen idol throughout North America and, at the same time, a menacing image of sexuality in the eyes of countless parents. His bodily movements, facial expressions (especially his peculiar raised lip twitch), hairstyle, and verbal drawl were emulated by male teens. Some continue to cling to the Elvis Presley model of physical appearance. Since Elvis' death in 1977, the "king of rock 'n' roll" lives on as a mythic hero, worshipped and venerated through television serials, Elvis impersonators, reissues of his records, and a host of memorabilia. Such is the emotional force of pop culture.

Following in Elvis' footsteps was Jerry Lee Lewis, who transformed the sensual innuendoes of Elvis' *All Shook Up* (1956) into blatant carnal sexuality in such hits as *Whole Lotta Shakin' Goin' On* (1957), *Great Balls of Fire* (1958), and *Breathless* (1958). Presley and Lewis thrilled teens and petrified parents. Fearing censorship and curtailment of sales, the record industry quickly responded by providing well-groomed male teen idols such as Frankie Avalon, Fabian, Paul Anka, Bobby Rydell, and Ricky Nelson, with their new "syrupy" sound, making rock 'n' roll more widely acceptable.

In the 1960s and early 1970s, rock 'n' roll music took a different route. It became, unexpectedly, an artistic medium for expressing revolutionary social and political ideas. It was no longer just music to dance to or to fall in love by. The hippie movement of the 1960s was propelled by rock 'n' roll. Its leaders included Bob Dylan, Joan Baez, Joe Cocker, Van Morrison, Simon and Garfunkel, the Mamas and the Papas, the Band, the Rolling

Stones, the Doors, Jimi Hendrix, the Byrds, Procul Harum, Pink Floyd, and the Beatles. These new voices denounced apathy, warmongering, racism, stereotyping, and other social ills.

The influence of the British rock group, the Beatles, to the course of this new movement, cannot be ignored. Coming out of the working-class slums of Liverpool, by the time they produced the album *Sergeant Pepper's Lonely Hearts Club Band* in 1967, the Beatles were raising rock 'n' roll to the level of high musical art. The musical revolution they started made the rock concert, especially the open-air concert, a momentous aesthetic and ideological event. Drugs were consumed openly at such concerts to induce or heighten the whole experience of the event. By the end of the decade, rock operas, such as *Tommy* (1969) by the Who, were considered serious works of musical art by mainstream classical music critics.

The 1970s and 1980s saw the further entrenchment of rock, but, once again, it caught the attention of society's moral guardians. Performers and bands such as Black Sabbath, Metallica, Motley Crüe, the Cult, Bon Jovi, Van Halen, Iron Maiden, Guns 'n' Roses, the Ramones, Talking Heads, and Blondie came often under the scrutiny of censorship-minded people, because of the explicit sexual and sinister themes they expressed, and because of the fashions they introduced—black clothes, pentagram pendants, and earrings for males. Of particular concern to society at large was the emergence of the punk movement. Those who called themselves "punks" were British teens who came, at first, from the working class. Feeling alienated from mainstream culture, they came forward to threaten the social order by inveighing violently against it through their music, actions, and lifestyle. They were anti-bourgeois and anti-capitalist. Their stage performances were deliberately violent and confrontational. They spat on their audiences, mutilated themselves with cutting instruments, damaged the props on stage and in the hall, and incited their audiences to do the same. The fashion trends they introduced emphasized degradation: chains, dog collars, black clothes, army boots, shaved heads, Mohican hairdos. Their music was intentionally chaotic. Musicians played notes, banged their guitars, shouted, burped, urinated, and bellowed at will on stage to a pulsating beat.

Running parallel to the punk movement, was "disco" music, epitomized in the 1978 movie, *Saturday Night Fever,* starring John Travolta. Attendance at a Saturday night disco, for those teens not part of the punk culture, became a rite celebrating sexuality. Bands and performers like

Chic, the Village People, Donna Summer, and KC & the Sunshine Band, catered to the amorous whims of their fashionable "hormone crowd," as some critics called the disco dancers.

Throughout the 1980s rock 'n' roll became increasingly diversified. There were rock styles for every taste—pop rockers (Elton John, Madonna, Wham, Duran Duran, Michael Jackson), jazz and blues rockers (Sting, Anita Baker, Steely Dan), country or blue-collar rockers (Allman Brothers, Lynyrd Skynyrd, Eric Clapton, the Eagles, Bruce Springsteen), and so on. But by the 1990s rock was starting to lose its edge and appeal among the younger generations. The rap movement that came to the forefront, especially among Afro-American teenagers, signaled a shift in musical idiom. The movement started in the dance halls of Harlem and South Bronx where, in the mid-1970s, the disk jockeys played an eclectic mix of funk, soul, and hard rock. The more enthusiastic audience members would sing-song rhymes, exhorting others to dance. These "rapping" sessions, which spread throughout New York clubs, became a major focus of African-American rock artists everywhere. In becoming part of pop culture, rap music vindicated the often-ignored role played by African-American music in the birth of rock. The rap scene of the 1990s also introduced many new fashion trends, including back-to-Africa dashikis, shell necklaces, Kangol caps, sweat suits, unlaced hi-top sneakers, gold chains, and capped teeth.

To summarize, the history of rock 'n' roll has been, in many ways, the history of pop culture—a culture of youth, even if its adherents are not necessarily young any more. But rock 'n' roll seems to be much less influential in shaping pop culture than it once was. The establishment of the Rock and Roll Hall of Fame and Museum, in Cleveland in 1995, is a sure sign that rock is increasingly perceived as "museum art" rather than as a social force. Pop culture trends have become eclectic and varied, and subject to a fast turnover. Pop artists come and go much more quickly than ever before. Neomania has become an intrinsic component of the modern psyche, as Barthes predicted.

TELEVISION

Television service was in place in several Western countries by the late 1930s. By the early 1940s there were 23 television stations operating in the United States. But it was not until the early 1950s that technology had advanced far enough to make it possible for virtually every North American household to afford a television set. By the mid-1950s television was becoming a force shaping all of society. TV personalities became household names and were transformed into icons. People increasingly began to plan their lives around their favorite television programs. Performers like Elvis Presley and the Beatles became instant cultural heroes after appearing on TV.

The role that television plays in our system of everyday life cannot be stressed enough. The character Archie Bunker of *All in the Family* sat constantly in front of a television set, reacting mindlessly to what was being shown. How emblematic this was! By the 1970s, television had become a fixture inside the household. From morning to late at night, television provided programs "to live by." Viewing the world through a television camera has led to a perspective of the world as montage. Consequently, we tend to gaze upon the real world as if it were a TV program. Day in and day out TV's fragmented images of life influence our overall view that reality is illusory.

Most people alive today cannot remember a time without a television set in their homes. Like the automobile at the turn of the century, television has changed society permanently. Demographic surveys now consistently show that people spend more time in front of television sets than they do working, that watching TV is bringing about a gradual decline in reading, and that TV satellite transmission is leading to the demise of the nation-state concept as ideas and images cross national boundaries daily through television channels. When asked about the stunning defeat of communism in eastern Europe, the Polish labor leader, Lech Walesa, was reported by the newspapers as saying that it "all came from the television set," implying that television undermined the stability of the communist world's relatively poor and largely sheltered lifestyle with images of consumer delights seen in Western programs and commercials. Television has indeed created a "global village," to use McLuhan's term,[9] shrinking the world into a global system of everyday life. Television now dictates the pose, the look, the walk, the talk, the overall presentation of self in society.

Like any type of privileged space—a platform, a pulpit, etc.—television creates mythical cultural heroes by simply "showing" them. Think of how you would react to your favorite television personality if he or she were to visit you in your own home. You certainly would not treat his or her presence in your house as you would that of any other stranger. You would feel his or her presence to constitute an event of momentous proportions, an almost unreal and other-worldly happening. TV personalities are perceived as deities by virtue of the fact that they are "seen" inside the mythical space created by television. TV personalities are the contemporary equivalents of the graven images of the Bible.

TV is where moral issues are now being showcased. Take, as an example, sex-related issues. The first bare female breasts appeared unintentionally on TV in 1950 when talk-show host Faye Emerson accidentally fell out of her plunging-neckline dress. The 1977 mini-series *Roots* was the first program to intentionally show breasts. TV's first pregnant character in prime time appeared in 1951 on *One Man's Family*, but Lucille Ball's pregnancy on *I Love Lucy* was featured in seven episodes without the word "pregnant" being mentioned once. The first TV couple shown sleeping in the same bed were Ozzie and Harriet in 1952. Actress Yvette Mimieux wore a scanty bikini and bared her navel in a 1961 episode of *Dr. Kildare*, no other navels were shown until the *Sonny and Cher Comedy Hour* in the 1970s when Cher put an end to that taboo. In 1968 *Star Trek* featured the first interracial kiss in an episode titled *Plato's Stepchildren*. The first divorced couple appeared in 1970 on *The Odd Couple*. In 1971, *All in the Family* brought the first homosexual characters into prime time; the same program dealt with the topic of rape in 1973. In 1983, an episode of *Bay City Blues* showed a locker room full of naked men. The first scene of women kissing was aired in 1991 on an episode of *L.A. Law*. In 1992 an episode of *Seinfeld* dealt with one of the more taboo subjects of all, masturbation. Since the early 1990s, topics such as sexual perversion, pornography, transsexualism, and the like are discussed matter-of-factly on both sitcoms and talk shows.

People make up their minds about the guilt or innocence of people by watching TV news programs. They see certain behaviors as laudable or damnable by tuning into a talk show. They experience the moral sentiments of rectitude and justice by viewing the capture of a criminal on real-life police programs. Sports events like the *World Series*, the *Super Bowl*, or the *Stanley Cup Playoffs* are transformed on television into Herculean struggles of mythic heroes. The John F. Kennedy and Lee Harvey Oswald assassinations, the Vietnam War, and the Watergate hearings have all been transformed into portentous and prophetic historical dramas, reminiscent of the great classical dramas of the past.

Television has become both the *maker* of history and its *documenter*. The horrific scenes coming out of the Vietnam War, which were transmitted into people's homes daily in the late 1960s and early 1970s, brought about an end to the war. It is truly incredible to contemplate that more people watched the wedding of England's Prince Charles and Princess Diana, and more recently Diana's tragic death, than ever before in human history. A riot that gets airtime becomes a momentous event; one that does not is ignored. This is why terrorists have always been more interested in simply "getting on the air," than in having their demands satisfied. The mere fact of getting on television imbues their cause with significance. Political and social protesters frequently inform the news media of their intentions to stage demonstrations, which are then carried out in front of the cameras. The invasion of Grenada and the Gulf War were documented by television. The military operations and conflicts were real events, but the reporting of these wars was orchestrated by a massive public-relations operation. Reporters were kept away from the action so that the news coverage could be edited and managed more effectively. The idea was to give the viewing public a military and social victory and, therefore, to allow Americans to feel good about themselves. Television takes such events and fashions them into dramatic stories; and we call them reality.

In semiotic terms, television can be characterized as a *social text,* an authoritative point of reference for evaluating real-life actions, behaviors, and events. To grasp this concept, imagine stepping back in time, living in some village in medieval Europe. How would you conceive and organize your daily routines in that village? The routines of your day, week, month, and year would no doubt be centered on a Christian view of life. Some of the contents of that Christian social text are still around today. This is why religious dates such as Christmas and Easter constitute regular cultural events. In medieval Europe, people went to church regularly, and lived by moral codes that were iterated in church sermons. The underlying theme of the medieval social text was that each day brought people closer and closer to their true destiny: salvation and an afterlife with God. Living according to this text imparted a feeling of emotional shelter. All human actions and natural events could be explained and understood in terms of this text.

With the scientific advances brought about by the Renaissance, the Enlightenment, and the Industrial Revolution, the Christian social text lost its grip on the system of everyday life. Today, unless someone has joined a religious community or has chosen to live by the dictates of the Bible or some other religious text, the social text by which people live is hardly religious. We organize our day around work commitments and social appointments, and only at those traditional "points" in the calendar (Christmas, Easter, etc.) do we synchronize our secular social text with the more traditional religious one. The need to partition the day into "time slots" is why we depend so heavily upon such devices and artifacts as clocks, watches, agendas, appointment books, and calendars. We would feel desperately lost without such things. In this regard, it is appropriate to note that in his 1726 novel, *Gulliver's Travels,* Jonathan Swift (1667–1745) satirized the reliance of modern (post-Renaissance) culture on the watch. The Lilliputians were intrigued and baffled that Gulliver did virtually nothing without consulting his watch. Today, most people would indeed deem it unthinkable to go out of the home without a watch. We always need to know "what time it is" in order to carry on the business of our daily life.

When television entered the scene in the 1950s, it almost instantly became the modern world's social text. With cable television and satellite dishes, this text now appears to be a highly individualistic one, tailored to meet the needs of individuals, rather than of society at large. But this is not completely true. Specialized information, children's, sports, exercise, movie, and other channels may appear to cater to special interests, but overall there is still a social pattern to television programming. By and large, morning television is geared to people heading off to work, school, or doing household chores. The emphasis in morning TV is thus on the news, on physical exercise programs, on educational and recreational programs for young children. Men or women who are at home and are in need of some kind of stimulation, recreation, or relaxation can tune in to the morning talk shows, quiz shows, and soap operas. In the same way that morning prayers provided medieval people with a meaningful act to start off the day, so too does morning TV programming provide a meaningful format for TV viewers to start their day. In the afternoon, rather than go out and chitchat with other villagers as did medieval people, people today can do virtually the same thing by viewing the complicated lives of soap opera characters or talk show guests. Talk shows in particular are TV's moral dramas, replacing the pulpit as the platform from which moral issues are discussed and sin is condemned publicly. The host has replaced the medieval priest, commenting morally on virtually every medical and psychological condition known to humanity.

The evening is reserved for family-oriented sitcoms, sports events, adventure programs, documentaries, movies, and the like, with moral and social messages for the entire family. When children are safely in bed, adult viewers can indulge their prurient curiosities with late-night talk shows and adult erotic channels (through pay TV). Under the cloak of darkness, and with "innocent eyes and ears" fast asleep, one can fantasize with social impunity about virtually anything under the sun.

OF CIGARETTES AND HIGH HEELS, AGAIN

My purpose in this book has been to illustrate what a semiotic study of the system of everyday life would entail, what things it would focus on. Its underlying premise has been that there is an innate tendency in all human beings to search for, and to make, *meaning* in the world. The task of the semiotician is to look everywhere for the "signs of life." As the philosopher Charles Peirce often remarked, they are indeed everywhere. My hope is that this excursus into semiotic analysis has engendered in the reader a questioning frame of mind with which to view his or her own society up close, unimpeded by the habits of thought that the reader may have formed growing up and living in that society. In a fundamental sense, semiotics is an exercise in *knowing oneself*.

I contrived my presentation of the subject matter of semiotics around an imaginary courtship display. The gestures, bodily postures, dialogue, and other features that characterize such displays testify to the fact that humans carry out their everyday life schemes with a skillful deployment of signs. This display also testifies to the fact that we live our lives like characters in a play, constantly rehearsing, acting out, and at times changing our social roles. Semiotics catalogues the features of the play's script. Our imaginary scene occurs in bars, restaurants, and cafés throughout North American society.

I must emphasize that the characters in my vignette, Cheryl and Ted, are prototypical characters. Changing their ages, race, ethnicity, or adapting the lifestyle codes they deployed in the vignette to meet contemporary standards—the widespread prohibition of smoking in public places, the hairstyles of the characters—will not change the basic message of this book. On the contrary, it will confirm one of its themes: that codes are dynamic, flexible systems, adaptable to the whims of individuals and entire societies.

The overarching theme of this book has been that systems of everyday life provide networks of shared meanings that define human cultures. Such networks have come about in our species, arguably, to make possible the formulation of answers to the basic metaphysical questions that haunt humans everywhere: Why are we here? Who or what put us here? What, if anything, can be done about it? Who am I? As philosopher Johan Huizinga has put it, these questions constitute the psychic foundations of cultural systems: "In God, nothing is empty of sense . . . so, the conviction of a transcendental meaning in all things seeks to formulate itself."[10] The goal of semiotics is, ultimately, to unravel how culture guides the human search for meaning and, thus, how it influences the ways in which people think and act. By seeing the answers of any one culture to the questions of existence as tied to that culture's meaning network, semiotics provides a strong form of intellectual immunization against accepting those answers as the only ones that can be devised.

Carl Jung, the great Swiss psychoanalyst, was fond of recounting how the system of everyday life had the power to affect even what one sees. During a visit to an island tribal culture that had never been exposed to illustrated magazines, he found that the people of that culture were unable to recognize the photographs in the magazines as visual representations of human beings. To his amazement, he discovered that the islanders perceived them, rather, as smudges on a surface. Jung understood perfectly well, however, that their erroneous interpretation of the photographs was not due to defects of intelligence or eyesight; on the contrary, the tribal members were clear-sighted and highly intelligent hunters. Jung understood that their primary assumptions were different from his own, and from those of individuals living in Western culture, because they had acquired a different signifying order that blocked them from perceiving the pictures as visual signs.

The system of everyday life is a powerful force in human life. It can even create particular kinds of disease. A case in point is *anorexia nervosa,* a psychophysiological disorder that is characterized by an abnormal fear of becoming obese, a distorted self-image, a persistent aversion to food, and severe weight loss. As incredible to the Western mind as it may appear, psychologists have found that there simply is no such thing as *anorexia nervosa* among some peoples, such as Malaysians and native Americans. As mentioned in a previous chapter, disease must be defined culturally. For example, in the lexicon of Western psychotherapy there is no mention of the condition called *zar* by the people of North Africa and the Middle East whereby a person is believed to be possessed by a spirit that causes him or her to laugh uncontrollably. Nor is there any mention of *latah,* a syndrome that Malaysian, Japanese, Indonesian, and Thai peoples believe results from sudden fright; nor of *dhat,* a state of severe anxiety associated with the discharge of semen and feelings of exhaustion, which is reported by East Indians, Sri Lankans, and some Chinese. There are indeed many syndromes that are not recognized by Western clinical practice. How would a psychotherapist treat what the Japanese call *taijin kyofusho,* a morbid dread that someone will do something that will embarrass other people?

The appeal of semiotics is that it is basically iconoclastic, and goes counter to several intellectual trends that have set the tone in our society and in our academies. The implicit argument in the foregoing discussion is that scientific-sounding terminology or explanations are not necessarily correct. Semiotics does not see an opposition between nature and culture. Rather, it sees them as the two sides of the same human equation. Recently, a school of thought has emerged that has attempted to emphasize biology at the expense of culture. Known as *evolutionary psychology,* its main claim is that culture is a product of biology. According to this perspective, human rituals such as kissing and flirting are explained as modern-day reflexes of animal mechanisms. Our feelings, thoughts, urges, sense of humor, artistic creations, and so on are all products of such mechanisms.

This point of view has gained widespread popularity beyond academia, in part as a result of the publication of accessible and widely publicized books by clever academicians like Desmond Morris,[11] Richard Dawkins,[12] and Stephen Pinker.[13] With great rhetorical deftness and aplomb, they portray cultures as collective, adaptive systems that emerged in the human species to enhance its survivability and future progress by replacing the functions of genes with those of mental units which Dawkins calls *memes*—a word he coined in direct imitation of the word *genes.* Memes are defined as replicating patterns of information (ideas, laws, clothing fashions, art works, etc.) and of behavior (marriage rites, love rituals, religious ceremonies, etc.) that people inherit directly from their cultural environments. Like genes, memes involve no intentionality on the part of the receiving human organism. Being part of culture, the human being takes them in unreflectively from birth, passing them on just as unreflectively to subsequent generations. The *memetic code* has thus become responsible for cultural progress and betterment. This clever proposal poses an obvious challenge to virtually everything that has been written on human nature in traditional philosophy, theology, and social science. If scholars like Dawkins are correct, then the search for meaning to existence beyond physical survival is essentially over. Any attempt to seek spiritual meaning to life would be explained as one of the intellectual effects of culturally inherited memes such as the *soul, God,* and *immortality.* To evolutionary psychologists, these memes have come about simply to help human beings cope with their particular form of consciousness, thus enhancing their collective ability to survive as a species.

The key figure behind this whole intellectual movement is the North American biologist E. O. Wilson (1929–), known for his work tracing the effects of natural selection on biological communities, especially on populations of insects, and for extending the idea of natural selection to human cultures. Since the mid-1950s, Wilson has maintained that social behaviors in humans are genetically based and that evolutionary processes favor those that enhance reproductive success and survival. Thus, characteristics such as heroism, altruism, aggressiveness, and male dominance should be understood as evolutionary outcomes, not in terms of social or psychic processes. Moreover, Wilson sees the creative capacities undergirding language, art, scientific thinking, and myth, as originating in genetic responses that help the human organism solve problems of survival and species continuity. As he has stated rather bluntly, "no matter how far culture may take us, the genes have culture on a leash."[14]

Obviously captivated by such rhetoric, popular magazine and TV science programs have come under the spell of this new paradigm. But what, one might ask, do such things as paintings, music, marriage rites, burial rites, really have to do with survival or reproductive success? There never has been, nor will there ever be, concrete evidence that language, art, music, science, or any of the other characteristic attributes of humanity are the remnants of animal mechanisms. Like all theories, evolutionary psychology is itself the product of a particular world-view. To paraphrase Foucault, human beings seek to understand and define their identities by ascribing them either to nature, human effort, or God. As others have done in the past, the evolutionary psychologists of today have placed most of their bets on nature.

This book has attempted to argue that the nature of *Homo sapiens* cannot be understood primarily in biological terms. The thoughts and actions of human beings are shaped by forces other than the instincts. The most powerful argument against reductionist evolutionary theories of humanity is the fact that humans can change anything they want, even the very systems of everyday life in which they are reared. Such systems can be compared to the default mode of computer software. This format can, of course, be changed intentionally by a human programmer, but if there are no changes made to the format, the computer will automatically operate according to its original format. Analogously, the signs acquired through culture make up the human being's default mode of representing and, thus, knowing the world. In the same way that a human programmer can always choose to change the computer's format so, too, the individual human being can decide to alter his or her own "personal signifying format" at any time. Indeed, throughout the lifecycle, there is a negotiation within each person between individually based and culturally based meaning-making. When the categories of the latter fail a human being in his or her search for new or more profound meanings, then the innate capacity for meaning kicks in to help him or her alter the default mode. This "way out" of the format is made possible by the human imagination—what the Italian philosopher Giambattista Vico called the *fantasia:* the creative force behind the great works of art, the great scientific discoveries, the profound ideas contemplated by philosophers, and, more to the point, cultural change.

Musical performances, stage plays, common discourse exchanges, ceremonies, and the like are always in flux, always being changed and developed to suit new ideas, new needs, new realities. There is no way to explain the human spirit. We can, of course, develop religious philosophies, mythical narratives, or scientific theories to explain it, but these are of our own making. The American-born British-naturalized poet, literary critic, dramatist, and winner of the Nobel Prize for literature, T. S. Eliot (1888–1965), who is best known for his poem *The Waste Land,* argued that knowledge of who we are starts with understanding the past, with comprehending the historical forces that have made us what we are today. These forces are unwittingly part of larger life forces to which, with our limited sensory apparatus and cognitive faculties, we have limited access.

This book has been inspired by Eliot's idea. We can know ourselves today only by knowing how we got here. The history of smoking, of words, of names, of rituals, of art works, tells us where our search for meaning has led. History is nothing if not a record of our search for meaning to life. Hopefully, this book has shed some light on how we search for meaning, and why we will continue to do so.

NOTES

CHAPTER 1

1. Source: *World Tobacco Market Report,* Euromonitor (Chicago, 1996).
2. Margaret Leroy, *Some Girls Do: Why Women Do and Don't Make the First Move* (London: Harper Collins, 1997).
3. Jordan Goodman, *Tobacco in History: The Cultures of Dependence* (London: Routledge, 1993).
4. Richard Klein, *Cigarettes Are Sublime* (Durham: Duke University Press, 1993).
5. Michael E. Starr, "The Marlboro Man: Cigarette Smoking and Masculinity in America," *Journal of Popular Culture* (1984), pp. 45–56.
6. According to the 1995 report of the U.S. Center for Tobacco Free Kids, nearly 35 percent of teenagers are smokers, many of whom started smoking around 13 years of age.
7. Marcel Danesi, *Cool: The Signs and Meanings of Adolescence* (Toronto: University of Toronto Press, 1994).
8. Susanne K. Langer, *Philosophy in a New Key* (Cambridge: Harvard University Press, 1948).
9. See F. M. Mondimore, *A Natural History of Homosexuality* (Baltimore: Johns Hopkins University Press, 1996).
10. An in-depth authoritative treatment of Charles Peirce's contribution to sign theory is the one by Roberta Kevelson, *Peirce, Science, Signs* (New York: Peter Lang, 1996).
11. William Rossi, *The Sex Lives of the Foot and Shoe* (New York: Dutton, 1976).
12. Valerie Steele, *Fetish: Fashion, Sex, and Power* (Oxford: Oxford University Press, 1996).
13. Erving Goffman, *The Presentation of Self in Everyday Life* (Garden City, Conn.: Doubleday, 1959).
14. Lillian Glass, *He Says, She Says* (New York: G. P. Putnam's Sons, 1992), pp. 46–8.
15. Mary Jenni, "Sex Differences in Carrying Behavior," *Perceptual and Motor Skills* 43 (1976), pp. 323–30.

16. Desmond Morris, *The Human Zoo* (London: Cape, 1969).
17. Ferdinand de Saussure, *Cours de linguistique générale* (Paris: Payot, 1916).
18. Umberto Eco, *A Theory of Semiotics* (Bloomington: Indiana University Press, 1976).
19. Morris, *The Human Zoo*, p. 5.
20. Susan Sontag, *Illness As Metaphor* (New York: Farrar, Straus & Giroux, 1978).
21. Liam Hudson, *The Cult of the Fact* (New York: Harper & Row, 1972).

CHAPTER 2

1. C. K. Ogden and I. A. Richards, *The Meaning of Meaning* (London: Routledge and Kegan Paul, 1923).
2. C. E. Osgood, G. J. Suci, and P. H. Tannenbaum, *The Measurement of Meaning* (Urbana: University of Illinois Press, 1957).
3. Thomas A. Sebeok, *Signs* (Toronto: University of Toronto Press, 1994).
4. See D. Schmandt-Besserat, "The Earliest Precursor of Writing," *Scientific American* 238 (1978), pp. 50–9.
5. David McNeill, *Hand and Mind: What Gestures Reveal about Thought* (Chicago: University of Chicago Press, 1992).

CHAPTER 3

1. Desmond Morris et al., *Gestures: Their Origins and Distributions* (London: Cape, 1979).
2. Paul Ekman and Wallace Friesen, *Unmasking the Face* (Englewood Cliffs, N. J.: Prentice-Hall, 1975).
3. Paul Ekman, *Telling Lies* (New York: Norton, 1985).
4. Helen E. Fisher, *Anatomy of Love* (New York: Norton, 1992), pp. 272–3.
5. Roger Wescott, *Sound and Sense* (Lake Bluff, Ill.: Jupiter Press, 1980).
6. See the interesting study of hairstyles by Grant McCracken, *Big Hair: A Journey into the Transformation of Self* (Toronto: Penguin, 1995).
7. Marshall McLuhan, *Understanding Media* (London: Routledge, 1964).
8. Erving Goffman, *The Presentation of Self in Everyday Life* (Garden City, Conn.: Doubleday, 1958).
9. Michel Foucault, *The History of Sexuality*, vol. 1 (London: Allen Lane, 1976).
10. Andrew Synnott, *The Body Social: Symbolism, Self and Society* (London: Routledge, 1993), p. 22.
11. L. S. Dubin, *The History of Beads* (New York: Abrams, 1987), p. 134.

12. Keith H. Basso, *Western Apache Language and Culture: Essays in Linguistic Anthropology* (Tucson: University of Arizona Press), pp. 15–24.

13. Barry Richards, *Disciplines of Delight: The Psychoanalysis of Popular Culture* (London: Free Association Books, 1994), pp. 70–1.

14. Marcel Danesi, *Cool: The Signs and Meanings of Adolescence* (Toronto: University of Toronto Press, 1994).

CHAPTER 4

1. Charles W. Morris, *Foundations of the Theory of Signs* (Chicago: Chicago University Press, 1938).

2. Julian Jaynes, *The Origin of Consciousness in the Breakdown of the Bicameral Mind* (Toronto: University of Toronto Press, 1975).

3. An in-depth synthesis of this line of work in linguistics, known more technically as *cognitive linguistics,* can be found in Gary B. Palmer, *Toward a Theory of Cultural Linguistics* (Austin: University of Texas Press, 1996).

4. Robert Levine, *A Geography of Time: The Temporal Misadventures of a Social Psychologist or How Every Culture Keeps Time Just a Little Bit Differently* (New York: Basic, 1997).

5. Ronald W. Langacker, *Concept, Image, and Symbol: The Cognitive Basis of Grammar* (Berlin: Mouton de Gruyter, 1990).

6. Roger W. Brown, *Psycholinguistics* (New York: Free Press, 1970), pp. 258–73.

7. The most in-depth theory of modeling systems in semiotics is the one by Thomas A. Sebeok, *Signs: An Introduction to Semiotics* (Toronto: University of Toronto Press, 1994).

8. F. M. Müller, *Lectures on the Science of Language* (London: Longmans, Green, 1861).

9. B. Alpher, "Feminine As the Unmarked Grammatical Gender: Buffalo Girls Are No Fools," *Australian Journal of Linguistics* 7 (1987), pp. 169–87.

10. Brent Berlin and Paul Kay, *Basic Color Terms* (Berkeley: University of California Press, 1969).

11. N. McNeill, "Colour and Colour Terminology," *Journal of Linguistics* 8 (1972), pp. 21–33.

12. A detailed treatment of color categories, as well as an up-to-date debate on the relation between color categories and perception, can be found in C. L. Hardin and Luisa Maffi, eds., *Color Categories in Thought and Language* (Cambridge: Cambridge University Press, 1997).

13. Robert J. Di Pietro, *Strategic Interaction* (Cambridge: Cambridge University Press, 1987).

14. Deborah Tannen, *Talking Voices* (Cambridge: Cambridge University Press, 1989), p. 24.
15. Marcel Danesi, *Cool: The Signs and Meanings of Adolescence* (Toronto: University of Toronto Press, 1994).
16. David McNeill, *Hand and Mind: What Gestures Reveal about Thought* (Chicago: University of Chicago Press, 1992).
17. R. A. Gardner and B. T. Gardner, "Teaching Sign Language to a Chimpanzee," *Science* 165 (1969), pp. 664–72.
18. D. Premack and A. J. Premack, *The Mind of an Ape* (New York: Norton, 1983).

CHAPTER 5

1. Giambattista Vico, *The New Science,* translated by Thomas G. Bergin and Max Fisch, 2d ed. (Ithaca: Cornell University Press, 1984), par. 821.
2. Ibid., par. 142.
3. Ibid., par. 144.
4. Ibid., par. 1106.
5. Ibid., par. 1106.
6. Ibid., par. 1106.
7. Ibid., par. 1108.
8. I. A. Richards, *The Philosophy of Rhetoric* (Oxford: Oxford University Press, 1936).
9. Solomon Asch, "On the Use of Metaphor in the Description of Persons," in *On Expressive Language,* ed. Heinz Werner (Worcester: Clark University Press, 1950), pp. 86–94.
10. W. Booth, "Metaphor as Rhetoric: The Problem of Evaluation," in *On Metaphor,* ed. S. Sacks (Chicago: University of Chicago Press, 1979), p. 47
11. John M. Kennedy, *Drawing and the Blind* (New Haven: Yale University Press, 1993).
12. Ellen Winner and Howard Gardner, "The Comprehension of Metaphor in Brain-Damaged Patients," *Brain* 100 (1977), pp. 717–29.
13. H. Pollio, et al., *The Poetics of Growth: Figurative Language in Psychology, Psychotherapy, and Education* (Hillsdale, N. J.: Lawrence Erlbaum Associates, 1977).
14. George Lakoff and Mark Johnson, *Metaphors We Live By* (Chicago: University of Chicago Press, 1980).
15. Walter J. Ong, *Interfaces of the Word: Studies in the Evolution of Consciousness and Culture* (Ithaca: Cornell University Press, 1977), p. 134.
16. George Lakoff, *Women, Fire, and Dangerous Things: What Categories Reveal about the Mind* (Chicago: University of Chicago Press, 1987); Mark John-

son, *The Body in the Mind: The Bodily Basis of Meaning, Imagination and Reason* (Chicago: University of Chicago Press, 1987).

17. Lakoff, *Women, Fire, and Dangerous Things*.

18. A panoramic survey of the major findings on metaphor can be found in Raymond W. Gibbs, *The Poetics of Mind: Figurative Thought, Language, and Understanding* (Cambridge: Cambridge University Press, 1994).

19. Lakoff and Johnson, *Metaphors We Live By*, pp. 35–40.

20. Linda Hutcheon, *Irony's Edge: The Theory and Politics of Irony* (London: Routledge, 1995).

21. Lakoff and Johnson, *Metaphors We Live By*, p. 49.

22. Marcel Danesi, *Cool: The Signs and Meanings of Adolescence* (Toronto: University of Toronto Press, 1994), pp. 105–6.

23. Alice Deignan, "Metaphors of Desire," in *Language and Desire*, ed. Keith Harvey and Celia Shalom (London: Routledge, 1997), p. 41. An in-depth treatment of love metaphors is the one by Zoltán Kövecses, *The Language of Love: The Semantics of Passion in Conversational English* (London: Associated University Presses, 1988).

24. Northrop Frye, *The Great Code: The Bible and Literature* (Toronto: Academic Press, 1981).

25. K. C. Cole, *Sympathetic Vibrations* (New York: Bantam, 1984).

CHAPTER 6

1. David Lodge, "Narration with Words," in *Images and Understanding*, ed. H. Barlow, C. Blakemore, and M. Weston–Smith (Cambridge: Cambridge University Press, 1990), p. 141.

2. Vladimir J. Propp, *Morphology of the Folktale* (Austin: University of Texas Press, 1928).

3. Algirdas J. Greimas, *On Meaning: Selected Essays in Semiotic Theory*, trans. Paul Perron and Frank Collins (Minneapolis: University of Minnesota Press, 1987).

4. Friedrich M. Müller, *Lectures on the Science of Language* (London: Longmans, Green, 1861).

5. Claude Lévi-Strauss, *La pensée sauvage* (Paris: Plon, 1962).

6. Roland Barthes, *Mythologies* (Paris: Seuil, 1957).

7. Claude Lévi-Strauss, *The Raw and the Cooked* (London: Cape, 1964).

CHAPTER 7

1. Edward T. Hall, *The Hidden Dimension* (New York: Doubleday, 1966).

2. See, for instance, Michael Argyle, *Bodily Communication* (New York: Methuen, 1988).

3. Desmond Morris, *The Human Zoo* (London: Cape, 1969).
4. Helen Colton, *The Gift of Touch* (New York: Putnam, 1983).
5. Robert Ardrey, *The Territorial Imperative* (New York: Atheneum, 1966).

CHAPTER 8

1. Helen E. Fisher, *Anatomy of Love* (New York: Norton, 1992), pp. 253–4.
2. Marshall McLuhan, *The Mechanical Bride: Folklore of Industrial Man* (New York: Vanguard, 1951).
3. Edward B. Tylor, *Primitive Culture* (London: Murray, 1871).

CHAPTER 9

1. Susanne K. Langer, *Problems of Art* (New York: Scribner's, 1957).

CHAPTER 10

1. Roland Barthes, *Mythologies* (Paris: Seuil, 1957) and *Système de la mode* (Paris: Seuil, 1967).
2. Cited in Marcel Danesi, *Interpreting Advertisements: A Semiotic Guide* (Ottawa: Legas Press, 1995), p. 16.
3. Vance Packard, *The Hidden Persuaders* (New York: McKay, 1957).
4. Brian Wilson Key, *The Age of Manipulation* (New York: Henry Holt, 1989), p. 13.
5. This opinion is based primarily on my own experience with advertisers and marketers as a consultant on the meanings that their ads generate and on the kinds of reactions that subjects have to them. This experience has given me a unique behind-the-scenes look at the whole advertising and marketing business.
6. Marshall McLuhan, *Understanding Media* (London: Routledge & Kegan Paul, 1964).
7. Andy Warhol was an American painter and filmmaker, who was a leader of the pop art movement. He attracted attention in the 1960s with exhibitions of pop art objects from daily life, such as his *Campbell's Soup Can* (1965).
8. Gail Sheehy, *New Passages* (New York: Ballantine, 1995).
9. McLuhan, *Understanding Media*.
10. Johan Huizinga, *The Waning of the Medieval Ages* (Garden City, Conn.: Doubleday, 1924), p. 202.
11. Desmond Morris, *The Human Zoo* (London: Cape, 1969).

12. Richard Dawkins, *The Selfish Gene* (Oxford: Oxford University Press, 1976), *The Blind Watchmaker* (Harlow: Longmans, 1987), *River Out of Eden: A Darwinian View of Life* (New York: Basic, 1985).

13. Stephen Pinker, *How the Mind Works* (New York: Norton, 1997).

14. E. O. Wilson and M. Harris, "Heredity versus Culture: A Debate," in *Anthropological Realities: Reading in the Science of Culture,* ed. J. Guillemin (New Brunswick, N. J.: Transaction Books, 1981), p. 464.

INDEX